The EVERYTHING®
Small Dogs Book

Dear Reader:

Small dogs have been part of my life as a professional dog groomer for more than thirty-five years. They are the perfect pets, just the right size to hold and cuddle, full of personality, and adorable in all their endless variety. I've said it in jest to the loving dog owners in my clientele, but these pint-size pets really do make perfect surrogate children. Doting on them is half the fun!

Small dogs are marvelously entertaining, and they make devoted companions to adults of any age and to children who have been taught to treat them with kindness and care. They fit in just about anywhere, suitable for any type of dwelling, from apartments, condos, and mobile homes to rambling estates. Although they are big on the "cuteness factor," small dogs need training to keep them from running the show. Some breeds are more dominant than others.

I hope you will find the information on the following pages helpful in finding the perfect small dog for you. From the elegant toy poodle to the spirited terrier breeds and happy hounds, you'll have a plethora to pick from. Though diminutive in size, all are capable of delivering huge amounts of joy to your life.

Kathy Salzberg

The EVERYTHING® Series

Editorial

Publishing Director	Gary M. Krebs
Associate Managing Editor	Laura M. Daly
Associate Copy Chief	Brett Palana-Shanahan
Acquisitions Editor	Kate Burgo
Development Editors	Karen Johnson Jacot
	Jessica LaPointe
Associate Production Editor	Casey Ebert

Production

Director of Manufacturing	Susan Beale
Associate Director of Production	Michelle Roy Kelly
Cover Design	Paul Beatrice
	Erick DaCosta
	Matt LeBlanc
Design and Layout	Colleen Cunningham
	Holly Curtis
	Erin Dawson
	Sorae Lee
Series Cover Artist	Barry Littmann

Visit the entire Everything® Series at *www.everything.com*

THE
EVERYTHING
SMALL DOGS
BOOK

Choose the perfect dog
to fit your living space

Kathy Salzberg

Adams Media
Avon, Massachusetts

To Rollie, my beloved French bulldog,
who taught me that good things come in small packages
and left me with an undying legacy of laughter and love.

An Everything® Series Book.
Everything® and everything.com® are registered trademarks of F+W Publications, Inc.

Published by Adams Media, an F+W Publications Company
57 Littlefield Street, Avon, MA 02322 U.S.A.
www.adamsmedia.com

ISBN: 1-59337-419-4
Printed in the United States of America.

J I H G F E D C B A

Library of Congress Cataloging-in-Publication Data
Salzberg, Kathy.
The everything small dogs book : choose the perfect dog to fit your living space / Kathy Salzberg.
p. cm. -- (The Everything series)
Includes bibliographical references.
ISBN 1-59337-419-4
1. Dogs. 2. Toy dogs. I. Title. II. Series.

SF427.S25 2006
636.76--dc22
2005026438

This publication is designed to provide accurate and authoritative information with regard to the subject matter covered. It is sold with the understanding that the publisher is not engaged in rendering legal, accounting, or other professional advice. If legal advice or other expert assistance is required, the services of a competent professional person should be sought.

—From a *Declaration of Principles* jointly adopted by a Committee of the American Bar Association and a Committee of Publishers and Associations

Many of the designations used by manufacturers and sellers to distinguish their products are claimed as trademarks. Where those designations appear in this book and Adams Media was aware of a trademark claim, the designations have been printed with initial capital letters.

This book is available at quantity discounts for bulk purchases.
For information, please call 1-800-872-5627.

Contents

Medical Emergencies / 139

Looking Good / 151

Housetraining / 167

Obedience Begins at Home / 181

Obedience 101: Off to School / 195

Acknowledgments

I would like to thank my daughter, best friend, and business partner, Missi Salzberg, without whose support I would have been unable to undertake this project. She took over many of my shifts at our business, The Village Groomer & Pet Supply, so I could be home at my keyboard doing what I love best—writing. I would also like to thank our amazing grooming staff, Anne Francis, Joey Charland, Kathy Duffus, Karen Boyden, Jimmy Beaucage, and Melanie Charron, for their dedication and the beautiful grooming that keeps our business going and growing, and our wonderful clients, both two-legged and four-legged, who have taught me so much over three decades of working with dogs. Thanks are also due to veterinary colleagues Denise Trapani, DVM, Michelle Salada, DVM, and Margo Roman, DVM, for medical information; and trainers Caryl A. Crouse, Nancy Bradley, and Fran and Mike Masters for sharing their time and expertise. Special thanks to my agent, June Clark, and my acquisitions editor at Adams Media, Kate Burgo. Thanks also to my son David, his wife Aline, my son Peter, his wife Julie, and my five grandkids for understanding why Nana Kathy was so busy with this project. Last but by no means least, eternal thanks to my late husband, David Salzberg, who taught me to love dogs with a passion and who supported me in all things.

The Top Ten Most Popular
Small Dog Breeds, according to
AKC Registration Statistics for 2004

1. Yorkshire terrier

2. Dachshund

3. Poodle (includes the toy, miniature, and standard varieties)

4. Shih tzu

5. Chihuahua

6. Miniature schnauzer

7. Pug

8. Pomeranian

9. Boston terrier

10. Maltese

Introduction

▶ Some say the world is divided into dog people and non-dog people. While that may be true, it is further divided into big dog people and small dog people. Big dog folks are the ones who say things like "I prefer real dogs" when you introduce them to your little shih tzu, or who smile condescendingly when you parade through the park with your Italian greyhound in its snowsuit.

It all boils down to stereotyping, but those of us who cherish pint-size pets can be as guilty of it as the next person. Of course we know that a dog is a dog regardless of its size. But let's admit it—we secretly delight in babying our diminutive dandies. It's all about love and nurturing, part of the reason we wanted a little dog in the first place, but we know in our heart of hearts that small dogs are every bit as courageous, loyal, and protective of their loved ones as the big boys are. All dogs need our companionship, proper nutrition, a warm place to sleep, a safe home, and lots of love and attention.

Small dogs have the same needs as large dogs. The tiny miniature pinscher must be trained and socialized, just like its big Doberman cousin. The perky Pomeranian needs its bouffant coat brushed as much as the chow chow. Although your Boston terrier may not need as much room to let off steam as the lanky Dalmatian, it still benefits greatly from a daily walk around the block.

As a professional dog groomer for three decades and a lifelong dog owner, I have come to love and appreciate the small dogs who have graced my home and my grooming table, bringing a smile to my face and teaching me what wonderful companions they can be. Each one has its own beauty, whether it be the perfectly sculpted bichon frise or the comical pug, who would rather stand on its head than get its nails trimmed.

I hope this book will help you find out if you really are a small dog person. It will debunk the myths about small dogs, detail their special needs, and help you decide if you have room for one in your home as well as in your heart.

If you do decide to join this select fraternity, I hope this book will help you select the right small dog for you and your family, steering you through introductory research on breeds and their history and instructing you on how and where to find your own small dog. It will also help you find the support systems that you will need: veterinary care, grooming, trainers, and caretakers.

If this book lights a spark in your heart, and you are successful in your quest, I wish you all the joy and love I have derived from the small dogs in my life. Like Dorothy and Toto, may you and your little dog skip down the Yellow Brick Road, sharing a long and happy life together.

E Chapter 1

Small Is Beautiful

Almost a third of the American Kennel Club's (AKC's) 153 breeds could be considered small dogs. With these pint-size pets spread throughout five of the seven AKC groups, twenty are tiny enough to be proud members of the Toy Group and all forty-eight will fit nicely in your lap. If you are considering adding a small dog to your family, you will be joining millions of other small-dog owners who know that, as with other things in life, good things come in small packages.

How Small Is Small?

Since there really is no official definition of "small" when it comes to canine companions, the designation must be a subjective one. For the purposes of this book, small means under twenty-five pounds and no taller than sixteen inches at the withers (shoulders). Of course, small dogs don't have to be purebred. Countless varieties of mixed-breed small dogs are among the most appealing and unique pets you could find.

As millions of devotees will attest, small is indeed beautiful. When it comes to the size of your dog, there is absolutely no correlation between its height and weight and the love and joy it will bring to your life.

For the prospective dog owner, the world of small dogs offers a delightful smorgasbord of sizes, personalities, coat types, and activity levels. There is amazing variety in this small world, from energetic sleek-coated beauties like the miniature pinscher to the scissor-sculpted bichon frise, which looks like it was plucked off the shelf at the toy store. Looking for the right small dog is a lot like choosing a mate: It all boils down to the looks and traits that you find appealing, plus that indefinable something that lights a spark in your heart.

The Case for Owning a Small Dog

Except for purchase price, which for pedigreed dogs of any size can range from a few hundred to a couple thousand dollars, it is cheaper to own a small dog. Small dogs eat less. Veterinary care usually costs less, and even essentials like crates and leashes are priced according to size. While grooming costs are not related to a dog's size, it is still easier and less expensive to maintain full-coated small dogs between grooming visits. You can place them on a tabletop or a counter for a primping session or pop them into the kitchen sink for a bath.

Small dogs obviously require a lot less space. If your rooms are less than spacious, they can stretch out on the rug without crowding you or your family. Whether you live in an apartment or a house in the suburbs, small dogs are a lot easier to house and manage than their larger counterparts.

Owning a small dog can also be your ticket to a new world of friendship. It's a place where owners bond and swap stories about their diminutive darlings, much like proud parents. A visit to the groomer or the vet, or a stroll through the park with your miniature dog on the end of the leash offers instant camaraderie with those who share your passion for these compact canines. Not only will you meet new friends, your dog will too. A cute little dog is a shy person's best calling card!

The health and fitness of the owner is an important consideration when choosing a dog. If you are an avid hiker or runner, you'll probably be happier with a medium-to-large athletic dog rather than a little dandy you'd have to stash in your backpack. But elderly citizens or any adult not in tip-top physical shape may find that a large exuberant dog may simply be too much to handle. Couch-potato people are content with couch-potato pets. People who are appalled by dog hair do best with a smooth-coated or nonshedding breed.

Alert!

All dogs start off as adorable little puppies, but when you're picking a pet, you need to know how big your four-footed baby will grow. Thousands of dogs end up at the shelter each year because they have grown too big or too unruly for their owners to handle. Before you select a dog, research its space and exercise requirements.

Small Is In

People are busier than ever, fast-tracking and multitasking their way through life. Young married couples postpone having children while they build their careers. Stay-at-home moms are in the minority. Empty-nesters miss their children when they have grown and flown, while senior citizens often deal with loneliness. But no matter where you are on life's journey, you still feel the need to nurture. Small dogs have become our babies. Doting owners of all ages love to pamper them, spending billions on supplies, food, treats, toys, grooming, training, and vet care. Small-dog owners often unashamedly lean toward anthropomorphism with their pocket-size canines. It goes with the territory.

Why Small Dogs Are Fun

Although all dogs are beautiful, the smallest of the species hold a special appeal for many of us. Like a doll or a teddy bear, they are just the right size to carry, cuddle, and care for. Small dogs come in an infinite variety, each with its own wonderful quirks and qualities. The small breed you choose to make your own will depend upon its personal appeal, your particular lifestyle, and a certain inexplicable chemistry. It's a lot like falling in love.

Small dogs are portable pets. The toy breeds can be picked up and toted along like a fashion accessory (think Paris Hilton and Tinkerbelle, her omnipresent Chihuahua). Even at the larger end of the small dog spectrum, most people would have no trouble carrying their dog indoors if it had physical problems. On the other hand, when large dogs experience physical disabilities or are recovering from surgery, managing the daily routine can become very challenging for adults who are not big and strong themselves.

Cute little canines bring out the doting parent in all of us. Most people can't help but respond to their comical antics and exuberant expressions of unconditional love. In the pet-care industry, it's not uncommon to see burly truck driver types talking baby talk to a shih tzu, poodle, or pug.

Essential

The world of Lassie and Timmy, where dogs ran free down on the farm, made for good television all those years ago, but things have changed. Both for their own safety and because of legal constraints like leash laws, our dogs stay home with us these days.

They make perfect playmates. Whether you're tossing a ball, playing tug-of-war with a rope toy, or making your petite pup sit up and beg for a biscuit, such activities activate our sense of fun and take our minds off the workaday world. No matter how old or how serious we may be, small dogs give us permission to play and be silly.

Understanding Small Dogs

One of the best things about small dogs is how bonded they become to their owners. It's no wonder some owners refer to their small companions as "Velcro dogs." Small dogs seem to need human companionship more than their big-breed brethren. It's nice to be needed. Whether you are watching television, preparing a meal, or sitting at the computer, your small dog will no doubt be nearby, parked strategically in case any morsels should happen to fall its way or snoozing happily under the desk. Small dogs are determined to monitor your every move and keep you company.

 **Question?**

Aren't little dogs really "sissy" dogs?
All dog breeds were developed for a particular purpose. Some small dogs are tough as nails because they had to be back in the days when they worked for a living. Don't be fooled by a small dog's diminutive stature. Pound for pound, some can be every bit as tough and fearless as their larger counterparts.

Understanding your small dog will be easier if you realize the reason for which it was bred. Although that original purpose may have been left far behind in its colorful past, its original function is still present inside that neat little four-footed package. It will play a big part in your dog's appearance, temperament, and activity level.

Terriers

These feisty characters are busy little rascals bred to "go to ground" in search of prey. This proclivity for digging makes them potential escape artists and adept rearrangers of the landscape. They are also highly territorial so they will often bark to announce your visitors. Some are more stubborn and strong-willed than others, but all have that spark of mischief and keen understanding that delights those who fancy these spirited dogs. Small members of the Terrier Group include the miniature schnauzer and West Highland white, as well as the Scottish, cairn, Border, wire fox, and Parson Russell terriers.

Scent Hounds

Scent hounds were bred to track game. Members of this group could be described as "a nose with a dog attached." They are independent, tough, and reliable, but they can also be stubborn. With that fabled nose always on the job, they are food- and scent- driven dogs. Dachshunds, the smallest members of the scent-hound pack, are always on the alert. That makes them good watch-dogs, so expect to hear a sharp bark from them when company arrives. Expect to find their little toys and chew bones buried in the couch cushions, too!

Non-Sporting Dogs

While the AKC's Working and Sporting Groups have no small dog members, the diverse category known as the Non-Sporting Group has them in abundance. The breeds in this group are the most varied collection in terms of size, coat, personality, and overall appearance. Some were bred strictly as companion dogs, a function they still happily fulfill.

Fact

The German word for "poodle," *Pudel*, refers to splashing in water. Despite their fancy-pants image, poodles originated from water dogs that were used to hunt waterfowl.

The poodle comes in three sizes, two of which fit the criteria for small dogs. Toy poodles stand ten inches or under at the shoulder, while miniatures measure fifteen inches at the same point. Available in a wide range of colors, their image is that of a fancy dog, though the larger European variety worked as retrievers. Today, they are superb in their role as companions. Properly groomed, this dog has an air of elegance and great dignity. Not a hothouse flower but a wonderful family dog, the poodle is clean, nonshedding, intelligent, and affectionate.

The American Eskimo resembles a white fox. It comes in three sizes, with the toy and the miniature fitting the small-dog designation. This handsome dog with its white double coat is curious and reserved with strangers. Popular as a circus dog in the early twentieth century, it is very bright and learns tricks quickly. True to its Northern roots, it loves cold weather and relishes a good romp in the snow.

The cheerful bichon frise was a lapdog of French royalty and was featured in several paintings by the Spanish artist Goya. It was bred to be a companion and it is still marvelous at its job. Happiest at the center of family life, bichons continue to be born people-pleasers who love children and require minimal space.

The smooth-coated Boston terrier is an easy-to-care-for little character that is also a companion through and through, the role for which it was bred. This American breed is happy and sensitive. Easily adapted to apartment or condo living, it gets along well with children and other pets.

Hailing from the temples around the sacred Tibetan city of Lhasa, the Lhasa apso was bred to be protective and fearless in its job of palace sentinel. Its beautiful coat is long and thick enough to have kept it warm in the high Himalayas. The Lhasa's dominant nature suited it well in its ancient role but makes it wary of strangers and children it does not know well.

Originally a boat dog from Belgium, the schipperke's name means "little captain," which suits this shiny black dog perfectly. That same alert nature that helped it guard the boat and keep vermin at bay makes it an ideal watchdog and companion who is reserved with strangers but devoted to its home and family.

Toys Are Us

When we come to the Toy Group, the name alone gives us pleasure, conjuring up the joys of childhood. Like the playthings of our youth, the small size and adorable expressions of these diminutive dogs fill us with delight. Despite their size, however, some toy dogs are tough little characters, and many are unsuitable for very young children. All are ideal companions for adults, especially apartment and condo dwellers, and they make great lap warmers on cold nights.

The toy breeds are the affenpinscher, Brussels griffon, cavalier King Charles spaniel, Chihuahua, Chinese crested, English toy spaniel, Havanese, Italian greyhound, Japanese Chin, Maltese, Manchester terrier, miniature pinscher, papillon, Pekingese, Pomeranian, pug, shih tzu, silky terrier, toy fox terrier, and Yorkshire terrier.

Among toy-breed idiosyncrasies are a feisty personality, such as that of the tiny Chihuahua who is not always fond of other breeds and can be nippy when feeling overwhelmed. This little dynamo comes in both a smooth-coated and longhaired version.

Not surprisingly, the most grooming-intensive toy breeds are the long-haired shih tzu, Havanese, and Maltese. They require lots of home care or regular trips to the groomer. If you do lots of brushing and combing at home, you can keep the coats of the Pomeranian, Japanese Chin, English toy spaniel, cavalier King Charles spaniel, papillon, silky terrier, and Yorkie in good condition, but occasional visits to the groomer are advisable for them as well. The harsh coats of the affenpinscher and Brussels griffon are easily maintained by brushing and occasional hand-stripping (plucking or pulling out dead hair.)

Fact

Toy dogs such as the Maltese, English toy spaniel, cavalier King Charles spaniel, papillon, and Japanese Chin were bred as companions for royalty and the aristocracy. These dainty little charmers remain fashionable accessories to this day, living love objects that like to be pampered.

For toy dogs, socializing is every bit as important as housebreaking. It helps them feel secure in the world. They need more protection from their owners than their larger brethren. Owners must be watchful of them in all situations involving other dogs and children. They can be more easily injured than their larger counterparts and they often feel more threatened in unfamiliar situations.

You can give your tiny dog confidence by making sure it meets lots of people and is comfortable being handled by others. Make plenty of trips to the park or mall, and sign up for a puppy kindergarten class. The more time you devote to "bringing up baby," the more you will be rewarded with a happy, well-socialized little dog to share your life.

Is a Small Dog Right for You?

Whether a small dog is appropriate for you depends on what you are looking for in a dog. If you need an intimidating guardian for your property, small is not a good choice. If you're looking for a running partner as you train for the marathon, small won't do. However, if you're in the market for a companion, playmate, and love object, small is terrific. Before you make a decision affecting you, your family, or another animal, consider some additional factors.

Regardless of its size, your dog will need training to make it a happy confident dog that you can take with you anywhere. While small dogs are admittedly easy to spoil, it is still easier to train a ten-pound dog than a 100-pound dog. Training goes hand in hand with the toy dog's need for protection. Mastering the basic obedience commands can save its life.

Just because you live in a small apartment or condo does not mean that any small dog will do. Some crave regular exercise, like the highly energetic Parson Russell terrier. For most, a daily walk around the block will fit the bill; for some, more energetic romps in the park or participation in dog sports such as hunting and tracking trials, agility, or fly ball would provide a great outlet for all that energy.

Grooming requirements and costs are another factor that must be taken into account. Some, like the shih tzu, poodle, and bichon frise, need a great deal of professional grooming. Do some research at local grooming salons to determine whether or not your budget will bear the cost of professional grooming.

There are also the costs of vet care and obedience training; pet sitters or boarding costs if you need to travel without your pet; licensing; food and treats (a necessity when training); home-grooming supplies and cleaning products (for those unavoidable accidents); flea and tick products; leashes and collars; and protective clothing for smooth-haired breeds in winter.

 **Fact**

Senior citizens and small dogs are a match made in heaven. Medical research has proven than pet ownership leads to lower blood pressure and lessened stress levels. Daily walks with a canine companion provide an opportunity for needed exercise and socialization. Small dogs offer companionship and security to seniors as well. No one can tell what size your dog is when it barks from behind a closed door at an unwelcome visitor!

Small Dogs in a Big World

Small dogs are like small children. Some of them don't realize the limitations that come with being small. But while children eventually stop thinking they can fly like Superman, your spunky little dog may think he's a superhero all his life. If your tiny dynamo thinks he can take on the pit bull down the block, you need to protect him from his oversized ego. All small dogs need to be monitored in all interactions with larger dogs they do not know. They can't be allowed outdoors on their own unless the yard is securely fenced. Sometimes a tiny tyke can look like prey to his big dog buddies. Similarly, small dogs can feel overwhelmed by boisterous, fast-moving children or other household pets.

Small Dogs and Children

Very young children are unpredictable. Out of sheer curiosity, they may poke your dog's eye, yank its tail, or take a treat out of its mouth. While pet ownership is a wonderful way to teach a child kindness and responsibility, children need to learn how to safely pick up a small dog, and they need to take care not to frighten it with boisterous actions. They also need to leave it alone when it is sleeping or eating. Dogs communicate through body language as well as by barking. Teaching children to understand the dog's signals that it is feeling threatened—growling, lip-curling, stiffening, retreating, and hiding—will make the situation safer for all concerned. Well-socialized dogs only bite when they feel they have no alternative. The adults in the family must supervise interactions between small children and dogs. It's up to you to direct the teaching process so that children will understand that their dog is a living creature, not a furry toy.

Question?

How can I get my little dog to be comfortable around children?
By exposing your small dog to children in small doses, you can socialize it to little humans. Of course, just as dogs need obedience training, kids do too. Because they can drop a small dog and cause permanent injury or worse, teach them the correct way to hold a puppy and how to walk it on a leash without dragging it around by the neck.

Some breeds like the Lhasa apso, Pekingese, or Chihuahua are not comfortable with highly active children. The tiniest breeds––the toy poodle, toy fox terrier, Yorkie, and silky terrier—could easily be injured if stepped upon or mishandled. Some are afraid of children's loud, high-pitched voices and wild running around. All small dogs need a place of their own—a bed, a basket, or their crate—where they will not be bothered and can take a restful time out.

Small Dogs and Other Companion Animals

It's not true that dogs and cats are natural-born enemies. Most will accept each other after an adjustment period, usually a week or two. Constant supervision is required when you first introduce them, and you may need to separate them. In such a situation, the cat will usually take it upon itself to disappear and sulk for a bit. (It's easier to introduce a kitten into a household that already has a small dog.)

 Fact

Keep in mind that terriers are ratters at heart. They were bred to hunt rodents, and they cannot distinguish between unwanted vermin and your pet hamster. Generally, if they can get hold of a mouse, gerbil, guinea pig, or bunny, they will. For this reason, terriers are not compatible housemates for these types of pets.

Dogs are pack animals, and it only takes two of them to make a pack. Many dog lovers would never keep just one because they know that dogs really do form strong bonds of friendship and keep each other company, playing together and curling up to snuggle and snooze when they get tired. If you are introducing a new dog into the home, you need to supervise the initial interactions. Feed the dogs separately, and show equal attention to each one. While some dogs have aggression issues and are better as "only children," in most cases, having more than one dog means canine companionship for both you and your pets.

Chapter 2

Popular Small Dog Breeds

Whether you're looking for a purebred dog with an impressive pedigree from a renowned breeder or a lovable mix of uncertain parentage from the local shelter, the search for the right dog does require a lot of thought and planning. Keep in mind that the breeds presented in this chapter represent only some of your numerous options. The good news is that doing your homework while you search can be fun.

Beginning Your Search

Each of the dogs described here has a dedicated following of fans who believe their small dog stands head and shoulders above the rest of the pack. When you check out the AKC link to a breed's parent club or conduct your own online search, you are bound to come up with plenty of Web sites devoted to each breed. You'll find lots of adorable photos, too!

 Question?

Don't little dogs tend to be nippy?
As far as nipping goes, small dogs do feel more inclined to protect themselves because of their size. People tend to overwhelm and intimidate them, clamoring to pick them up and cuddle them. Children look upon them as stuffed toys that don't need batteries. If small dogs are allowed to get to know people before being picked up and passed around, and if they are raised to be self-confident, they will be far less inclined to nip their admirers.

Of course there are also numerous dog breeds from around the world and here in the United States that are not recognized by the AKC. Two such up-and-coming small breeds to add to our list are the Coton de Tulear, a dog from Madagascar that is similar to the bichon, and the Bolognese, a toy-size fluffball from Italy.

Popular Small Purebreds

According to the AKC, the most popular small dogs are the dachshund, Yorkie, poodle, shih tzu, Chihuahua, miniature schnauzer, pug, Pomeranian, Boston terrier, and miniature pinscher. But dogs go in and out of fashion, and closely nipping at their heels in popularity are the Maltese, Welsh corgi, bichon frise, and West Highland white.

Also currently surging in demand are the "doodle" or "designer" dogs, mixes of poodles and every breed under the sun. The large breed Labradoodle (Labrador retriever and poodle mix) and Goldendoodle (golden retriever and poodle) are now in high demand, but smaller doodles have been around for years. Although the practice has always been frowned upon by serious dog people, dog owners have always paired up little dogs of differing pedigrees. These smaller mixes are now riding a wave of popularity on the tails of their bigger doodle counterparts.

Groomers have long been familiar with the popular Cocker-Poo, a small- to medium-size mix of cocker spaniel and poodle that comes in the full spectrum of poodle colors. Then there is the Schnoodle (miniature schnauzer/poodle), Peke-a-Poo (Pekingese/poodle), Yorki-Poo (Yorkshire terrier/poodle), Chi-Poo (Chihuahua/poodle), Shi-Poo (shih tzu/poodle), Malti-Poo (Maltese/poodle), Bich-Poo (bichon frise/poodle), Lhasa-Poo (Lhasa apso/poodle), and Westi-Poo (West Highland white/poodle).

Alert!

If you decide on the ever-popular Chihuahua, your dog should always be in your care, not allowed to play unsupervised outdoors.

In addition to their unique teddy-bear looks, these dogs are nonshedding, a prized legacy from their poodle parent. If you are one of the millions who suffer from allergies and asthma, the idea of owning a hypoallergenic dog could be very appealing.

Because poodle mixes obviously don't come with a pedigree, there is no guarantee they will not shed. Sometimes it takes a few generations of selective breeding to produce a truly hypoallergenic dog. If you want a known quantity, several nonshedding small purebreds are available, including the poodle, bichon frise, and Maltese.

You also now routinely see such canine concoctions as Chia-Pins (Chihuahua/miniature pinscher), Buggles (beagle/pug), Bugs (Boston terrier/pug), Dorgis (dachshund/corgi), Chitzus (Chihuahua/shih tzu), and Shi-Lhas (shih tzu/Lhasas)

While mixing pure breeds is considered indiscriminate by devoted breeders and the AKC, combining different breeds is nothing new. When you research the history of any breed, you will find a diverse cast of ancestors that added size, color, coat type, spirit, and spunk to create the breeds we know today. There is also the factor known as "hybrid vigor." Because mixes (known less flatteringly as mongrels or mutts) come from different breeds, they are less likely to inherit breed-specific health maladies such as hip dysplasia, problems with their liver, eyesight, heart, or kidneys, or the high incidence of cancer now prevalent in some breeds that share closely bred foundation stock.

 Essential

Regardless of which dogs are being bred, it's important for the breeder to know their medical histories. Some inexperienced people are jumping on the doodle-dog bandwagon without screening for health problems and temperament issues. Although there are no guarantees that any dog will be free of health problems, you need to consider the unpredictability factor and ask for references about other pups sold by that breeder when considering such a designer pup.

Unlike doodle dogs, most mixed-breed pups are the result of accidental breeding. Sadly, the shelters are full of these dogs, and the small ones are usually adopted first. Mutts are an all-American tradition with an appeal all their own. When you adopt one, you'll be saving a life as well as gaining a wonderful pet.

American Kennel Club Breed Standards

The standard of a particular breed is nothing more than a written description of how an ideal dog of that breed should look, move, and behave. The breed standard details a group of characteristics that define a particular breed, covering size, proportion, carriage, details of the head and body, coat, color, and personality.

The breed standard is an ideal of perfection. Just like the people who love them, not many dogs are perfect, but a dog need not be perfect to win points toward a championship at an AKC-sanctioned show. In reality, the show dog is not really in competition with its peers but with the judge's interpretation of the perfect breed specimen and how that dog measures up. Although the AKC is the largest and best-known registry of purebred dogs, hundreds of breeds throughout the world do not have AKC recognition.

Those breeds officially recognized by the AKC are cataloged in an AKC studbook. Prior recognition by other registries would help prove that a breed has been well established, a big factor in gaining AKC recognition. Before the AKC considers adding a breed to its registry, its board of directors must be convinced that there is sufficient interest and widespread activity within that breed. If it meets those criteria, the breed is first admitted to the Miscellaneous Class. Although they may compete in conformation shows, these dogs are only allowed to compete within the Miscellaneous Class and are not eligible for championship points. Dogs can compete against other purebreds in regular classes and work toward AKC championships.

When it comes to dog breeds, humans have been pretty busy for thousands of years. Some breeds can be traced back to the Roman Empire or ancient Egypt, some to the Middle Ages and the palaces of emperors and kings. All breeds were developed for particular purposes such as herding, hunting, pulling sleds, hauling carts, or serving as treasured companions, a role every dog deserves. When we study the origins of the small breeds, we discover a fascinating history as diverse as these dogs themselves.

Popular Toy Breeds

Toy dogs are primarily companion pets. Many of these breeds started out much larger and heavier than they are today and have been bred down to the small sizes we now know and enjoy. Generations of selective breeding have produced this cast of lovable munchkins for you to explore, in alphabetical order.

Affenpinscher

Dubbed the monkey dog because of its flat nose, round eyes, jutting jaw, and whiskery face, this scruffy toy terrier originated in seventeenth-century Germany, where it was probably crossed with small pinschers and used to hunt vermin. Impish in personality, it makes a great dog for families with older children and needs little exercise. Its hard shaggy coat, usually black or gray, requires regular brushing and occasional tidying up. A mercurial little charmer, the affenpinscher's mood can range from stubborn to playful to deeply affectionate—all within a half hour or so!

Brussels Griffon

Another terrier-type toy, at eight to twelve pounds this little gamin is a bit sturdier than the affenpinscher, one of its probable forbears back in Belgium. The Brussels griffon comes in a smooth variety, but the wire-coated version is better known. Its hard coat, usually red but also beige, black, and tan and black, needs regular brushing and occasional hand-stripping. Its gremlin-face needs occasional tidying to accentuate its domed skull, neat ears, and sparkling eyes. Easy to train and always amusing, the Brussels griffon needs minimal exercise and makes a good family pet but can be wary of young children.

 Fact

Originally a peasant's dog, the Brussels griffon was an avid ratter used in the stable that grew popular as it rode around seated next to the driver in hansom cabs.

Chihuahua

Named for its home state in Mexico where it was discovered in 1850, this is the oldest purebred North American dog. Available in both a smooth and long-coated version and usually weighing no more than six pounds, the Chihuahua makes the perfect portable pet, if you spend time on proper socialization. The smooth variety needs only a weekly rub from a rubber curry, the longhaired version a good weekly brushing. This tiny companion can be litter-box trained and beyond loving attention, a cozy spot to curl up, and a warm winter coat, its needs are minimal. Not a good choice if you have small children, the Chihuahua feels safest and happiest with adults and may be nippy when it feels threatened.

Chinese Crested

Available in hairless and powderpuff varieties, this ancient breed is now virtually extinct in its native land. Fortunately, these affectionate companions accompanied Chinese explorers and traders to far-flung ports. The hairless version of the Chinese crested is not completely naked. It has a tuft on its head––its namesake crest––a plume on its tail, and shaggy socks, but the rest of its smooth body needs regular moisturizing and sunscreen when it goes outdoors.

Alert!

The skin of the hairless Chinese crested needs to be moisturized and protected with sunscreen. This dog also needs a coat in cold weather.

Weighing up to ten pounds and no taller than thirteen inches, the Chinese crested like to grasp toys with their paws and hug their owners. Due to their unusual appearance, these dogs are an acquired taste, but they make wonderful pets. Burlesque queen Gypsy Rose Lee was an avid fancier and breeder.

English Toy Spaniel

Similar to the cavalier King Charles smaller but smaller at ten to eleven inches and eight to fourteen pounds, the toy spaniel's long silky coat comes in four colors: Blenheim (red and white); ruby; Prince Charles (white with black-and-tan markings); and King Charles (black and tan). It needs brushing twice a week. The quintessential lap dog, the toy spaniel's roots are in the Orient, but its greatest popularity came in fifteenth- and six-teenth-century Europe where it was the beloved "comforter dog" of royalty, including Mary, Queen of Scots. Its intelligence, trainability, and gentle disposition make the toy spaniel a great family pet, but children must be taught to be very gentle with this little dog.

Italian Greyhound

Standing thirteen to fifteen inches tall and weighing about eight pounds, the smallest of the sight hounds was bred down from larger counterparts that were popular in ancient Egypt where greyhounds were mummified and carved into tombs. The miniature Italian version was bred to be the darling of aristocratic ladies, including princesses and queens. It enjoyed hunting small game and still delights in a good run. Elegant, lovable, and easy to train, this streamlined pet needs warm clothing in winter and is highly adaptable to apartment living. Its grooming needs are as basic as it gets—a weekly wipe-down with a chamois cloth. It's too delicate for roughhouse play with children and can be timid with strangers.

Japanese Chin

Originating in Asia, the Japanese Chin was bred as a lapdog for the imperial aristocracy. Once fed only on rice and sake to keep them tiny, dogs of this breed now come in two sizes—over or under seven pounds—but smaller is still considered better. Most frequently seen in black and white but also available in a variety of colors, the Japanese Chin's profuse coat needs brushing several times a week. With their trademark high-stepping gait, Chins make charming companions, perfect apartment dwellers that do well with older children.

 Fact

Commodore Matthew Perry presented Queen Victoria with a breeding pair of Japanese Chins. Credited with opening Japan to international trade in the mid-nineteenth century, Perry was a devoted dog lover who also introduced the Japanese spaniel to the Western world.

Maltese

Whether descended from terriers, spaniels, or a bichon prototype, this ancient snow-white breed was said to have been brought to Malta by Phoenician sailors around 1000 B.C. Bred as companions, they were the lap and sleeve dogs of royalty. Playful and full of personality, this glamorous dog has a flowing single coat worn parted down its back, with its head traditionally styled in two topknots. It does not shed but is high-maintenance in terms of grooming, needing frequent brushing and combing to keep those tresses from tangling. To make life easier, many pet owners keep it trimmed. This gorgeous little dog with the coal-black eyes stands four to six inches tall and weighs from four to six pounds. Great in small quarters and with children who have been taught to handle it properly, the Maltese's exercise needs can be met by indoor play and occasional walks.

Miniature Pinscher

Tenth in popularity among small dogs, the "min-pin" is a big dog in a small package. It was bred down to its tiny size (ten pounds, ten to twelve-and-a-half inches) from the German pinscher in the late 1800s. There may have been some dachshund and Italian greyhound genes in the mix as well. With its prancing gait and show-off tendencies, this dog is a natural in the show ring. Its coat is smooth as glass and comes in black, black and tan, or red. Its ears are either erect or cropped, and its tail docked like the larger pinschers. Min-pins are not lapdogs. They are a challenge to train because they try to outwit you but are lively, mischievous, and protective. While they don't dislike children, they will not tolerate mishandling.

Papillon

Another living toy of European royalty, the papillon's name means "butterfly" in French. Originally known as a Continental toy or dwarf spaniel, it began endearing itself to the ladies of the Spanish court back in the twelfth century. Its popularity spread throughout Europe and especially to France, where its fanciers included Madame Pompadour and Marie Antoinette, but this symbol of the ruling classes was nearly wiped out after the French Revolution. There are several theories explaining how the papillon acquired its trademark "butterfly" look with the erect fringed ears. One says it was inter-bred with the spitz and possibly the Chihuahua, while another theory maintains prick-eared spaniels were culled and selectively interbred to achieve this result.

The drop-eared version of the breed, known as the phalene (French for moth, rather than butterfly) is now quite rare. Papillons love to bark and be with people. Their coats require regular brushing and combing to keep mats at bay. Weighing eight to ten pounds, this dog does well in most climates and living situations. It loves children but they must be taught that it really is a dog, not a toy.

Pekingese

Named for the city where they were held sacred, these dogs were members of the imperial court for eight centuries. At one point, 4,000 eunuchs were assigned the sole purpose of breeding and raising these living icons, also known as Lion Dogs. When the British sacked Peking in 1860, all of the Pekingese dogs were ordered destroyed so that none would fall into the hands of the invaders. Two survivors were brought back to England and presented to Queen Victoria.

Standing six to ten inches tall and weighing under fourteen pounds, the Pekingese has an unforgettable look, a flowing bundle of fur floating along with a rolling gait. Its thick double coat demands daily brushing and broad head, fringed ears, pushed in nose, and distinctive wrinkles give them a unique appearance. Self-assured, strong-willed, and choosy in its affections, the Peke is not suitable for a family with children but can live quite happily in any space with a devoted owner. It does well with little exercise, especially in hot weather when its short muzzle can cause difficulty in breathing.

Pomeranian

The smallest of the Northern breeds, the Pomeranian is a four-legged fluffball with its thick double coat, small pointed ears, and bushy curled tail up over its back. Originating in the Baltic region known as Pomerania, this tiny toy spitz dog captivated Queen Victoria when it was brought to England, and the Pom soon became a favorite of the noble ladies. Only nine inches tall and weighing under five pounds, most Poms are solid-colored in white, black, brown, or orange. The breed's bouffant coat does best with daily brushing, and its exercise needs are minimal. A good little watchdog that is affectionate with its owners, it is mistrustful of strangers and wary of children.

Pug

Another unique and ancient dog from China, where it flourished before 400 B.C., the pug was first documented in Buddhist monasteries in Tibet. Brought to Holland by traders from the Dutch East India Company, it became the official dog of the House of Orange. Two centuries later, a pug named Fortune was the treasured companion of Napoleon's wife, the empress Josephine. Pugs were brought back to England after the sacking of Peking along with other prized canine booty, the Pekingese and shih tzu. Devotees included the Duke and Duchess of Windsor as well as Winston Churchill.

Compact in build, this endearing dog with its round wrinkled face and curled tail comes in fawn and black. It stands ten to eleven inches tall and weighs fourteen to eighteen pounds. It lives to please its family and thrives on love and attention, though it will hold a grudge if mistreated. The pug is great with children but prone to breathing problems in warm weather and obesity if overindulged. Its short coat sheds profusely, requiring regular attention with a curry brush.

Shih Tzu

With roots in Tibet stretching back to the first century, this exquisite dog with the flowing coat was brought to China in the seventeenth century, where it became a favorite in the Imperial courts. Called the chrysanthemum dog because of the way its facial hair sprouts in all directions, the shih tzu is a dwarf version of the Tibetan terrier, possibly with the Pekingese and Lhasa apso. The breed was all but destroyed during the British sacking of Peking in 1860, and the remnants were nearly eliminated a second time after the 1949 Communist takeover, but somehow the shih tzu was saved from extinction. Less wary than the Lhasa, the shih tzu is a living love object with a bit of the clown in its personality. At nine to ten inches in height and weighing nine to sixteen pounds, it comes in a rainbow of colors. The shih tzu is neither the easiest dog to train nor the best watchdog, but its personality overrules its drawbacks, the biggest of which is the maintenance of its coat. If kept long, the coat requires daily brushing, so many owners make life easier by keeping their shih tzu in a shorter trim. A small apartment and a daily walk or play session will suit this dog just fine.

Silky Terrier

Often confused with the Yorkshire terrier, the silky terrier was developed in Australia by crossing the Yorkie with the Australian terrier. This tough little tyke was a formidable hunter of mice and other small mammals. With larger ears and a longer muzzle than the Yorkie, it stands nine inches tall and weighs under ten pounds. Its longer back is a likely result of crossbreeding with Skye and Dandie Dinmont terriers. The silky's silvery hair is worn parted down the middle and falls to its knees, not draping to the floor like the Yorkie coat, but it needs the same frequent brushing and combing to keep it tangle-free. Loyal and territorial, the silky likes to bark as it guards the home and can be aggressive to strange people and other dogs. It adores children, as long as they treat it with care.

Toy Fox Terrier

Newly recognized by the AKC as a separate breed, the toy fox is a smaller version of the smooth fox terrier. Tiny at under seven pounds, tricolored and smooth-coated, it's also known as the Amer-Toy. Wash-and-wear pets that fulfill their own exercise needs, these jaunty little sprites couldn't be better suited to apartment living, but they retain the instincts of the tough little ratters they once were. The Web site of the American Toy Fox Terrier Club states: "The TFT is a big dog in a little package. He considers himself 'Superdog,' making it clear that he has a huge ego, and will dominate almost every situation." The breed's sharp intelligence and keen hearing make this a great service dog for the physically challenged and hearing-impaired. With its erect ears and little stub tail, the toy fox makes an endearing companion but should not be paired with very young children.

Yorkshire Terrier

This diminutive dandy had humble beginnings as a ratter among the farmers, miners, and weavers of Scotland, who developed the breed from a conglomeration of Scottish and English terriers, some of which are now extinct, and probably the Maltese as well. The Scotsmen brought the little dogs with them to Yorkshire, England, and the rest is history. Although it is among the most beautiful of dogs with its silky flowing coat, the Yorkie retains a true terrier temperament, fearless, feisty, and bold. Kept long, its coat requires daily brushing, so many owners opt for a shorter, easier-to-maintain trim. A busybody that keeps tabs on its family, the Yorkie is playful and mischievous. Although under seven pounds and only nine inches tall, the Yorkie thinks it's a big dog and relishes the role of ferocious watchdog. Born black and tan, in adulthood the black coat turns steel blue, and most Yorkies sport a topknot to keep the hair out of their eyes. A fine companion and therapy dog, it has been a great favorite in the United States since it arrived here in the late 1800s. Due to its size, small children pose a threat to its safety.

Toy Poodle

The smallest of the three poodle varieties, the toy poodle was bred down from its larger and older cousins in France during the eighteenth century. Affectionate, smart, and clean as a whistle, this dog loves to play and be with its people. Its coat comes in blue, black, gray, silver, chocolate, apricot, café au lait, and cream. It should be professionally groomed every four to six weeks if you want the true poodle look. Besides its fancy show styles, the coat can be kept in shorter and more manageable pet trims, sometimes groomed to look like a tiny teddy bear. The toy poodle stands ten inches tall and weighs under ten pounds but some breeders have produced an even smaller version known as the teacup poodle. Smaller is not necessarily better; some of these tinier pets can be fragile and unhealthy. The toy poodle is a wonderful pet for older children who treat it with respect and makes a great therapy dog.

Chapter 3

A Little More to Love

Larger than the toys, a wide variety of dogs are still small enough to be part of the small dog family. These include many members of the Terrier Group, spunky dogs bred to banish vermin. Are the terriers terrible or terrific? It all depends on whether their alert and spunky personalities strike a chord in your heart. We also have guard dogs, those who got by on their looks alone, and breeds that survived on pure determination.

American Eskimo

This breed comes in three sizes, standard, miniature, and toy. The latter two fit our criteria, with the toy measuring nine to twelve inches and the miniature from twelve to fifteen inches at the withers. Usually snow-white but sometimes cream colored, this breed is America's version of the spitz, bearing all the hallmarks of a typical Nordic dog: prick ears, a thick double coat, and a bushy tail carried proudly over its back. The AKC standard describes it as "intelligent, alert, and friendly, although slightly conservative."

A natural watchdog, the Eskie is protective of its family and often shy with strangers. Once a popular circus dog, it learns tricks easily and excels in obedience training, which will also provide needed socialization. The Eskie is a snow bunny, with a double coat that acts as its snowsuit and needs lots of brushing, especially in the spring and fall when it sheds profusely.

Bichon Frise

Now riding a crest of popularity, the bichon frise is an adorable white puffball with a storied history of ups and downs. In the 1300s, sailors brought these dogs back to Europe from Tenerife. In France, Spain, and Italy, it became the darling of royalty, but after the French Revolution these dogs found themselves out on the streets, where only the strong survived. The bichon's winning personality and lovable nature helped it find new niches as an organ grinder's dog and circus performer.

 Essential

The bichon's history as a trendy trade item, royal plaything, circus dog, and street performer predated its role as a "yuppie puppy" status symbol of the 1980s. Today, it is appreciated for simply being itself—a cute and curly pet whose cheerful personality lifts the spirits of everyone it meets.

The bichon still loves the limelight, thriving on attention and always ready to entertain. With its dark eyes and black nose framed by a fluffy white face, members of this breed are beautiful, clean, and nonshedding. The bichon is easy to train but so sensitive that it needs a gentle hand. Sturdy and playful, it gets along with everyone, including other pets. To look its best, it needs daily brushing and professional styling every four to six weeks.

Dachshund

The number-one small breed in the United States, the dachshund comes in two sizes and three coat types. The miniature weighs nine to eleven pounds, in line with our definition of a small dog. Both versions come in smooth, wirehaired, or longhaired coat types and are available in a rainbow of single colors, two-color combinations, dapples, and brindles. Its grooming needs depend on coat type, from the low-maintenance smooth version to the setter-like coat of the longhair, which should be brushed daily, to the coarse-coated wirehair, which must occasionally be hand-stripped.

 **Fact**

The dachshund's ancestors were bred in Germany more than three centuries ago. Their original purpose was to dig their way into badger holes in search of their quarry.

Called a sausage dog, hot dog, and wiener dog, the Doxie will bring a smile to your face with its comical demeanor and winning personality. As originally developed, it was one formidable hunter, killing badgers that weighed as much as forty-five pounds. With that low-slung body perfectly suited for tunneling underground, it will happily dig up your flower bed in pursuit of who knows what. This mighty mite is versatile, excelling in obedience, tracking, agility, field trials, Earthdog events, and therapy work. Although the Doxie is a great family dog, children need to be taught how to handle it because its long back makes it prone to back problems.

Havanese

Another dog from the bichon family of the Mediterranean, the Havanese was brought to Cuba on merchant ships. Similar in size to the bichon frise, its coat is wavy rather than curly and varies in color from white to beige, brown, and gray. These dogs have a full-flowing coat, a style that requires plenty of upkeep to keep them from tangling.

Happy and lovable, the Havanese are growing in popularity as family pets. They are highly intelligent and will generally do fine in homes with other dogs. They aren't noisy dogs and they are easy to train. Clean and nonshedding, they do well in small spaces, but they crave daily exercise.

Lhasa Apso

With a history tracing back to 800 B.C. in its native Tibet, these dogs were symbols of good luck, exchanged as gifts but never sold. Bred to be sentinels at palaces and monasteries, these Lion Dogs still retain a wariness of strangers and use their sharp bark to announce visitors.

The Lhasa apso stands ten to eleven inches tall, with a flowing coat that comes in many colors. Glamorous in the show ring, these dogs require daily grooming especially their coats are kept long. They make good dogs for owners who won't let them dominate the household and are usually not compatible with small children.

 Fact

The Lhasa apso was first brought to the United States as a gift from the Dalai Lama.

Lowchen

In its traditional lion clip with shorn back and bouffant mane and chest, this is another dog associated with the King of Beasts. Originating in the

Mediterranean as a bichon type, this companion breed was developed in France and a favorite of fifteenth-century Florentine nobles. Almost extinct in the twentieth century, the breed was resurrected by Belgian fanciers. The lowchen is still rather rare but is gaining in popularity as a wonderful companion with a winning disposition. At eight to eighteen pounds, the unique-looking breed is under thirteen inches in height.

Lively and playful, the lowchen doesn't require a lot of exercise. It tends to be a long-living dog, and is peaceful and gentle. However, it is not well suited to small children. It needs a lot of loving attention, and frequent brushing and combing. The lowchen also tends to be pricey compared to other small breeds.

Miniature Schnauzer

Sixth in popularity for small dogs in the United States, the miniature schnauzer is named for its bearded muzzle (schnauze). Back in Germany, it was a ratter and watchdog, bred down from the standard schnauzer with affenpinscher in the mix as well. Standing twelve to fourteen inches tall at around fourteen pounds, its appearance is distinctive with its silver, salt-and-pepper, black-and-silver, or solid black coat, well-muscled body, and expressive face. Its appeal is based upon its handsome looks, fun-loving personality, high intelligence, and solid devotion to its family. It is sturdy enough to enjoy romping with children, thriving on such physical activity to keep it in high spirits. Highly sensitive to its owner's moods, its training should be consistent but gentle.

Schipperke

This black dog from Belgium earned its name, which translates to "little captain of the boat," on the canals of Flanders, where it served the dual purpose of guard dog and catcher of vermin. Tailless either by birth or through docking, the schipperke is handsome with its glossy black coat, pointed ears, and foxy face. It is bred in three sizes, all of which are under twenty pounds. Its coat is of several lengths, defined in the breed standard as having a thick ruff around the neck, a shorter cape over the shoulders, a "jabot" across the chest, and "culottes" on its rear thighs.

Waterproof with a downy layer underneath, the Skip needs regular brushing. Nosy and curious, the breed retains its watchdog tendencies, being reserved with strangers but patient and affectionate within the family circle. The smaller version is best for apartment living.

 **fact**

Documented as far back as the Middle Ages and evolved from Northern spitz dogs of Viking days, the schipperke is seen in many Flemish paintings.

Spaniels

Like terriers, spaniels were originally bred to be hunting dogs. They are active and excitable and would be a good choice for active owners who enjoy taking them out for regular exercise. They need frequent brushing, so unless you are prepared to spend time grooming them or to take them to a professional groomer, they probably aren't the best choice for you. Spaniels tend to show more submissive behavior than other breeds, so they aren't overly aggressive or hard to manage, although they need firm discipline.

Cavalier King Charles Spaniel

Growing in popularity in the United States as more people become familiar with this beautiful small spaniel, the cavalier King Charles fulfills all the criteria for a great family pet. It was named for "Cavalier" King Charles II, who ruled Great Britain in the 1700s. The breed was brought back from the point of extinction in the early twentieth century. Like all small spaniels that were the lap- and foot-warmers of nobility, it probably had ancient Oriental toy breeds as well as sporting spaniels in its ancestry.

At twelve to thirteen inches tall, this spaniel weighs ten to eighteen pounds. A daily walk or play session will fulfill its exercise requirements. Its gently waving silken coat needs frequent brushing and is worn naturally, not clipped. Usually seen in the red-and-white coloration, the cavalier King Charles also comes in a variety of colors and combinations. Steadfast in its devotion to family, patient and loving with children, it does well in obedience and adapts to any situation.

Tibetan Spaniel

Loving and bright, in ancient times this breed was both a revered watchdog and a treasured companion, roles it excels at to this day, standing ten inches tall and weighing nine to fifteen pounds. Its thick medium-length coat, usually golden but also seen in other colors and combinations, does well with a weekly brushing. The Tibetan spaniel likes children and other pets, is easy to train and eager to please, and a daily walk or romp in the yard will keep it fit and happy. This breed remains one of the best-kept secrets of the small dog world.

Terriers

Most terriers are small dogs. Because they were originally used to hunt, especially for vermin, they are energetic diggers. Their lively hunting nature also makes them prone to chasing anything that moves. Sturdy and muscular, terriers require a fair amount of exercise. In general, their temperaments are easygoing, and they adapt well to the sometimes-chaotic demands of city living.

Australian Terrier

Like most short-legged terrier breeds, this terrier's ancestors came from Scotland and England. Brought to Australia with early settlers, its rough-and-ready persona and all-around working skills were developed in the outback where it hunted, guarded the homestead, and even herded sheep. Small in stature at ten inches tall and twelve to fourteen pounds, and blue and tan or sandy in color, its rugged coat is maintained by weekly brushing and occasional hand-stripping to preserve its hard texture. Confident and affectionate, the Aussie terrier makes a great housedog and enjoys children. It needs frequent walks and backyard romps to keep it happy. This breed can be a bit stubborn, and its history as a ratter could cause problems if other household pets include any members of the rodent family.

Border Terrier

Among the oldest of the terrier breeds, the Border was an all-around farm dog with the versatility to hunt badgers and otters as well as to guard the home and keep vermin at bay. Originating in the hardscrabble hill country between England and Scotland, it has adapted well to city life.

At ten inches in height and weighing eleven or twelve pounds, its coat is red to wheaten, grizzle with tan, or blue with tan. Its harsh dense coat should be brushed weekly and may be hand-stripped but should not be clippered. Affectionate and plucky, this dog's adventurous nature may cause it to wander, and it can show aggression to dogs it does not know but it makes a great family pet.

Boston Terrier

With its sleek coat and unflappable disposition, it makes an exceptional companion for older children and adults of any age. Grooming is minimal for this wash-and-wear dog that weighs under twenty-five pounds. It loves to play and have a daily walk.

Question?

Did Boston terriers really come from Boston?
Bred in the United States, this little gentleman of the dog world was developed in the city for which it was named for in the 1870s. The refined Boston terrier's ancestors were originally bred for pit fighting.

Bred from larger bulldogs and terriers, it exhibits none of the aggression of its fighting forbears but is confident enough not to back down when challenged. It does not do well with temperature extremes, being subject to heatstroke in hot weather and needing the protection of a coat or sweater in cold climates. It is easy to train and eager to please.

Cairn Terrier

Named for a pile of rocks used as boundary markers in the Scottish Highlands, this dog dates back 500 years in its native land. Those rock piles made perfect hiding places for foxes, badgers, and other wild creatures, and these scrappy terriers were dispatched by the Scottish lairds to dig in and kill such quarry. Sturdy and rough-coated, the cairn terrier needs regular brushing but should retain its trademark tousled look. Like their hunting ancestors, they still love to dig and will live happily in a busy household with children or as the devoted companion of a single adult.

Dandie Dinmont Terrier

This short-legged long-backed terrier hails from the borderlands between England and Scotland, where it was bred in the 1600s to hunt badgers and otters. Only eight to eleven inches tall and almost twice as long, it sports a fluffy topknot, tasseled ears, and large expressive eyes. Its silvery hair is part crisp and part silky and requires regular brushing and occasional hand-stripping. A bit stubborn and too independent to be a lapdog, the Dandie retains the personality of a tough little terrier but loves its family and relishes walks and outdoor play, especially with children.

Fox Terrier

Seen in two versions, smooth and wire, both were bred to be hunting terriers, carried on horseback to be set loose once the hound pack had cornered its quarry.

At sixteen to eighteen pounds and standing around fifteen inches tall, the fox terrier has remained unchanged since its heyday in England in centuries past. The smooth variety needs little in the way of grooming, but to maintain its rough coat, the wire version should be brushed twice a week and hand-stripped every few months. Many owners opt to have these handsome dogs clippered instead. Clean and lively, fox terriers like to bark. They love children and need lots of exercise to keep them occupied.

Lakeland Terrier

From the lake districts of northern England, this dog was bred to be a no-nonsense working terrier that went to ground after the fox and killed it where it lived. Also called the Patterdale terrier, its wiry coat comes in combinations of brown, black, and blue. It is groomed like the wire fox but has a distinct fall of hair between its eyes. Standing thirteen to fifteen inches in height, it weighs seventeen pounds. A down-to-earth dog that needs regular brushing, the Lakeland is good with children and has lots of energy and personality.

Manchester Terrier

This elegant black-and-tan dog comes in two sizes, both fitting our guidelines as small dogs. The toy version weighs seven to twelve pounds, while the larger weighs in under twenty-two pounds. Developed in Manchester, England, from the black-and-tan terrier and the whippet, this dog was a courser (racer) and a ratter par excellence. Its smooth glossy coat, intelligence, and watchdog tendencies make it a good choice for almost any situation, but the toy variety needs protection from young children.

Norfolk and Norwich Terriers

These little terriers are the same size, at ten inches in height and eleven to twelve pounds, with the drop-eared Norfolk terrier originally considered a variety of the erect-eared Norwich. Both are now separate breeds, with an identical history in England where they were farm dogs and hunters. Once they made it to the United States, they were used in packs to go to ground after prey after the foxhounds had done their job. When these happy little red-to-wheaten dogs are kept in natural coat, they need regular brushing and occasionally hand-stripping. They make good housedogs, are even-tempered with children, and can live happily in the city if frequently walked to burn off their terrier energy.

Parson Russell Terrier

One of the most active and exuberant of the terriers, this dog formerly known as the Jack Russell terrier is bred in both a smooth and rough-coated variety and is natural in appearance. It was bred for its narrow chest to fit into burrows, and enough leg and body length to run swiftly on the hunt. From twelve to fifteen inches in height and around twenty-five pounds, it is predominantly white, with black and/or tan markings. This bold and friendly breed is athletic and clever and can climb or dig its way out of just about anywhere. Around the house, it is playful, attentive, and affectionate but it so spirited that it will constantly test and surprise you.

 **Fact**

Jack Russell terriers (recently renamed Parson Russell terriers) were used in the hunt, flushing foxes from their dens, and hunting and killing rats.

Scottish Terrier

Originally bred in the Aberdeen area, the Scottie is a strong-willed and energetic terrier that once employed its hunting skills against rats, foxes, and weasels, pursuing them into their burrows. Standing ten inches tall at about twenty pounds, it cuts a striking figure with its long beard, prominent eyebrows, sharply pointed ears, and alert demeanor. With its wiry topcoat and dense undercoat, the Scottie requires frequent grooming. One of the more dominant terriers, it needs a firm hand in training and is not always tolerant of children. It is adaptable to apartment living as long as it gets lots of walks.

Sealyham Terrier

The same height and weight as the Scottie, this stout-hearted dog originated on the estate of Captain John Edwardes in Sealyham, Wales, where it hunted everything from rats to polecats. Dignified in appearance with drop ears and a distinctive fall of hair cascading down its nose, the Sealyham enjoys people and has a great sense of humor. They do well in obedience training with owners who command their respect.

Although the Sealy makes a great companion, it is a willful dog that will not tolerate teasing or rough handling from children. Its weather-resistant double coat comes in white or white with lemon, tan, or gray markings on its head and ears. The Sealy's coat needs frequent brushing and professional grooming every few months.

Skye Terrier

Hailing from the Isle of Skye in Scotland's Hebrides Islands, this low-slung long-backed dog is a hard worker that dates back to the seventeenth century. Standing ten inches tall and weighing about twenty pounds, the Skye terrier was bred to be a ferocious hunter of vermin. It later gained popularity as a royal companion in Victorian England. Its flowing coat is parted down the middle of its back and falls over its eyes. Tough-minded with a need for outdoor romps and long walks, the Skye terrier makes a loyal companion that usually bonds to one favorite person. An excellent watchdog, it is not the best choice for families with small children.

Welsh Terrier

This black-and-tan terrier from Wales looks like a miniature Airedale, with the same kind of wiry coat that is hand-stripped for the show ring. Always a sporting terrier, it was bred as a ratter that also hunted badgers and otters. Weighing twenty pounds and standing fifteen inches tall, its legs were long enough to keep up with the horses and it could climb the rugged hills and swim the streams as well. This handsome dog is good-natured enough to be a great family pet and a lovable buddy for children, but its family should be able to match its love of play and high energy. As long as its exercise needs are met, the Welshie can live happily in any setting.

West Highland White Terrier

The Westie has been known by many names: Highlander, white Scottish terrier, Poltalloch terrier, and Roseneath terrier, after the estate of an early fancier, the Duke of Argyll. Like most terriers, it was bred to track, unearth, and destroy vermin, but its engaging personality and hardy character has made the Westie a prized companion as well. At ten to eleven inches tall and around twenty pounds, with its flashy white coat, dark eyes, black button nose, pointed ears, and round dish of a face, it looks the way it is: cheerful, curious, and plucky. It needs a good brush-out once a week. The Westie can be a trickster during training, and it thrives on toys, games, and outdoor fun to keep it from getting into mischief. Clean and friendly, it makes a great family pet in all situations.

Chapter 4

Choosing the Right Small Breed

Dogs are individuals, just like the people who love them. Their personalities are influenced by several factors: breed, genetic inheritance, health, socialization, and the way they are treated. As you begin your search for the right small dog, you need to take all these factors into consideration. When looking for that canine/human match made in heaven, remember that you play a big part in the equation, too!

Researching Small Dog Breeds

Surfing the AKC Web site, attending a dog show (or watching one on television), taking a trip to the local grooming salon, observing a dog obedience class, or supporting a dog-walking fundraiser in the park will give you an overview of small dogs in all their wonderful variety. Talking to dog-owning friends and reading books on the subject will further expand your knowledge. Dog breeds did not just happen randomly. Each breed was carefully developed with a specific purpose in mind. When considering a small dog, you should think long and hard about why its particular breed came into being.

Terriers: Terrific or Terrible?

The answer to this question depends on your point of view. Their name derives from the Latin *terra*, meaning "earth." This alludes to their intended function, to dig into the ground in search of vermin. The small terrier breeds are all genetically predisposed with this hunting drive. It makes them aggressive in pursuit of prey, whether it's a squirrel in your backyard, a squeaky toy, the neighbor's cat, or the dog next to it at obedience class.

 fact

Small terriers and dachshunds can be rewarded for just being themselves in AKC-sanctioned Earthdog trials, earning titles for their inborn talent at going to ground in pursuit of rats (caged for humane reasons) or scent-laden artificial quarry.

Thankfully, not many of us have a vermin problem these days, but these little dogs remain focused on their mission. After all, it was their reason for living back in the days when they had to earn their keep. It makes them strong-willed and fearless; many were pitted against quarry two or three times their size. Mixing it up with badgers, foxes, otters, weasels, and rats was a tough duty, often a matter of life or death for these little warriors. Consequently, they also developed a high tolerance for pain. Some have wiry coats that protected them like a suit of armor as they launched themselves into the bramble bushes or tunneled underground in hot pursuit.

Small terriers still have feisty personalities. If you are attracted to such spirited companions, you will admire their spunk and delight in their toughness. On the other hand, if you want a docile companion that is a snap to train, you may think these little characters have an attitude problem. In general, terriers make wonderful, fun-loving pets. But when it comes to training, they require owners who appreciate their lively personalities and whose determination matches their own. If that person is you, get busy doing your homework, researching the small terrier breeds.

Essential

Because small terriers love to dig, they will be happy to unearth those bulbs you just planted and to dig their way to freedom. A fenced-in yard is wonderful, as long as you make sure there are no gaps a small dog can squeeze through. A wire-mesh barrier along the bottom of the fence can keep your little Houdini at home.

Terriers vary in terms of size, coat care, degree of independence and dominance, compatibility with children, and need for exercise. The AKC Web site (*www.akc.org*) is a great place to learn about them. As already noted, the terriers have a group of their own, but a few tiny members are also found in the Toy Group: the Yorkshire, silky, toy fox, and toy Manchester terriers. In that same group are also a couple of small dogs with a healthy dose of terrier in their genetic makeup. For instance, the affenpinscher and Brussels griffon both used to hunt vermin in their early days. These droll little characters owe their impish personalities and harsh coats to their terrier heritage.

Toys and Companions

Many toys were bred to be companions, status symbols of the ruling classes that were themselves pampered like royalty. These breeds were not created to be single-minded and purposeful like terriers, hunters, or herders. Consequently, they do not have the built-in attention span of their hardworking canine counterparts.

It's not that toy breeds didn't have a job. Their purpose in life was to look drop-dead beautiful or captivatingly cute, to serve as fashionable accessories, to warm the bed at night, and, since they were often presented as gifts or bribes, to grease the wheels of the social system. Their "trophy dog" past does not necessarily make them the dim bulbs of the dog world. In the hands of a devoted owner, they can easily master the rudiments of obedience training. Your single-minded focus upon your small companion will help sharpen its own focus, helping it to master the task at hand.

Companion dogs were also bred to entertain. This makes them lively, responsive, and playful in temperament. It also makes us happy to have little buddies that are sensitive to our every mood. They have the inbred ability to cheer us up no matter what else is going on in our lives. It's their history—they were supposed to be the life of the party, not wallflowers or bores!

Fact

According to tradition in ancient China, four Pekingese were chosen as the emperor's royal bodyguards. Two walked ahead as he made his way down the palace halls, their sharp barks announcing his arrival. The other two followed behind, the hem of the emperor's flowing robe held firmly in their mouths.

In the Toy Group, the cavalier King Charles, English toy spaniel, Tibetan spaniel, Japanese Chin, Chinese crested, Havanese, Maltese, papillon, Pomeranian, pug, and shih tzu are great companions, lovable playmates, and effective lap-warmers. In the Non-Sporting Group, small dogs bred for this social butterfly/love-object role are the bichon frise, poodle, and Low-chen. The Lhasa apso served a dual role as palace sentinel and treasured companion and still has the tendency to guard and protect, as does the schipperke, the famed boat dog of Belgium, and the American Eskimo, a good companion and excellent watchdog. The Pekingese retains its air of royalty and still enjoys being worshiped and pampered.

Poodles have their own unique history. Evolved from large-size hunting retrievers into darlings of European royalty as they were bred down in size, they becoming living objets d'art in the court of Louis XVI of France. Circus dogs, truffle hunters, fashion statements, and companions of kings and queens, poodles still rank high in popularity, making graceful, clean, and affectionate pets. The Bolognese and Coton de Tulear, not yet recognized as AKC breeds, also fit nicely into this companion category. Other toy breeds to consider are the Chihuahua and Italian greyhound, both true companions with unique personalities.

Factors to Consider

Choosing the breed that most appeals to you is a highly individual matter. Many factors play into your decision to focus upon a particular breed. Looks, temperament, size, coat type and grooming requirements, sex, age, health issues, and how it will fit into your particular lifestyle are important considerations.

There's no need to stress out about your decision, however. Several breeds will likely fill the bill, easily capturing your heart. This is a process that will be both educational and fun-filled as you learn about these wonderful small companions in all their variety. Let's begin with the head-turning factor.

Looks

Usually, the first thing that draws us to a particular breed is its appearance. Some of us are awestruck by the majestic coat of the Maltese, shih tzu, or Lhasa apso. Some are smitten by the tragic-comic face and stubby body of the pug as it ambles along with its rolling gait. The art deco elegance of the Italian greyhound or the regal appearance of the cavalier King Charles spaniel may attract us, or we may be drawn to the seal-like sleekness of the min-pin or Manchester terrier.

Some are delighted by smallness; the tinier the better. If so, the Yorkie, toy fox terrier, and Chihuahua may be the perfect pocket-size pet. Some are impressed by the poodle in all its perfectly coiffed perfection, while others might be turned off by that same fancy-pants image. Some fall hard for a cute little puppy in the pet shop. Some are infatuated by a dog breed spotted in a movie or television sitcom. Physical attraction is a highly subjective thing, but it may light the spark that draws you to a particular breed.

Temperament

This has to do with your own activity level as well as the dog in question. Are you a peppy person who would love a little live wire to run around the yard with you and your children, or are you the type whose idea of aerobic exercise is puttering around the apartment? Are you a homebody who craves a little love object to keep you company? Would combing the tresses of a tiny dog be as much fun for you as playing with a doll come to life?

Or are you in the market for a tail-wagging goodwill ambassador, a dog that befriends everyone it meets? If you must work long hours, you're probably looking for a laid-back little buddy that won't shred the sofa when it's left home alone.

Alert!

Many small terriers, tiny toy breeds, or small dogs bred to guard and protect have little tolerance for small children, whose high activity levels can make them cranky and nippy. A tiny dog's reaction to such a rowdy ruckus can range from quivering under the bed to a full-fledged panic attack to an aggressive attack mode.

Perhaps you would like a little partner to take to obedience classes. This "sport of dogs" provides a needed outlet for a dog's energy and desire to learn and gives both of you a great sense of accomplishment. Small dogs are no slouches when it comes to winning obedience titles, and they are more fun to watch than the big breeds as they sit, stay, come, and heel in total concentration. You might consider one of the following smarty-pants breeds:

- Dachshunds
- Poodles
- Chihuahuas
- Cavalier King Charles spaniels
- Pomeranians
- Papillons
- Yorkshire terriers
- Pugs
- Chinese crested
- Boston terriers
- Shih tzu
- Miniature pinschers
- Havanese
- Italian greyhounds

Serious competitors can keep going to earn advanced obedience titles, with the cream of the crop taking it all the way to national competition. There are lots of ways to keep your new best friend occupied if you have the time and desire to compete. Such activities also provide a wonderful way to make friends who share your passion for dogs.

Size

It's important to know how big that pup will grow before you bring it home. If you live in an apartment or condo, most small dogs will fit right in, but some are more high-spirited than others. The liveliest of the little guys are such terriers as the wire and smooth fox, Parson Russell, Manchester, and Lakeland. They are fairly active indoors and do best with forty-five minutes a day of outdoor walking or playing.

Question?

Will a small dog be comfortable in my apartment?
Small dogs can live happily wherever their owners live, as long as pets are allowed. They can always find a place to curl up and be comfy, usually on your lap or close by your side.

Another consideration is weight. If you must climb stairs, you may want a dog that can easily do so too or that won't be too heavy to carry. A Chihuahua, Yorkie, Pomeranian, toy fox terrier, English toy spaniel, Japanese Chin, or papillon would be easier to tote than a pug, Scottie, Westie, or Boston terrier.

Coat Type

A dog's coat type is a major consideration in picking your pup. While all dogs benefit from regular grooming, some coats demand far more time and attention than others. If you get a dog that's a heavy shedder––the American Eskimo, pug, or schipperke, for example––you'll need to brush it a few times a week to keep that hair from accumulating, turning to solid clumps in the coat known to groomers as "packing." If you get a full-coated breed and you want to keep its hair long, it will need daily brushing and combing to keep from becoming matted. If you pick a dog that needs professional trimming to look the way it's supposed to–like the poodle, bichon frise, miniature schnauzer, Scottie, or Westie––it will need to see the groomer at least every six weeks. At $30 to $45 per session depending upon your breed, region, and groomer's pricing, plan to spend from $360 to $540 per year if your dog needs professional trimming on a four-to-six-week basis. (See Chapter 10 to learn more about grooming requirements and home maintenance that can cut down on costs.) Grooming-wise, the easiest keepers are the smooth-coated breeds—the min-pin, smooth dachshund, Manchester terrier, smooth and toy fox terrier, Italian greyhound, and Boston terrier.

Question?

What dog would be good for someone with allergies?
If you or anyone in your household suffers from allergies, a nonshedding dog would suit you best. Consider the poodle, bichon frise, Maltese, and Chinese crested, or a dog you are certain is a poodle/terrier mix. The miniature schnauzer as well as the wire fox, Lakeland, and Welsh terrier are also good choices as they rarely shed.

Sex

For dogs of most breeds that are neutered or spayed, there is little or no difference in personality or temperament between males and females. Unless you plan to show and/or breed your dog, having it fixed is the best course of action. Intact or unneutered males are more aggressive, and they like to mark territory by urinating indoors and out on a walk. If they catch the scent of a female in heat, they can become obsessed to the point of not even caring about their food. Intact males are also inclined to wander off looking for romance.

Unless spayed, a bitch or female dog comes into heat, or estrus, twice a year. This is when she can get pregnant, so if you don't want a litter of little surprises from a neighborhood suitor, you must keep her confined. You can outfit her with a sanitary garment and give her pills to lessen that scent that drives the boys wild but realistically, you should never let her out of your sight. Usually lasting ten days, her heat will be accompanied by bleeding, also controlled by a pair of doggie britches or sanitary belt with removable pads.

Age

While there is nothing more appealing than a puppy, they are very labor-intensive in terms of housebreaking, training, and socializing. In its early days, a pup cannot go more than a few hours between meals and potty trips.

For some of us, raising our dogs from babyhood is an integral part of the experience and we wouldn't miss it for the world. For others, adopting a mature dog from a rescue group, breeder, or shelter may be a better alternative. You would be getting a dog that is already people-oriented and housebroken, beyond the demanding stages of puppyhood and adolescence—as a bonus, it may have had some obedience training as well. You also may be saving a life by adopting such a pet.

Health Issues

Purebred dogs of any breed all originate from the same gene pool. Because of this common ancestry, some breeds have a high incidence of hereditary health problems. Responsible breeders work to screen out such problems in the dogs they produce. Before you purchase a pup, it is vitally important to research any known hereditary problems that occur in the breed you are considering.

Short-muzzled dogs like the pug, Boston terrier, and Pekingese, for example, are at high risk for heatstroke, a life-threatening situation. (A dog's normal temperature is 101 to 102.5 degrees but when overheated, it can shoot up as high as 109, causing permanent organ damage even if the dog is resuscitated.) These dogs have trouble breathing in warm weather, so their activity should be restricted. They also tend to snuffle and snore, but true fanciers find that endearing!

In addition, the pug's pushed-in face puts it at risk if it needs anesthesia for surgery or even teeth cleaning. Most also need veterinary intervention when they whelp, often requiring a Caesarian section rather than a normal delivery. Their large protruding eyes are vulnerable to injury and infection, and the breed is also prone to skin problems. Like all breeds with facial wrinkles, they are also susceptible to entropion, the inversion of the eyelid that can cause severe irritation, a condition that can be corrected by surgery.

Miniature schnauzers are prone to von Willebrands disease, a problem related to blood clotting that can cause complications or require surgery when giving birth. Pancreatitis, Cushing's disease, cataracts, urinary tract infections, and a skin condition known as schnauzer bumps are also prevalent in this breed.

Essential

Many small breeds are susceptible to periodontal disease, so dental care is a must. In addition to soft food, they need chew toys and hard kibble to help remove the plaque that leads to gingivitis.

Tracheal collapse is common among small and toy breed dogs, especially as they age. With this condition, the normally rigid trachea or windpipe becomes softer and weaker, lessening the air supply to the lungs. Impaired breathing can occur after strenuous activity, stress, or overexcitement and can range from a mild discomfort and coughing to a life-threatening situation.

Blocked tear ducts occur frequently in the Maltese and shih tzu, causing tear staining. Facial hair that is constantly moist becomes a breeding ground for yeast and bacteria, resulting in a reddish-brown stain. Treatment of blocked ducts can vary from irrigation by the vet to surgery to reopen them. Cataracts are often seen in bichon frises, poodles, and Boston terriers.

Poodles are also prone to patellar luxation, a dislocation of the kneecap seen in other small breeds as well. Along with dachshunds and schnauzers, they also have a high incidence of epilepsy.

Dachshunds, Lhasa apsos, and other long-backed breeds are prone to degenerative disc disease, treatable by anti-inflammatory medication and/or surgery. Endocardiosis, a valve problem with the heart that can eventually lead to heart failure, is often seen in small breeds, as is Legg-Calve-Perthes disease, a malformation of the hip and thighbone.

Some small dogs are born with skin disorder called atopy, or allergic dermatitis. Puppies that scratch incessantly need to be taken to the vet for a diagnosis. Sometimes their discomfort and chewing at themselves can be caused by an allergic reaction to food or a substance in their environment. Some breeds are also prone to mange, a skin disease carried by mites detectable only under the vet's microscope. Although the condition may correct itself over time, such a pup would benefit from treatments to relieve the itch.

Doing your homework on a particular breed's health issues can save you a lot of heartache and money. You can educate yourself further by talking to a vet about the breed you are considering, consulting a breeder, and researching these issues online. Responsible breeders carefully select their breeding stock to keep hereditary conditions like hip dysplasia, eye problems, seizure disorder (epilepsy), brucellosis (a venereal disease), thyroid, and autoimmune diseases from their line if these conditions occur in breeds they produce.

Narrowing the Selection

Once you have made your list of the breeds you like, it's time to narrow down your options to find out which one suits you best. After considering the factors outlined in Chapter 1, such as children, space, and cost, you can rule out any breeds that seem inappropriate or unappealing. You can use an online search engine to get help finding your perfect match by entering the keywords "dog breed selector" or "dog breed quiz." You can also find any number of books on the subject.

If you have young children, you have probably ruled out the Chihuahua, Pekingese, Lhasa apso, and Scottish terrier for temperament reasons, along with all of the toy breeds except the pug. With school-age children, you may be considering the miniature schnauzer, miniature poodle, bichon frise, dachshund, shih tzu, Brussels griffon, pug, Boston terrier, West Highland white, cairn terrier, Border terrier, Australian terrier, Welsh terrier, cavalier King Charles spaniel, Tibetan spaniel, or schipperke. Many mixed breeds also make great family pets.

If you are a city dweller in a high-rise building or a senior citizen, your pick may be one of the toys. These petite pets can be litter-box trained, eliminating late-night elevator trips outside for their potty calls. Other highly adaptable pets that don't need a great deal of exercise are the Boston terrier, bichon frise, poodle, Chinese crested, and lowchen. If you think housebreaking and training a pup would present too much of a challenge, consider adopting an adult dog from a breed rescue group or a shelter.

If your budget would buckle under the grooming costs of longhaired breeds or those requiring regular precision styling by a professional groomer, consider the short- and smooth-coated breeds like the pug, Boston terrier, Chinese crested, min-pin, Manchester terrier, smooth fox terrier, smooth dachshund, Italian greyhound, or the short-haired Chihuahua.

If you want a lively little companion that is always up for a romp or a play session, perhaps the Parson Russell, fox, Border, Welsh, or Lakeland terriers or the American Eskimo would fill the bill. If you don't have a fenced backyard, these are probably not for you. When it comes to humorous little characters that will always bring a smile to your face, you can't beat the pug, min-pin, affenpinscher, Brussels griffon, Boston terrier, or dachshund. If elegance and glamour turn you on, it's hard to beat the Japanese Chin, Maltese, shih tzu, Lhasa apso, Havanese, papillon, English toy spaniel, cavalier King Charles spaniel, or Italian greyhound.

When You Think You're Ready

You're starting to get excited. You've got one special breed on your mind and you're getting a bit impatient to bring that baby home. Slow down. This is a good time to review your homework and answer some vital questions:

- Is everyone in your household onboard with this decision?
- Will you have time to housebreak, exercise, and train this new family member?
- Are your surroundings safe for the new arrival?
- Are you ready to make a lifelong commitment to this pet?

Remember that timing is everything. This is a decision that you will have to live with for many years, so don't make the jump until you are ready. Most breeders shy away from selling puppies at Christmas. The holiday season is just too hectic for you to give your new little family member the attention it deserves, and there are too many dangerous distractions, including Christmas ornaments, tinsel, lights that could be chewed, sweets and people treats that could make it sick, plus a revolving door of company. In all this activity, a pup could easily get injured or lost in the shuffle. Similarly, if you anticipate moving in the next several months, you would do well to wait until after you relocate. If winters are severe in your region, you'd be better off waiting for milder weather when housebreaking would be a lot easier on both you and your pup.

Chapter 5

Finding a Small Dog

You may already know exactly what kind of small dog you want to add to your family, or you may prefer to select a small dog from whatever is available at your local animal shelter. This chapter will help you find your new little friend, whether it's a mature dog from a shelter or a puppy from a trusted friend.

Local Animal Shelters

Animal shelters are run by counties, cities, towns, and private agencies. Sometimes a municipality will contract out these services to a shelter run by a humane organization, which takes in stray dogs and those turned in by their owners, making them available for adoption if they have not been claimed, usually after a week or ten days. By law, such publicly funded shelters need only to keep a dog an additional ten days before it may be euthanized.

Most dogs that end up in the shelter are beyond puppyhood. They are housebroken and have varying degrees of socialization and training. Like those available through breeder referral services, they have been given up for a myriad of reasons, ranging from misfortune and necessity to the purely frivolous. ("He grew too big.") Once at the shelter, they receive the basics in vet care, including vaccinations. Some shelters spay or neuter, while others offer discount certificates for the surgery to those who adopt. Microchipping for permanent identification is also becoming common for shelter pets.

 **Fact**

Thousands of mixed-breed small dogs are produced accidentally each year and end up at the shelter waiting for a home. Each one is unique and adorable, often more hardy than their purebred counterparts.

Obtaining a shelter dog should not be looked upon as a poor substitute for getting a purebred dog from a breeder. Even Hollywood trainers go looking for future canine stars at the shelter. (When *Benji* creator Joe Camp wanted to cast a new star for his 2002 sequel *Benji Returns: From Rags to Riches*, he conducted a three-month nationwide search for a shaggy little look-alike at shelters.)

Many pets are surrendered to the shelter because of behavior problems. When possible, shelter personnel work with such dogs to correct these problems to make them more adoptable. Due to budget and space constraints, this is far more likely to happen when services are contracted out to a humane society facility or when pets are held in a privately run shelter.

According to the Massachusetts Society for the Prevention of Cruelty to Animals (MSPCA), before you adopt a shelter pet, to ensure that you and the animal are a good fit, you should do the following:

- Spend some time with the dog that you are interested in. All members of the household should meet the prospective new family member (this includes your current dog, if you are looking to add a new dog).
- Complete an adoption application, and discuss it with an adoption counselor. This usually takes about forty-five minutes.
- If you are a homeowner, show proof of ownership (e.g., mortgage or tax bills).
- If you rent, have your landlord's written consent to bring an animal onto the property. This information will be verified before sending a new dog home.
- Be certain that you are financially able to provide for the animal's needs. This includes food, supplies, licensing, and veterinary care.
- Be certain that you have adequate time to spend with your new pet. This includes training, exercising, grooming, and loving.
- Understand that in order to give a dog the best possible chance for a good home, no animal may be placed on hold. You will need to complete the adoption process before that dog can be guaranteed to you.

The usual fee for adopting a dog at the shelter is around $100. When making a match, both parties need to participate in the process, so be sure to ask the shelter personnel a few questions yourself:

- Do you have any history on this dog?
- Has it been spayed or neutered?
- Does it get along with other dogs?
- What vaccinations has it had?
- Has it had any health problems while at the shelter?
- Has it had any training here, or can you refer me to a trainer?
- Do you have experts available for behavior consultations if I need them?
- If the adoption doesn't work out, can I bring it back?

Alert!

To learn of adoptable animals from shelters and rescue groups locally and nationally, visit *www.petfinder.com*. Here you can search almost 200,000 adoptable pets from all over the country.

Newspaper Ads

There is no hard-and-fast rule on this, but reputable breeders do not usually advertise their pups in the newspaper. They often have a waiting list of people lined up to purchase their puppies before the next litter is born. If you decide to go the classified-ad route, carefully check out the pup's parentage, living conditions, and health before you reach for that checkbook. You also need to remember that people who sell puppies through the newspaper can say anything they want to about themselves and their dogs because few buyers check out their credentials. There is no great savings to be had, either. A pedigreed pup from a reputable breeder usually costs about as much as one from the classifieds or pet store. If you do pay considerably less for your purebred pup, down the road you may end up paying the difference plus a lot more in vet bills when health problems arise.

If you call one of these advertisers, find out how long they have been breeding dogs. This might be a litter that was a surprise or it was bred to let their children experience the miracle of birth. On the other hand, if they are breeding the mother every time she comes into heat, that's not good either. A breeding bitch needs time to recover. She is not supposed to be a money-making machine.

Often those advertising litters in the newspaper fall into the backyard-breeder category. Many small-breed puppies are produced by amateurs. They mate dogs without regard to breed standards, potential genetic problems in the breed, or temperament. You can get lucky and find a good dog this way, but it's a big gamble.

When breeders discuss their dog's lineage, are there AKC champions in its immediate background? Any pup whose parents are registered with the AKC is eligible for registration; however, just because a pup has registration papers does not mean it is a worthy specimen of the breed.

 **Fact**

When an ad states that a puppy has "papers," that should mean that both parents are purebred and registered with the AKC. When a litter is whelped, the breeder gets registration papers for each of the new puppies, which the breeder and new owner must complete and mail in to the AKC. Your puppy's registration will not be completed until this is done.

Some ads might mention OFA certification. The OFA is the Orthopedic Foundation of America, an organization that maintains a registry of dogs with hip and elbow dysplasia. Dogs whose X rays show they are clear of these conditions are called OFA-certified. This is generally a problem with larger breeds, but no puppy is eligible to be certified until it is two years old. If the parents have what it known as OFA clearances, that's a good indication the pup will not end up with dysplasia, but it is not a guarantee.

If you have discovered that your breed of choice is prone to hereditary eye problems, you should find out if your potential pup has had a Canine Eye Registration Foundation or CERF exam. Performed by a board-certified member of the American College of Veterinary Ophthalmologists, this test screens for cataracts and retinal dysplasia, and results are recorded in a national registry. CERF exams are good for one year only. For breeds in which eye problems are an issue, a breeder should at least be able to show that the pup's mother has had a current CERF exam.

When you visit the premises, is it a clean environment? Obviously, you will get to see the mother dog and possibly the father as well. Are they healthy and friendly? Are the pups being raised as part of the breeder's family so they will be well socialized, or are they kept in isolation? Are there all kinds of pups running around, or just the breed you are looking for? When several different breeds are on the premises, that person is most likely not an individual breeder but might be working with a broker for puppy mills.

Wonderful puppies come from diverse breeding situations, but as you shop around, the more knowledge you bring with you, the better.

Pet Stores

Pet stores are like automobile dealerships. They are in the business of selling a commodity and making money—in their case, on puppies. We live in a free enterprise system, and these are legitimate businesses. However, when you buy a puppy at a pet store, you need to realize that the contract you will receive covering the animal's health and the store's policy of returning a pup is written more to protect the pet store than to protect you.

Pet stores get their pups from commercial breeding kennels, most of which are located in the Midwest, and many of which fit into the infamous category of puppy mills. These are wholesale breeding operations that breed their bitches every time they come into heat and keep their dogs in the worst possible conditions. Such breeders are unlikely to know or care about the breed standard or to breed with breed betterment or sound temperament in mind.

These kennels sell their pups to a broker, who in turn sells them to pet stores or chains. The pups are crated and shipped to the stores when they are as young as four weeks of age and are sold when they are six to twelve weeks old.

Under federal law, commercial breeding kennels are required to be licensed by the United States Department of Agriculture (USDA). If such an operation is convicted of fraudulent practices or inhumane conditions under the Animal Welfare Act, its license can be withdrawn. Due to understaffing and difficulty in enforcement, this rarely happens. Obviously, there is no way for you to know what kind of environment produced that adorable little puppy you fell in love with at the pet store.

Potential problems with pet store pups do not stop there. Once they arrive at the pet store, the conditions under which dogs are kept there may lead to infections and illnesses. Even though the law requires that the puppies be examined by a vet and given a clean bill of health before they are sold, in many cases this exam is perfunctory, sometimes no more than a rubber-stamping of a pen full of pups. Even if the young dogs appear to be healthy, they may be incubating diseases picked up after they arrived at the store. Like human infants, puppies' immune systems are not yet fully developed, so they are susceptible to a wide variety of illnesses.

Alert!

In Massachusetts, a 2004 *Boston Herald* series of stories revealed numerous incidents of vets allowing sick dogs to be sold to the public by prescribing medications to animals they had not examined, with drugs administered by store clerks. Illnesses present in these pups included upper respiratory infections, pneumonia, parvovirus, kennel cough, and intestinal parasites highly communicable to humans.

State law allows consumers to return sick puppies, but most stores will offer a credit, not a full refund. Often the purchaser has already bonded with the pup and is fearful that it will be euthanized if they bring it back. Increasingly common, these puppy "lemon laws" enable dog purchasers to return a sick or dead puppy for a refund or replacement, and some offer the option of keeping the dog and being reimbursed for its medical care. Check with your state's Department of Consumer Affairs or with the AKC to find out about such protection.

The amount of socialization the pup has had is another consideration. It is important to spend time with the dog you are considering and observe its reactions to you and other animals. A dog that seems shy and fearful or overly aggressive may lack socialization or have inbred temperament problems. Pet-store clerks usually work for low wages and are not breeding experts, so they may not be equipped to answer your questions about the dog you are considering. Pet-store and puppy-mill puppies are often weaned, shipped, and sold so young that they do not have a chance to develop the social skills needed by every dog, large or small. If a pup is weaned and shipped to the pet store at five or six weeks of age, it has not had sufficient time to develop a personality and to learn important social skills. Without a mother's guidance and the chance to grow and learn, the puppy often develops behavior problems.

While some pet stores are clean and are run by caring people, you need to proceed with caution if this is the route you choose to get your dog. First and foremost, make sure the pup has been examined by a local veterinarian who is also accessible to you. Ask where it came from and if it has been registered with the AKC, an indication that at least the breeder's USDA license has not been revoked for unethical practices or unsanitary conditions. Ask to see genetic clearances on its breeding stock, and request a copy. Go over the store's contract to find out what kind of protection is offered if your pup should get sick or die.

If pet-store personnel are unable or unwilling to answer your questions, it's best to continue your search elsewhere. Your goal is to get a dog that will grow into a happy, healthy example of the breed you've chosen. If you don't find that puppy there, at least you have broadened your knowledge as you continue your search.

Family, Friends, and Freebies

For thousands of us, the neighbor down the street or the relative who loves dogs is our number-one source for obtaining a puppy. Sometimes the asking price for these dogs is just enough to cover vet bills. Getting a puppy this way has its good points. Obviously, the pup's mother is on the premises, and if the sire is nearby, that's another plus. These canine parents are your best predictors of what your puppy will grow up to be, both in looks and temperament.

You hate to stick your friend or relative with the label "backyard breeder," but the reality is that amateur breeders like these usually do no screening for possible health problems in their breed (if they are purebred pups). They may be blissfully ignorant of such matters. They know their little mother dog is cute as a button but may have no inkling of her breed standard. Temperament is another big factor. While Aunt Mary's little terrier bitch may be a sweetheart, the male they bred her with could be the poster dog for hyperactivity, aggression, or fear-induced shyness.

That is not to say that having a dog given to you won't have a happy ending. Often reputable breeders place their retired champions or breeding dogs past their prime with people they know will take good care of them, without charging for the dog. Groomers and vets often act as matchmakers, too, finding good homes for small dogs whose owners have died, gone into a nursing home, or have serious personal problems that make it impossible for them to keep a dog. Sometimes fate steps in, and a stray dog finds you. If you've checked with the animal control officer and a week or so passes without the four-legged urchin that wandered into your yard being claimed, you've got yourself a free pet.

On the whole, though, most animal-care professionals take a very dim view of "free to a good home" ads, in print or online. Although those who place such ads are probably well intentioned, the dogs they give away could fall into the hands of the wrong people. They could end up abandoned, turned into a shelter, or badly neglected. A person who has to make no investment to obtain a dog may not be committed enough to keep it. Many people do not value something they get for nothing, even if it is an innocent animal. Paying a fee, even if it goes to an animal-related charity, demonstrates a commitment to being a responsible owner.

Some scenarios are even worse. That seemingly nice person who shows up for a free puppy could be a "buncher," someone who sells dogs to research labs, as bait for fighting dogs, as live food for exotic pets, or to a puppy mill to become a breeding machine.

Unless an owner is placing the pup or adult dog with a trusted friend or family member, giving away a living creature is not wise.

Alert!

There's no such thing as a "free" pet. When you add up the costs of food, supplies, vet care, training, and grooming, plus the commitment of time and love you will need to provide, there are many costs involved, not all of them monetary.

If you do respond to such an ad for a freebie, proceed with caution. There is usually a reason why someone wants to give a dog away. Be observant, and ask lots of questions. The dog may have medical or behavior problems. Obtaining a dog this way is a big gamble. At best, it's a chancy proposition for dog and owner alike.

Breed Rescue

Most parent clubs listed for individual breeds on the AKC Web site also have a link to rescue organizations for their breed. These groups work hard to find homes for dogs that can no longer remain with their families because of illness, death, divorce, relocation, allergy issues, or because a person had no idea what they were getting into when they brought the dog into their life.

Rescue workers take in purebred dogs from animal shelters or from individuals who can no longer care for them. Some are well organized and well funded, while others may consist of a single individual or small group that makes this activity a huge priority in their lives. Most provide foster care for their rescued dogs, either in private homes or at their own facility, while waiting for the right owner to come along. Those who do not have space for foster care may simply provide referrals.

Rescued dogs are spayed or neutered before they are placed. Dedicated rescuers work hard to clear up any health problems and impart some basic obedience training in these dogs. They screen the dogs for behavior problems and screen prospective adopters, too, ensuring a good fit between dog and owner. Because the dogs they deal with have already been given up or abandoned, rescuers go to great lengths to ensure it doesn't happen again.

In order to make a good match with you and your rescued dog, you first fill out a questionnaire. The rescue group wants to know why you want to adopt, what kind of a living situation you have, whether you have children (and their ages, if you do), and whether you are able and willing to provide the exercise and veterinary care your dog will require. Most require references, and some make home visits. This evaluation process continues when you meet the dog and they watch your initial interactions.

Some rescue dogs have been scarred and traumatized by abuse and neglect. Building the bonds of love and trust takes a lot of patience and understanding, but when a good match is made, it makes it all worthwhile.

Chapter 6

Working with a Breeder

Dogs joined humans at the campfire some 10,000 years ago. As people migrated over the globe, dogs went along, pulling sleds, tracking game, herding stock, towing fishing lines, carrying cargo, charging into battle, even providing a source of food and clothing. It was from all these roles played by Canis domesticus that modern breeds evolved.

Dogs and humans share a common history, and reputable breeders—those who devote their lives to preserving and maintaining individual breeds—are carrying on this age-old tradition. When you're looking for a purebred pup, the most common advice you hear is to go to a responsible breeder. You've already put a lot of time into your search. If you know someone who has a wonderful dog of the same breed, ask where that dog came from. You can also ask the dog pros in your community, such as vets, trainers, and groomers. These dog devotees know a good specimen when they see one, and they are also good judges of temperament. Area kennel clubs are another good source of information on finding a good breeder.

Question?

What is a reputable breeder?
Reputable breeders are your best source for purebred dogs because they are involved in breeding for the love of the dogs, not for the money. Your pup's parents will have been carefully selected to produce a puppy that carries the parent's best traits while minimizing their faults.

Though the AKC is not in the business of breeding and selling puppies, it does offer comprehensive help in locating responsible breeders. At its Web site, *www.akc.org*, you can access your particular breed and find a link to the parent club. These national clubs are devoted to the breed they love, preserving, promoting, and protecting it. They offer breeder referral services to prospective dog owners. When you call or e-mail, the contact persons you reach may be breeders or volunteers who will put you in touch with those who have puppies available.

The AKC site also offers links to help you find a local club for your breed. Then there are the breed rescue and on-line breeders' classifieds links, as well as print ads from the *AKC Gazette* for you to investigate. The AKC also has a customer service number (919) 233-9767, where you can request information about breeders.

A good breeder's mission is to advance and improve the breed with each litter they produce. Their goal is a physically and mentally sound dog, as fine an example of that breed as possible. When you get your puppy from a breeder like this, you form a friendship, and you learn a lot in the process.

Finding an Ethical Breeder

You will learn a lot in your search for the right breeder. Take your time, and visit more than one. It is vital for you to deal with a breeder who you can trust, and that kind of relationship takes time to develop.

Your first contact with a breeder may be over the phone, followed up by a visit to their home or kennel. You should first get to see the pup's dam and sometimes its sire (mom and dad) without the irresistible distraction of their puppies. Meeting the parents first will not only keep you from falling in love at first sight with their adorable offspring but also give you a chance to observe their temperament. If they seem overly aggressive or fearfully shy, that's a huge red flag.

You should also ask to see the parents' pedigrees. Puppies coming from generations of titled champions will usually grow up to be good examples of the breed. Check out the breeder's prize ribbons and trophies. These are the A's on a breeder's report card and no doubt they will be prominently displayed for all the world to see.

When you find the right breeder, you will become part of an extended family. In most cases, it will become a lifelong relationship. Reputable breeders will be there for you when questions arise and when health issues come up during all stages of your dog's life. Their joy in their dogs is infectious, making dog ownership more pleasurable for you, too.

 Essential

A good breeder raises pups in a home environment with lots of love and attention, helping to socialize their canine youngsters in the process.

When you visit a breeder, you will get a feel for their operation and for the kind of care they provide. Look beyond the puppies. Are the premises clean and safe? Does the breeder and his or her family exhibit affection for their dogs? Are the pups clean, lively, and happy? Pups should look well nourished and show no signs of illness. Runny noses, teary eyes, sparse coats, skin conditions, fleas, or loose stools are indications that these babies are not healthy or well cared for.

First and foremost, a reputable breeder does not breed dogs primarily to make money. The preservation and betterment of their chosen breed is uppermost. They usually offer one or two breeds, producing a few litters a year. They screen the dogs they breed and the pups that are produced, and they offer health guarantees against genetic diseases common to that breed, including replacing that pup if such a disease should occur. If a pup does not work out in its new home for any reason, they will take it back.

Reputable breeders evaluate their puppies to see which ones are show quality and which are pet quality (usually costing less than show prospects). Pet-quality pups are by no means inferior or undesirable. Usually for cosmetic reasons like coloring, size, or conformation faults, the breeder has determined that they should not be bred, but as their name implies, these dogs make fine pets. Reputable breeders are interested in improving their breed. They will answer all of your questions and willingly provide references from other owners of their dogs.

Finally, a reputable breeder will be just as interested in checking out your suitability as an owner. Sometimes this can rub a prospective dog owner the wrong way, but it shouldn't. Although the breeder's attitude may seem somewhat picky and overprotective, keep in mind that any concerns spring from finding the best situation for the dogs.

 Fact

Reputable breeders often sell pet-quality puppies with a spay/neuter contract. This means that in the interest of breed betterment and preventing pet overpopulation, they will not sell you that puppy unless you sign a paper agreeing not to breed it.

What to Ask a Breeder

An ethical breeder will also be willing to answer any questions you may have. After all, you both seek the same goal: the best match for owner and pup. Some questions you should ask include the following:

- How long have you been breeding these dogs?
- Do you and your dogs participate in any dog sports? (Conformation, obedience, agility, and field trials are some examples. Such activities show an ongoing appreciation for the breed as well as the desire to keep increasing knowledge.)
- What kind of a contract do you provide?
- Do you provide a health guarantee?
- What is your policy on taking back a puppy or replacing it if it gets sick?
- Will you help us pick the puppy that suits us best?
- Do you provide references from others who have purchased your puppies?
- What health problems are common in this breed?
- What kind of genetic testing have you done on the parents? Will you provide copies of those clearances?
- What shots will the pup have had before you sell it? What about deworming?
- How big will the puppy grow as an adult?
- At what age is this breed considered mature?
- What are its nutritional needs? Do you recommend a specific diet?
- How much activity will this dog need?
- Will it be protective of my family?
- Will it get along well with other pets?
- What would you recommend for obedience training?
- What will its grooming needs be? Can I groom it myself, or will I need a professional?
- When can I take my puppy home?

Because the betterment of the breed is vital to a responsible breeder, they usually sell pet-quality puppies with a spay/neuter contract. It is up to you to be equally ethical and fulfill your part of this agreement. They also provide the puppy's first shots.

Reputable breeders view the puppies they produce as family members too. If they cannot sell or place one of their pups for any reason, they will keep it. Because they will be screening you as well, be prepared for their interest in the kind of home you will be providing to their baby.

Questions You Will Need to Answer

A reputable breeder is just as concerned about what kind of owner you will be as you are about his or her qualifications. For that reason, you should welcome, rather than be offended by, any personal questions the breeder may ask you about the kind of home you are going to provide for the dog being relinquished to your care. Be prepared to answer the following questions during your meeting:

- Do you have children and if so, what are their ages? (For safety reasons, many breeders of toy and small-breed dogs will not sell their pups to people with small children.)
- Have you ever owned a dog before? What breed was it, and how long did it live?
- What is your living situation? If you rent, can you provide proof that the landlord allows dogs? If you are living in an apartment or condo, are you aware of your responsibilities regarding noise level and cleaning up after your dog?
- If you own your home, do you have a fenced yard?
- Does your community have a leash law?
- Can you afford vet care, licensing, food, supplies, training, boarding, and grooming for this dog?
- How active are you? Can you meet this dog's exercise needs?

Not all questions need to be verbalized. The breeder will also be observing you and your family as you interact with the puppy. Like protective parents, they need to be assured that their canine offspring will be in a safe and loving environment when it leaves their care.

The Process

Once you have made your pick, most breeders will let you make frequent visits to your puppy before it is old enough to leave its mother and siblings and go home with you. This helps socialize the puppy and builds the bond between you and this future family member. While the pup is with its mother, it is growing in confidence and strength as well as size. Rough-and-tumble play with its littermates is instructive as the pup learns the difference between playing and hurting its siblings and becomes more socialized in the process.

Puppies' eyes open at about two weeks of age, and their ears open completely by three weeks. They can move around fairly well by four weeks. Until then, most of their time is spent feeding and sleeping. After four weeks, they begin exploring their surroundings and engage in puppy play with their littermates. Small-breed puppies in particular need more time with their mother and siblings and sometimes are not ready for their new home until twelve to sixteen weeks.

Before they leave the nest, they need to develop the three S's: size, strength, and socialization. Toy breeds may not be hardy enough to get their vaccinations until they are well beyond that six-week birthday. This is another huge benefit that comes with choosing a knowledgeable breeder.

 Fact

Between the sixth and twelfth weeks of life, puppies start learning how to be dogs. As they wrestle and roughhouse, they are experimenting with behavior displays ranging from tough competitiveness to tender affection.

Finding a Healthy Dog

Aside from that indefinable thing called chemistry, consider the basic signs of good health. Your first criteria in picking a puppy should be selecting one that is healthy and sound. Here's what to look for:

- Eyes should be open, clear, and clean, without redness, tearing, or discharge, brightly radiating the pup's healthy curiosity about its world.
- Ears should be clean and wax-free. If the ear canal is dirty, smelly, swollen, or tender to the touch, an infection may be present.
- The nose, that all-important little button, should be clean and moist. If it's drippy, has a discharge, or if the puppy is sneezing, this could indicate an allergy or upper respiratory infection.
- In the mouth, baby teeth should be clean and white, breath fresh, gums and tongue pink and moist, and jaws not misaligned (puppies should not have a noticeable overbite or underbite).
- Well-fed puppies have nice round bellies and a protective layer of fat, but if the tummy is hard and distended, this could indicate the presence of worms. Ribs should not be visible but should be discernible to your touch.
- The pup's skin is a velvety suit it is growing into. It should be supple and a bit loose, not flaky, dry, or leathery. A healthy coat is free of bare spots, redness, or flea infestation.
- The pup should not exhibit pain or tenderness as you go over its body with your hands. Its joints should not be sore or swollen, and it should walk with a normal gait.
- The odor, if a pup is clean and healthy, should be the warm and wonderful smell of a fresh puppy.

We've covered the basics of choosing a healthy puppy. In addition to the obvious signs of good health, you need to carefully check your little dog for congenital defects. Some are repairable by surgery, but you may ask the breeder to consider reducing the price if you'll be faced with this expense.

On male pups, check to see if both testicles have descended from the abdomen into the scrotum. When they have not, the condition is called testicular retention.

Undescended testicles can be removed when the dog is mature, but such a dog can never be bred or shown. Neutering is advisable because this is a hereditary trait. Left untreated, retention of the testicles can lead to testicular cancer. If you have your heart set on a small dog with such a condition, talk to the breeder about adjusting the price and discuss the matter with your own vet.

 fact

A male dog with one undescended testicle is called a monorchid, while one with both testicles in the abdomen is referred to as a cryptorchid.

You can spot a sound robust little dog without much trouble. However, the only way to make sure your pup is in good health is to take it to your own vet while it is still under the breeder's guarantee. If your vet detects a health problem and advises you to return the puppy to the breeder, you should follow this advice. It may be hard for you, but owning a dog with major disabilities will be an even bigger heartbreak down the road. Your best chance for sharing a long and happy life with your new dog is to start off with a healthy puppy.

Choosing Your Puppy

If you have already established a relationship with a breeder you trust, you are halfway home. You've already done a lot of homework, asking a lot of questions and witnessing firsthand the care and dedication it takes to raise puppies. But you may still be playing "eenie, meenie, miney, moe." Which one of these marvelous little creatures should you pick for yourself?

Temperament

Your dog's personality is just as important as its health. Just watching a litter of puppies interact with each other will provide a lot of clues to their personalities. You can spot the bully in the bunch, the most dominant pup, and the shyest member, remaining somewhat removed from the fray. Are you looking for a spunky little ball of mischief or a quiet little pal?

Get down to their level. Sit on the floor with the pups, not grabbing or reaching for them, and see how they react to you. Call to them or tap on the floor to get their attention. A curious pup will toddle over to investigate, maybe even climbing into your lap to give you wet kisses or bowing down, inviting you to play. A shy one will hold back while a more independent youngster will take its sweet time approaching you.

Toss a puppy-size ball or a toy to see which one gets it first. When you make a sudden noise like clapping or snapping your fingers, you'll see which ones seem afraid and run away and which boldly approach to see what you're up to.

Essential

If you get down on the floor with the litter and act like a big puppy yourself, you'll get to know these youngsters better, helping you pick the one that's right for you.

Now it's time for one-on-one with members of this little brood. When you hold the pups, which one seems to be most comfortable with you? (If you're not sure how to hold it safely and comfortably, ask the breeder.) Can you cradle it like a baby and tickle its tummy or does it try to squirm out of your arms? Take your time in getting to know each one of these little individuals. You don't have to make up your mind the first time you visit them.

Even if you find yourself falling for one over the others, involve your family members to help with the selection process as well. Ideally, everyone in your household needs to be part of the decision because ultimately, you will all have to live with it. You'll need all the help you can get to raise this puppy, and the more people who love it, the happier it will be.

Following a Breeder's Advice

Already aware of the diverse personalities within the litter, the breeder may steer you toward one they feel matches you best. Of course, you'll need to feel that the decision is yours as well. Naturally, breeders spend far more time observing the behavior of their puppies, learning which are mischievous, bossy, and independent, or shy, sweet, and submissive; which will require a soft reassuring approach to thrive; and which will need owners who establish their leadership from day one. Remain open to the breeder's valuable input as you observe, listen, and learn before choosing.

Will the Dog Be a Companion or Show Dog?

Most litters bred by reputable breeders produce both pet- and show-quality pups. Pet-quality puppies are not bargain-basement knockoffs or litter leftovers. They have had the same care, dedication, and money put into their planning and raising as their show-quality littermates. They also share the same impressive lineage.

Often, people looking for a puppy are under the impression that "pet quality" means a dog of lesser value. In truth, it merely means that the breeder has decided that this particular pup will not come close enough to the breed standard—the official ideal of perfection—to become a champion in the ring. Campaigning a dog to its AKC championship takes a tremendous amount of time and money, so unless breeders are fairly confident that a dog stands a good chance of winning, they would much prefer to see it in a loving home as a valued pet.

Fact

For a reputable breeder, each breeding is carefully planned to advance the kennel's line. Unless a dog has the look and personality they aim to perpetuate, it is deemed a pet and sold with a limited registration. In other words, it will neither be shown in conformation nor bred.

If a breeder wants to maintain breeding rights on your dog, you may face conflicts down the road. On the whole, contracts of this type benefit the breeder more than the person who is the dog's primary caretaker. Once you have bonded to your dog, you may resent fulfilling your agreed-upon obligation. If you view it as your entry into the exciting world of AKC championships, this kind of agreement may suit you very well, but proceed with caution.

Be careful of contracts that sell a puppy for the full purchase price and require it to be bred, with the breeder keeping the puppies. Breeding a litter requires a huge commitment of time, energy, and responsibility on your part. Both emotional and monetary costs are involved. Think long and hard before you become involved in such a co-ownership contract.

Male or Female?

In small and toy dogs that are spayed or neutered, gender differences are not a huge concern. Ask your breeder about personality differences in their male and female dogs. In some breeds, males may be more stubborn and dominant. Females tend to be a bit smaller in size and less inclined to wander, but since no small dogs should ever be running around unsupervised, that really is a moot point.

In any case, if you are not planning to breed your dog, spaying and neutering has significant health benefits as well. It prevents mammary and uterine cancer in females and testicular and prostate cancer in males. It also prevents accidental litters, which can be disastrous for tiny female dogs impregnated by larger canines, and cuts down on the male's aggressive tendencies and habit of marking territory by urinating, inside and out. Whichever sex you choose, your dog may be spayed or neutered at six months of age.

 Fact

Sex differences in small dogs are a matter of personal preference. Whether a male or female dog is more affectionate or aggressive depends more upon its individual personality than its gender.

Some people believe that female dogs are easier to train and male dogs are more likely to challenge your authority. Again, this varies widely within specific breeds. Since there are enormous personality differences in dogs of both sexes, the question of how much males differ from females remains open to debate.

Buying Multiple Dogs

If you are considering acquiring two small dogs, the sex question becomes more important. On the whole, two male dogs will compete to be leader of the pack, and that can lead to fighting. This is more common with males that have not been neutered, but it also has a bearing on the degree of aggression and submission of the two males in question. Usually, getting a male and a female and having them both fixed or having two spayed females works out best. They will keep each other company while you are away and become the best of friends. You may have to monitor feeding to make sure one doesn't gobble up the other's share of food. You will also have two dogs to housebreak and train, double the work of just one. Since two heads are better than one at thinking up fun things to do, you will also have double the mischief. But many dog lovers wouldn't dream of having only one dog, looking upon two little dogs as twice as much fun.

Question?

Can I trust my dog to play safely with other dogs?
In a multidog household, it's important to monitor the behavior of pets, especially if they are diverse in size. An overexuberant Lab could easily injure a small-boned canine housemate in rough play. In dog parks where pets are allowed to run off lead, your cairn terrier may look like prey to a fleet-footed greyhound.

Adding a new small dog to a household that already has an older dog can be a chancy proposition. For safety's sake, the older dog must not be much larger or stronger than the new arrival. Some older dogs are like some older people; they don't have as much tolerance for youthful high jinks as they once did. A pesky little puppy that always wants to play could really get on an older dog's nerves. Some older dogs will exhibit personality changes when you bring a young one into your home, either growing depressed and retreating from the family circle or becoming jealous and more demanding of your attention.

Puppy Paperwork

You're itching to get your hands on that special little puppy, but the transaction will not be complete until you've done all the paperwork, including the forms described in the following sections.

Contract

The contract is much more than a bill of sale. It does specify price and terms of payment, but it also spells out when the pup can go home with you, how health issues will be dealt with—including stated time limits for guarantees––and the breeder's requirements for spaying and neutering. The contract may also require that the dog come back to the breeder if for any reason you are unable to care for it. Study this guarantee closely before you sign it, and know your options. Make sure it allows enough time for you to take the pup to your own vet for a complete checkup while the health guarantee is still in effect.

Pedigree

This is your puppy's family tree, tracing back over two or three generations. It includes any championships earned in conformation (show dog titles), obedience and agility titles, as well achievements in other dog sports and health clearances for genetic issues associated with the breed.

Registration

The AKC will register any puppy produced by AKC-registered parents. When you buy a dog represented as AKC-registrable, you should receive an application form filled out by the breeder. You can register by mail or online (with the proper fee), after which you will receive your registration certificate. In addition to the basic registration, packages offering pet health insurance, training videos, and AKC magazine subscriptions are also available.

Health "Certs"

This important piece of paper spells out the guarantee under which your pup can be returned if a health problem should crop up. It also documents the kinds of genetic testing and screening that has been done to guarantee that your dog does not have any breed-specific heritable conditions. The health guarantee limit provided by a breeder varies between a few days to several months. For example, if heritable eye diseases are common in the breed you are purchasing, you should receive a Canine Eye Registration Foundation (CERF) report on your pup's parents and, if possible, on the puppy as well. Responsible breeders have such puppies examined by a canine ophthalmologist before they go to their new homes. CERF certs are good for twelve months, after which the dog must be reexamined to maintain its registration.

If there is a frequent occurrence of hip or elbow dysplasia in your pup's breed, you should also receive an Orthopedic Foundation of America (OFA) report on the parent dogs. These problems affect large dog breeds far more often than the smaller canines, but if such problems have cropped up in your dog's line, such screening is a must. This screening cannot be performed until a dog is two years of age, but if the sire and dam have such clearances, chances are good the pup will not develop these debilitating conditions. Other certifications are available for heart, thyroid, and von Willebrands disease, a blood-clotting disorder.

Health Records

This packet will include your pup's "birth certificate," documenting the date and time of its arrival, and a listing of its veterinary examinations to date, including shots and deworming. When you bring your puppy to your own vet, which you should do promptly once you bring it home, take this along so your vet will know the pup's health history.

Chapter 7

Bringing Your New
Dog Home

The day that you bring your new puppy
or older dog home will be a big one in
your life, but it will be even more momen-
tous for this new little family member.
Have that camera ready! The better prepared you are for this wonderful event,
the less stressful and more enjoyable it will
be. Taking a few preparatory steps to get
ready for your new little friend will make
the transition much easier for everyone.

Preparing for Pickup

The pup will be leaving the comfort and familiarity of the nest, where it has been warmly nestled with its mother and littermates for the first few months of its life. Entering the vast new world of your home will be like a trip to a distant galaxy for this little sprite. Even if you are adopting an older dog, the transition to a new environment may be stressful and scary. You need to be reassuring as it makes this transition.

If you are getting a puppy from a breeder, visiting your puppy several times before it is weaned will familiarize it with your presence—your face, voice, touch, and, most importantly, your smell.

 Fact

A dog's smelling ability is the most highly developed of all its senses. With about twenty-five more olfactory receptors than humans, a dog's sense of smell is 1,000 to 10,000 times more powerful than ours.

A dog's nose is hardwired to its brain. As it sniffs every blade of grass and patch of pavement out on its daily walk, it is catching up on the news. You can harness this key to your dog's learning ability to ease its adjustment into your home. A few days before you are scheduled to pick up the pup, bring an old blanket or towel to the breeder and ask to have the mother dog's tummy wiped down with it to capture her scent. Leave this blankie with the puppy until pickup day, and then wrap the new arrival up in it for the trip home with you.

Bringing a new dog into your home will affect every member of the household. Ideally, all family members have been part of the decision before you acquired this pet. If you have children, they should also have visited their new buddy prior to its arrival and have been instructed in the proper way to act around this little creature. The small fry in the family are no doubt excited about their new pet, but they need to be reminded to curb their enthusiasm. Small dogs can be high-strung, and they are easily stressed by a lot of noise and excitement. Tell your children their job will be to make the little newcomer feel safe and secure in your home. They must also be taught not to bother the dog when it is eating or sleeping.

Before you bring your new dog home, take the time to rally the troops once more to let them know what's in store and what they can do to help. This is a good time to set some ground rules about pet care. Remind them that rough handling and wild behavior involving yelling and racing around will not be allowed. Discuss each person's responsibilities, such as who will be feeding, exercising, and potty-training the new dog, as well as how everyone can help with socializing and cleanup chores.

If you are adopting an older dog from a breed rescue or a shelter, expect a transition period before it settles in. First traumatized by being uprooted from its original home, then placed in the shelter setting, and now finding itself in yet another strange environment with you, it may take a few weeks for the dog's true personality to shine through.

At bedtime, the dog will feel more secure if it is rooming in with an adult. Even though it looks like a little stuffed toy, the children should not be allowed to carry your dog around or take it into bed with them. If they dropped it and it became injured or worse, you would bear the dual responsibility for the pup getting hurt and the child's heavy burden of guilt. All interactions must be supervised between any dog, especially a new one, and very young children.

Shopping for Supplies

The pet supply store is doggie wonderland. You could spend a fortune on an endless array of items for your dog there. It's best to do some research before you walk down those aisles, bedazzled by the amazing plethora of pet products. Throughout your dog's life, you'll have fun spoiling your new best friend with toys, treats, and stylish accessories. For starters, though, just concentrate on the things you'll really need. Before embarking upon that shopping spree, make a list of the basics so you won't bust your budget on unnecessary items.

Collars

For the small dog, a lightweight nylon ribbon collar of woven or braided nylon with a stainless steel buckle works well, as does an adjustable nylon snap collar with a plastic lock-and-release closure. Like cat safety collars, some snap collars will break away if your pup gets stuck on something. Don't spend a lot of money on your baby's first collar, as it may be quickly outgrown. For comfort for most toy breeds, it should be very narrow—around half to three-quarters of an inch in width. To get the proper fit, measure the pup's neck and add two inches. If it doesn't hang loose after you close it and you can fit two fingers underneath it, you've got the right size. Check frequently to make sure the pup has not outgrown it. You'll also need a fine-mesh stainless steel or nylon training collar once the pup begins its training, soon after you bring it home. Also known as choke collars, when used humanely and correctly these should never choke your dog.

ID Tags

For safety's sake, your dog will need an ID tag to fasten to that new collar. These come in small sizes, in plastic or stainless steel, and are usually available at pet supply stores or grooming salons where you purchase and pay for these items, then send in a form and have the tag mailed to you within two weeks. There are also do-it-yourself plastic tags and nylon ID collars that come embroidered with your dog's name and your telephone number. Another way to guarantee that your dog will be permanently identifiable is to have your vet implant a microchip when it goes for its shots.

Fact

Microchipping is the best way to protect your dog from becoming homeless, with all the heartbreak that ensues. The procedure hurts no more than getting a shot, involving the injection of a tiny capsule—about the size of a grain of rice—under the skin. A scanner reads the digital information on that chip, and whoever finds your dog can call the microchip company for your identifying information so your dog can be safely returned.

Leashes

Woven or braided nylon leashes come in six-foot and four-foot lengths and should be the same width as the pup's collar. (Wider leashes are too heavy for smaller breeds.) For walking around the block, the four-foot variety is fine, while the six-footer is better for obedience work. Leather leashes, which cost quite a bit more, also come in narrow widths. If it's thin enough, the six-foot length works well for training a small dog. Another popular variation is a retractable lead that reels in and out of its plastic handle. Once you get the hang of its brake-and-lock system, these enable you to walk your dog at your side or give it plenty of room to romp in the woods or at the beach.

Dishes

Your small dog won't need huge dishes, but they should be big enough to contain enough food and water to meet its needs. When filled with water, extra-large dishes are dangerous for tiny dogs because they could fall in and not be able to get out. Stainless steel, plastic, or ceramic crockery are all dishwasher-safe. They should be stable in case the puppy decides to play with them instead of eating or drinking. A stainless steel water cup that attaches to the crate door is also a good idea for times when the pup is home alone.

A Crate

Besides the gentle and reassuring welcome you and your family will provide, the most important thing your pup or adult dog will need is a warm safe place of its own, preferably a fiberglass or wire crate. A pup is an active, tiny presence underfoot, so you will need this place of respite as much as the puppy does. (Stepping or sitting on this little creature could cripple or kill it, so it's vital to know where that pup is at all times.)

Like the scent markers you will use to ease the transition, the crate taps into another age-old need in your dog: the den instinct inherited from its wolf ancestors. The crate will be its safety zone, away from the hustle and bustle of the household between playtime, feeding, and potty calls, as well as a soothing place to sleep at night. Pad it softly with a washable mat and a towel or blanket that carries your scent. The crate should be big enough for the pup to stretch out, turn around, and stand up in, but not too roomy. Because the pup will be transferring its primary bond to you, its new care-giver, the best place for its crate at night will be right next to your bed. This will also make it easier to make those nighttime potty runs.

Because yours is a very small dog, the crate it uses for solitude and sleeping can also serve as its travel crate. The most popular fiberglass crates are sold unassembled, so be sure to put it together before you bring that baby home. Make sure it closes securely and does not have any sharp edges that could hurt the pup. Line it with an imitation sheepskin or cotton pil-low-type mat to make it comfy, and buy a spare for when that one is in the wash. Crates are priced according to size—another benefit of owning a small dog!

Housebreaking Materials

If you are planning to have an indoor potty area for your small dog, either during the initial housebreaking period or as a permanent arrange-ment, have these supplies on hand:

- Housebreaking pads are disposable, highly absorbent, and treated with pheromones that act as scent markers, directing your pup to relieve itself in the right spot if you are paper-training indoors.
- Newspapers—and lots of them! The area where you put them down can be reduced as your little one catches on.
- Dog litter (scent-treated and featuring larger particles than kitty lit-ter) if you are using a litterbox for indoor housetraining.
- A low-sided litterbox, allowing the pup to get in and out with ease.
- A baby gate, to keep your untrained puppy out of areas that are off-limits in your home.
- Stain-and-odor-removing cleaners—because accidents will happen! The best ones feature enzymes that digest bacteria rather than just covering up the odor. Low-sudsing, they can also be used in your carpet-cleaning machine.
- A pooper-scooper for potty patrol outdoors.
- Disposable poop bags, a must at home and wherever you go with your little pet.

fact

Pheromones are naturally produced chemicals that give off scented signals capable of changing mood and behavior. The pheromones in your dog's urine give other dogs information about territory, gender, and even rank. For example, when a female dog is in heat, she releases pheromones detectable by male dogs in your neighborhood (and a few miles beyond!).

Beds

In addition to its crate, it's nice to have a bed for your dog, as a casual resting place and to discourage it from sleeping on the furniture where it can shed or someone might accidentally sit on it. Dog beds come in a wide variety of styles. For a puppy, the most important features are safety and ease of cleaning.

Baby Gates

You will sometimes want to confine your little dog to the kitchen or to some other puppy-proofed room, so one or two plastic mesh pressure-mounted gates will make life easier for you and safer for the pup. They come in different widths, adjustable to fit in any doorway or stairway without having to install any hardware. Beyond stability, the most important feature of such a gate is the size of the mesh openings. Avoid wooden accordion-style or vertical slat gates. The small pup's head could get caught between those slats, and it could be strangled.

Car Safety

Your little bundle of joy should not be allowed to bounce about in the car when you travel. You wouldn't dream of letting a small child ride without their car seat or safety belt, and your puppy shouldn't, either. Initially, you can use the crate, safely placed on the floor or on the seat, restrained with the seat belt. When the puppy gets a bit larger, you can fit it with its own car seat complete with safety belt. You can also buy a seat belt made just for dogs, available in a wide range of sizes.

Exercise Pen

Lightweight foldable wire pens—called exercise or x-pens by dog show folks—open into six- or eight-sided play areas for your dog. They are available in a wide variety of sizes, starting as small as two feet by two feet. They can be used indoors or out when you want to keep the dog safely confined and are available in wire or plastic. Like playpens for human babies, they come in handy for home and travel.

Toys

Buying toys for a puppy is like buying toys for a human baby. Keep it simple. You want to avoid small parts that could come off and choke the youngster. Stuffed toys are fun, but watch out for those that squeak—some breeds will try to "kill" squeaky toys and rip that squeaker out, possibly swallowing it in the process. Chew toys made of nylon or hard rubber, including those you can stuff with puppy-size treats, are a safe bet and will be useful when your pup is teething. Rubber balls are fun to chase and help your puppy learn how to retrieve, while foam balls are unsafe because they can be shredded and swallowed. Your new puppy is too young for real bones or hooves, and you should avoid rawhide unless you can supervise. A piece ingested by your pup could cause it to choke. Rope toys also require supervision, and tug-of-war games with feisty pups encourage aggressive behavior.

Grooming Supplies

For the small pup, you will need a gentle slicker brush for medium-or long-coated breeds or a rubber curry for smooth coats. The slicker comes with wire bristles embedded in a rubber backing. For long or fluffy coats, a double-sided stainless steel comb will be needed as well. Small-size nail clippers like those used for cats work best on toy and tiny breeds, and a jar of styptic powder is a good idea in case you should nick a nail. A mild tearless shampoo, crème rinse, some ear wash, and cotton balls will round out your basic grooming kit.

Food

If you got your dog from a breeder, you will probably go home with a starter bag of the food used at the kennel. Even if you decide to switch to another food, you will need to wean the pup slowly over a five-day period to prevent stomach upsets. Start by mixing only a spoonful or two of the new food and build up the ratio from there until you are serving only the food you prefer.

Enzymatic Cleaner

Accidents are bound to happen with any new dog. Using enzymes that actually digest the dirt- and odor-causing bacteria, this type of cleaner is best for removing stains from floors, carpets, and upholstery. It also removes the odor of urine and feces, scent markers that will keep your dog returning to relieve itself on the same spot next time.

Locating a Veterinarian

Within a few days of bringing your puppy home, you will need to visit your vet for that all-important first health checkup. Although you may have received a health guarantee and health record from the breeder, your own vet may discover problems that need addressing and should be documented in case you need legal evidence to enforce any guarantees down the road. Treatment of congenital problems or diseases can be extremely costly, so this exam is necessary for your own protection and for the health of your dog.

 Essential

Your puppy transaction will not be complete until it has been thoroughly examined by your own vet.

If you do not have a vet, ask your dog-owning friends, a local groomer, or the breeder for suggestions. Make sure the vet has plenty of experience with toy and small breeds. Bring along your puppy's health records, and ask any questions that pop up. Until the pup has completed its vaccination schedule, you will want to keep it home with your family because it is in the process of losing the immunity protection provided by its mother. During the gap in this protection, it will be highly susceptible to germs and diseases.

The entire subject of dog vaccinations is in flux at present, the general belief now being that dogs no longer need yearly vaccine boosters as the protection given by immunization lasts longer than previously thought. In addition, overvaccinating can be destructive to a dog's immune system. Toy, small, and elderly dogs often react adversely to vaccines, sometimes running a low-grade fever, experiencing muscle pain, and being generally exhausted for as long as two days after receiving their shots. At present, there is a philosophical split between traditional and holistic or homeopathic vets in the delivery of medical care for pets. You need to ask your prospective vet where he or she falls in regard to the changing protocols regarding vaccinations as well as all aspects of veterinary care.

Vaccinations against parvovirus, distemper, hepatitis, and leptospirosis do not take effect immediately. Full immunity takes one to two weeks to develop.

Toy and small-breed pups usually start being vaccinated at six to eight weeks of age, and they are given boosters every two to three weeks until they are four months old. In line with current research and the trend toward holistic care, many vets no longer advise combination shots of vaccines for distemper, hepatitis, leptospirosis, parainfluenza, and parvovirus for dogs in general and especially for small dogs.

No matter what vaccination schedule you and your vet decide upon, your dog needs to lead a sheltered life until it is fully protected against these diseases. Avoid puppy kindergarten, play groups, the neighbor's dog, the grooming salon, the public park, and any other places the young pup is at risk of picking up bacterial and viral infections. An occasional car ride to get it used to travel and to ward off nervous car sickness is a good idea, but other than that, the puppy can get all the attention and socialization it needs at home with you.

You will also want to ask prospective vets other questions about their practice:

- Are they general practitioners, or do they have certain specialties?
- What kinds of surgery do they provide? Are they affiliated with any teaching hospitals?
- Do they give to the community, offering their services to humane societies or rescue groups?
- What about emergency care when they are not available?
- What are the costs for their services?

Finally, you will want to feel a certain bond with this important health-care provider. Call it bedside manner or personality style, it helps to feel like you are on the same wavelength and that your vet sincerely cares about all aspects of your dog's life. Choose a vet as though you and your dog are establishing a lifelong friendship as well as a doctor/patient relationship.

Pet-Proofing the House and Yard

Like toddlers, puppies get into everything! You never know where their curiosity will lead them. Before you bring that baby home, take a good look around your house and see what you can put out of harm's way, including electric and Venetian blind cords, throw pillows, houseplants and artificial flowers, plastic toys, that prized photo album on the coffee table, your leather slippers, and those new running shoes. Everyday items such as string, pens, pencils, yarn, and elastic bands can be hazardous if chewed and swallowed by your dog. Things you would never suspect would be fun to chew—the remote control, DVDs, and scented candles—can be highly inviting to those busy little jaws. Make sure cleaning supplies are in locked cabinets, and get in the habit of putting dirty clothes in the hamper immediately.

If it smells like you, the pup might want to chew it. A baby gate or two will keep the puppy from rooms in which you don't want it roaming freely.

 **Essential**

Until a puppy is housebroken, it should not have the run of the house. It needs to earn that privilege!

Next, check out your yard. Look for spots in the fence where a tiny dog could squeeze through to escape. You can eliminate these gaps by running a barrier of wire mesh or chicken wire along the bottom of the fence. Make sure all gates close tightly.

Lawn- and pest-control chemicals can be fatal to a dog. Not using them at all is your safest bet, but if you must, they need to be well watered into the soil. Keep your dog away from the area for forty-eight hours after use. Have a potty area on the fringe of your yard where no such substances are ever used, and take the pup to this preferred potty spot to do its business from day one.

Swimming pools and other water features must be safely fenced off. Rubber hoses and bicycle tires are fun to chew, so remove them as well. Lock any toxic chemicals, cleaning compounds, sharp tools, and garden supplies in your garage or shed. These preventive measures will be well worth your while, making it more fun for you and your family to enjoy outdoor activities with your new little dog.

One final word of caution: Even if your yard is fenced and puppy-proofed, it is not a good idea to let the puppy out unsupervised. Leaving a puppy out unattended or risking injury with a tie-out or cable is simply not safe or wise. In areas with a coyote population, remember that your small dog would make a tasty meal for these wild predators. Keep an eye on your pup when it's out in the yard, and use a leash when you take it anywhere away from home.

Picking Up Your New Pooch

Because you and your new dog need time to get to know one another, plan to bring your dog home on the start of a weekend or during a vacation period so you'll be able to give the new arrival the time and attention it deserves. You'll also need this time to get used to being a new dog owner.

It would be best to have someone else accompany you for the pickup trip. Before you leave for home with the dog, make sure you walk it so it can relieve itself. Dogs often urinate or defecate when they get nervous. If you are getting the pup from the breeder, the all-important blankie (a piece of fabric impregnated with the mother's scent) should already be at the breeder's house. You should wrap the pup in it to be held in someone's lap or tuck it in a pet carrier or crate for the trip home. If it's cold outside, the blanket will also keep the pup from becoming chilled. Not only will an extra person help calm the puppy down, it will also make the car ride less traumatic, preventing travel-related stress and possible car sickness.

On the ride home, the person holding the puppy should speak reassuringly and pat it lovingly. Once you arrive home, take your new dog to the designated potty area for another try at doing its business before you go indoors. If it does, you're off to a good start, so offer lots of praise! You'll want to begin housebreaking right away, and this is your first opportunity. In winter, or if you live in a high-rise apartment, you may opt to paper-train or litter train your small dog rather than constantly take it outside. If that is the case, you should already have those needed supplies on hand as well as a designated indoor potty area for your new little housemate.

The First Day at Home

Once indoors, the new arrival will probably want to sniff its way around the house. Put it down and let it explore to its heart's content. As already noted, dogs learn a lot through their sense of smell and this is the first way your dog will familiarize itself with its new surroundings. As it explores, praise the pup using its own name as well as the words it will always love to hear: "good boy" or "good girl."

Naturally, everyone is excited. This is the day they have been waiting for. It's time for your household members to officially greet the new dog and welcome it into the family. Its arrival is also an important time to establish a predictable routine to make your dog feel secure and to make the job of integrating it into your household that much easier.

 **Fact**

During your puppy's first five months of life, it will soak up information like a sponge. Your behavior and attitude in this crucial time will shape your dog's confidence, socialization, and ability to trust the humans in its life.

Take it slow and easy. When you bring your new dog home, the first thing family members will want to do is pick it up and take turns passing it around. They may want to invite their friends over to meet the pup as well. It's understandable. You don't want to squelch their joy and pride, but it's best not to pass the dog around like a football or overwhelm it with hordes of new people. Explain that this is an important time to share within your own family circle. As it gets used to its new home, there will be plenty of time to show your dog off to friends and neighbors.

After the little dog has performed its sniffing ritual, it's a good time to let each household member take turns getting to know the new arrival, stroking it and talking softly to it as you hold it and then holding it themselves if they are old enough to do so safely. This is a good time to review puppy safety, going over the following points with your own version of show-and-tell:

- **Picking up the puppy safely:** Place one hand under its chest, holding its body against yours with its front legs dangling down between the fingers of your other hand. It will feel secure against your body. If the pup is too wiggly or squirmy, place it safely on the floor. Never drop it or let it jump!
- **Holding the pup:** You love it to pieces, but don't hug or squeeze it too hard. You could hurt the puppy, causing it to defend itself by

scratching, nipping, or trying to get away from you. Supervise very young children at all times.

- **The name game:** Use its name often as you talk to the pup. It will soon catch on that hearing its name means it's time for food, affection, a trip outside, or a play or training session. Calling its name as you get it to follow you around is also a subtle way to establish yourself as the leader of the pack from day one.
- **Using a leash:** Getting a puppy used to walking on a leash will take lots of patience, but it is the first step in obedience training. You should never drag it, poke it, or pull on any part of its body.
- **Food do's and don'ts:** Do not feed the dog from your plate or tease it with food. The processed and seasoned foods that we eat can make a puppy sick. Feeding it table scraps will teach it to be a beggar and a picky eater. It will prefer people food instead of the quality dog food it needs.
- **No hitting!** Even if the puppy acts fresh and nippy, as they all do occasionally, physical punishment is a big no-no. Hitting a dog with your hand or a newspaper will teach it to bite to defend itself or become afraid and distrustful of its own family.
- **Private time:** Do not bother the pup if it is sleeping or eating. A new puppy is like a new baby brother or sister. It needs lots of rest.

Holding the puppy is a huge part of the all-important bonding ritual. Everyone should get their share of puppy licks and kisses!

Alert!

Children who are noisy and out of control around puppies can cause them to be fearful or defensive, biting and growling to protect themselves. Conversely, children who are afraid of a puppy can teach the dog that it pays to be a bully and that nipping and misbehaving will allow it to get its way.

The items on your pup's daily to-do list will be potty calls, eating, drinking, playing, resting, training, grooming, and socializing. That's quite an agenda for a pint-size dog!

Once you have been playing with your new dog for an hour or so on that first day, take it back to the potty area. Remember that puppies usually need to relieve themselves every two hours or so and approximately half an hour after a meal. Give lots of praise if the mission is accomplished!

You have shown the puppy where it will go potty. The breeder has probably instructed you on the feeding schedule so if it is due for a meal, it's time to show your pup where it will eat. The breeder probably sent some food home with you. Toy and small-breed dogs can eat only a small amount of food at a time. Don't overfeed. Read the recommended amount on the bag of dog food. Initially, small-breed pups need to be fed several times a day because their tummies are so small. Feeding your pup on a regular schedule will help you manage its potty trips. To prevent accidents, feed it, and crate it for thirty minutes, then it's potty time once more. If not, it's time for some rest in its crate.

The crate will be kept near you at night. During the day, it can be placed in a quiet corner where the dog can sense the presence of family but be removed from the hubbub of activity to get its needed rest. Along with that all-important blanket with its mother's aroma, place one of your own unwashed T-shirts or socks inside the crate to add to the newcomer's comfy, scent-laden refuge when it's safely tucked away.

When you crate your dog for the first time, throw in some treats or a chew toy along with those all-important scented articles and then go about your business. It's fine for you and your family members to be busy nearby, but don't hover over the crate. The pup needs to get used to its little den. If it cries or whines, speak soothingly but let it be. It is probably tired from all the excitement of its homecoming and needs a rest. If you open the door and let it out every time it cries, it will soon learn that when it makes noise, you'll come running. It will eventually settle down, chew its toy, and take a snooze.

Puppy Behavior 101

Puppies are unpredictable, and they all get into trouble at one time or another. Establishing a routine for mealtime, playtime, resting, potty calls, and training will set limits for your new little friend and help it learn what's expected of it. Getting your dog used to its new life with you is a one-day-at-a-time process. Some days you'll make progress, and some days you won't, but you will need to be patient and keep your sense of humor.

Puppies are curious. They are very mouthy and will chew on whatever is at hand, from your cell phone to your new gloves. They always want to play, expressing this wish by pouncing, bouncing, rolling over, jumping up on you, and chasing anything that moves. They have short attention spans, so what totally fascinates them one minute can become totally boring the next. They like to vocalize, growling, yipping, and barking when they play, whining and crying when they feel lonely or neglected. They need lots of sleep and frequent potty walks.

They thrive on praise, love, and attention and are confused and frightened by angry outbursts and chaotic situations. Sure, there's a lot of ground to be covered on this journey through puppyhood, but as they master the rudiments of housebreaking, training, and socialization in their day-to-day routine with you, they will eventually get a handle on what is expected of them. Like small children, they do best when their caregivers are in charge, setting limits to make them feel secure in their world.

Adult Small Dog Behavior

Every adult dog that ends up in rescue programs or at the shelter has its own story of how it got there, and none of them are happy tales. When you take in an adult dog, you need to be aware that your home is at least its third place of residence.

When they are in the shelter, dogs don't always display their true personalities. They may be grieving, traumatized, or terrified by the changes in their lives or the by noise of that environment. Expect your older dog to need time, love, and understanding before it feels at home with you and your family. If it has had any behavior problems at the shelter, spend time with a counselor or behaviorist before you take it home so you can learn how to help it overcome these issues. Good shelters and rescue programs take the time to match their canine adoptees with suitable owners, so learn as much as you can about your dog's history before you bring it home.

 **Fact**

Adult dogs are the best choice for those who don't have the time or patience that a puppy requires. When you choose a shelter dog, you are also saving a life!

Unlike puppies, adult dogs are usually housebroken and socialized. They don't feel the need to chew on everything they can get their teeth into like puppies do. Some may even have mastered basic obedience. Furthermore, there is no truth to the old adage that you can't teach an old dog new tricks. With time and patience, adult dogs can master both basic obedience and pet tricks. Like puppies, they do best with a routine. Teaching them early on to recognize you as their leader helps them feel safe and secure in their new environment. They also thrive on praise. Like puppies, harsh treatment can make them fearful, withdrawn, defensive, or aggressive. Expect to witness your adult adoptee's true personality emerge into full bloom as it learns it has found a safe and loving home with you.

Chapter 8

Feeding Small Dogs

When it comes to taking care of a new puppy's nutritional needs, you'll need to take up where its mother left off. She will be a tough act to follow. During the first two days of its life, she provided powerful antibodies in her colostrum, the highly nutritional fluid she produced until her milk came in. After that, her milk met your pup's nutritional needs. The job of meeting your puppy's nutritional requirements is now up to you. If yours is an adult small dog, its dietary needs differ greatly from those of a puppy, but providing the proper nutrition is still vital to how it looks and feels.

Basic Dog Nutrition

Just like the people who love them, dogs need a balanced diet with the right amounts of protein, fat, carbohydrates, vitamins, minerals, and trace elements to keep them healthy. Dog diets are like those of their owners. They go through cycles in popularity according to the latest trends in nutritional knowledge. The table-scrap diet or commercial dog food in vogue when you owned your first dog as a child are now considered inadequate and outdated. Today, there is much controversy about dogs' dietary needs. Some experts view dogs as carnivores, while others consider them omnivores that do best with a wide spectrum of foods, including protein, grains, vegetables, fruits, and other natural substances. Those who espouse the omnivore theory note that when our dogs' progenitors had to survive on what they hunted, they ate much more than just meat. They also consumed the bones, internal organs, stomach contents, skin, and hair of their prey, providing them with essential nutrients that would be lacking in a meat-only diet.

Current Trends in Dog Nutrition

The current trend in dog nutrition favors whole foods. Minimally processed, whole foods get their name because they contain no nutritionally useless by-products. In other words, the less processed they are and the fewer chemical additives they contain, the better. Many owners also now opt to feed their dogs raw foods, supplementing with essential fatty acids, fruits, veggies, vitamins, and probiotics, enzymes that keep the flora of the dog's relatively short intestinal tract in balance to prevent gas, diarrhea, and constipation.

What are by-products, anyway? According to the Association of American Feed Control Officials (AAFCO), they are "nonrendered clean parts of carcasses of slaughtered animals." This would include heads, tails, feet, horns, hooves, beaks, feathers, hide, viscera (internal organs e.g., the heart, lungs, thorax, and intestines.) By-products are not necessarily bad. After all, dogs in their primitive state ate such items when they killed their own food. But in a high-quality dog diet, whether based on meat, poultry, or fish, the main protein source should be the real deal, not the stuff that gets thrown away when food is processed for human consumption.

When you read the ingredients of today's premium dog food, along with the protein and grain sources listed, you may be surprised to see such ingredients as fish oils, sweet potatoes, eggs, blueberries, cranberries, carrots, spinach, alfalfa, yogurt, flaxseed, and a host of vitamins and minerals. Chalk it up to advances in veterinary nutritional science. Over the last twenty-five years, we have learned to fine-tune the nutritional needs of our canine companions, adapting their food to suit their size, age, activity level, and physiology.

 **fact**

The dog food industry is now highly specialized, with an ever-growing variety of foods targeted toward puppies, adult dogs, working dogs, overweight dogs, canine senior citizens, and dogs with allergy problems. There are even breed-specific formulas, such as the one for bulldogs that alleviates their well-known gas problem.

Essential Nutrients

Dogs need a myriad of essential nutrients every day. Water tops the list. The loss of only 10 percent of a dog's body water can cause death. Next comes protein, the raw material for bones, muscle, nerve structure, and all other living tissue. The best proteins contain the essential amino acids that synthesize them, making them usable. Next comes fat, the fuel burned for energy and a big taste factor as well. Fats vary in nutritional value depending upon the content of essential fatty acids. These include omega-6, found mainly in vegetable oils, and omega-3, found in fish oil. Both are important for keeping cells healthy and for nourishing the skin and coat. Carbohydrates are available in the simple sugars found in fruits, milk, and honey (simple carbohydrates), as well as in starches and dietary fibers found in plants, including grains (complex carbohydrates). Also required in a balanced dog food is a full range of vitamins, minerals, and trace elements.

Whether you buy your dog's food or make it yourself, it is essential to provide a balanced diet appropriate for your dog's size, age, and physical condition. The right diet will have a huge bearing on your dog's quality of life and longevity.

Special Nutritional Needs of Small Dogs

Most of a small-breed puppy's growth occurs in the first six months of its life. At ten months it will be full-grown, having multiplied its birth weight by twenty months. To fuel this rapid growth, a proper ratio of protein, fat, vitamins, and minerals must be provided. Compared to their larger brethren, small dogs also have a higher metabolism, the process by which food is converted into energy within the dog's body. To further complicate matters, they lack the energy reserves of their larger counterparts as well.

 Fact

Per pound of body weight, toy and small-breed dogs have much larger energy requirements than large and medium-size dogs. A 6.5-pound dog needs 300 calories per day, twice as much per pound as the 130-pound giant who needs 3,000 calories daily.

Regardless of size, all puppies thrive on the same basic nutrients as adult dogs. Because of their speedy growth rate, the smaller breeds crave them in proportionately larger quantities. The energy requirement of a small-breed pup is two to four times that of an adult small dog. Puppies also need more protein and minerals for healthy bones and teeth. During their first six months of life, a small-breed pup gains about twenty grams per day. They may look like tiny toys, but these little tykes are actually the fuel-burning racecars of the canine world! Their speedy metabolism also makes them more prone to dehydration, so having a ready water supply is critical.

Quantity

Small dogs have less room in their stomachs than their medium- and large-breed counterparts. Still, they need to eat large amounts of food in relation to their body weight. To accomplish this, they need small meals, eaten several times a day until they are six months old. These mini-meals need to be high in calories and energy-dense. Growing up that fast takes lots of energy, and small dogs grow proportionately as much during their first year of life as we do in our first seventeen years.

Small dogs that do not eat on a regular schedule are also subject to blood sugar peaks and drops, causing their energy level to fluctuate dramatically. If your small dog has a finicky appetite, leave dry food in its bowl and let it feed whenever it pleases (a method known as free feeding). Canned or raw foods left out for long periods of time will spoil or attract bugs and bacteria, so free feeding works best with dry food. Spoiled food can cause gastroenteritis, resulting in gas, abdominal cramps, vomiting, and diarrhea. At ten months of age, the little tyke can graduate to adult food but will always require two meals a day. Buy smaller bags of dog food. Even with all those mini-meals, small dogs eat much less than larger ones and food left in the bag for a long period can spoil or deteriorate in taste and nutritional quality.

When you first bring that small pup home, follow the breeder's example. Feed the same food on the same schedule to help ease the transition. If you decide to change food, do so gradually, increasing the proportion of the new food over a week's time so that you won't cause any stomach upsets. For picky eaters, you can make meals more interesting by adding a spoonful of canned dog food to the dry. If you're cooking lean meats or veggies, you may also add a little—repeat, *little*—bit of your food to the dry. Just avoid feeding the dog from your plate. We love to baby our small dogs, but sharing your own meal from the dinner table leads to constant begging and poor eating habits for your dog.

The amount of food you give your dog depends on its size, weight, and activity level, the same factors that affect our food intake. The suggested amount is always printed on the label of the dry food bag and will increase with the dog's age and size. Note that amounts refer to "per day," not "per feeding"! Water intake will also depend on the dog's activity level.

Digestion

Small-breed dogs and puppies have a very limited capacity to digest starch. They lack our digestive enzymes and have a much shorter digestive tract. The grains and starches in their dog food turn into glucose, which is sugar. Too much of it can lead to hypoglycemia, hyperactivity, and diabetes. Watch that carb count when you read dog food package labels. A diet consisting of low starch and high meat protein works best for them.

Today's best dry foods have more digestible grains like barley, oatmeal, and brown rice for their carbohydrate base and more fresh fruits and vegetables as well, lowering their starch content. Corn, soy, and white rice are inexpensive grain sources for the dog food manufacturer, but they are not easily processed by the dog's system.

All meat proteins are not the same, either. In addition to the common protein sources of beef, lamb, and poultry, some foods now contain duck, turkey, and fish. Raw foods branch out even further, featuring rabbit, duck, mackerel, salmon, goat, quail, venison, ostrich, buffalo, and kangaroo. This plethora of proteins is offered not only for variety but to quell allergies to common meat sources now on the rise in dogs.

Bite-size pieces make the best dry food for small dogs. Your dog may have difficulty eating chunks that are too large or too hard. To make it easier for the dog to pick them up, the kibble or extruded pellets need to be small enough to fit those milk teeth and small jaws. Some premium dog foods offer special formulations for small dogs, some of which are breed-specific to suit your little dog.

 Essential

Lively and rapidly growing small-breed pups need twice the energy of adult dogs. Their higher metabolism rate and fast-developing bones, muscles, and immune systems require the right mix of nutrients to fuel this growth spurt. Their smaller mouths and tummies need the right size kibble for easy chewing and digestion.

Today's best premium foods offer our dogs much more than the basic meat and grain. They draw upon the nutrients provided by fruits and vegetables and are fortified with vitamins, beta carotene, amino acids, and probiotics, leading to higher absorption rates of vitamins and minerals.

Look for brands that do not contain large proportions of by-products, corn meal, corn bran or corn flour, white rice, or rendered animal fats. Look for natural preservatives like vitamin E, rather than chemicals like ethoxiquin, and avoid artificial food colorings.

Another thing to look for is human-grade meat, poultry, and fish protein sources. Your small dog will thrive on a healthy diet of whole foods, but it won't flourish on food stuffed with by-products, fillers, and chemicals.

Types of Diets

Dog foods come in four types: canned (also called wet or moist), dry, semi-moist, and raw (frozen). Choosing the right one or a balanced combination is up to you, so you need to understand the pros and cons of each type. The food you select should be nutritionally geared to your dog's age, condition, and health history. Your budget is a consideration as well, but keep in mind that bargain-basement dog foods may lead to higher vet bills down the road.

Canned Food

Canned dog food consists of 60 to 85 percent water. Brands vary widely in quality as well as in protein sources, cereals, and other ingredients, so you need to do your homework before you buy. Premium brands offer good protein sources as well as sufficient vegetable fiber content, and some are further enhanced by vegetables and fruits. Small dogs that eat a canned food diet must also have hard chewy food, treats, or toys as well to aid in teething, to satisfy their need to chew, and to keep their teeth and gums healthy. If the canned food you choose has a high meat content, feed it mixed with a little dry kibble.

Dry Food

These foods vary in texture and size of the particles, from gravel-like kibble to extruded forms that look like breakfast cereal, uniform in shape. Their moisture content is usually 10 to 12 percent. Dry foods have most of the moisture removed and are therefore more economical than canned.

They may be eaten dry or mixed with water, canned food, or raw food, but remember that when your dog chews its dry food, it is also cleaning its teeth and gums. Since many small breeds are prone to problems with their teeth, plain dry is better for their dental health. Its hard and crunchy texture helps satisfy the pup's need to chew as well.

Semi-Moist Food

High in sugar and preservatives, semi-moist foods usually contain 40 percent water and high sugar levels. Their chewy consistency is sometimes provided by propylene glycol, a chemical compound used as an emulsifier, which has been linked to severe health problems in cats. Artificial food coloring makes these foods look like real meat or cheese, a marketing strategy aimed at owners, not pets. Most dogs love this doggie fast food, but all that the sugar can contribute to obesity and dental problems.

Alert!

Obesity puts a small dog at higher risk, placing stress on its heart, joints, lungs, kidneys, and liver. Like overweight people, overweight dogs are far more prone to develop diabetes. Carrying excess poundage on its small frame depletes the dog's energy and makes surgery riskier as well.

Raw Food

The latest thing in feeding, raw dog foods have emerged during the last decade as one of the strongest trends in the dog food arena. Their popularity reflects a growing belief that our dogs need a raw, natural diet like their ancestors ate to achieve maximum health and vitality. Accompanying this theory is the opinion that commercial dog foods do not supply the nutrients our dogs need. A new generation of consumers is now questioning the belief that all dog food comes prepackaged and that as dog owners, our only role is to open that can or bag and serve it up.

One of the earliest proponents of the raw diet was Dr. Ian Billinghurst, an Australian veterinarian who instituted what he termed the *Biologically Appropriate Raw Food*, or BARF, diet. This is Billinghurst's recipe for returning our dogs to their evolutionary roots. It relies on raw meaty bones and ground up vegetables and organ meats. The diet is further enhanced by a myriad of supplements such as vitamins, essential fatty acids, probiotics, kelp, alfalfa, and herbs.

The raw-food revolution's appeal is based on the belief that many of today's dog diseases and allergies are directly linked to commercial dog foods, most of which contain substandard meats and lack essential live enzymes, vitamins, and other nutrients. It is further fueled by the desire of many dog owners to take back the responsibility for dietary decision making from mass manufacturers. (Of course, numerous companies producing these raw foods have sprung up all over.)

Raw diets are said to simulate the menu that nature intended for canine carnivores. Dogs have a shorter digestive tract, designed to quickly process the food that they eat before harmful bacteria can multiply and cause problems (the reason a dog can eat a rotting carcass without getting sick). Their jaws and teeth are designed to rip and tear, not to move side to side in a grinding motion like ours do as we chew. Human saliva contains enzymes that start breaking down our food before we even swallow it, but dogs have no such enzyme in their saliva. All of their digestion takes place in their stomach. Among the benefits claimed by raw-diet enthusiasts are a decrease in common canine illnesses, longer lives, and less dental disease.

The raw-food revolution is not without its detractors. Some warn that feeding uncooked meats calls for vigilant preparation and storage to prevent the spread of deadly bacteria like salmonella and E. coli. Spoiled raw food can make a dog very ill.

Feeding raw food is also a lot more work. For the dog owner, a large part of the popularity of prepared commercial dog foods is their convenience. Homemade and commercial raw diets need to be tweaked with all sorts of supplements to make them nutritionally balanced. For your dog's sake, such a switch should not be undertaken lightly. It's another area that calls for lots of homework.

 Essential

Whatever diet you choose, make sure that your dog always has plenty of water available. Wash its bowls daily, and don't feed your dog from your own plates. Along with its own special place to eat, a dog should have its own dishes.

Reading Dog Food Labels

When shopping for the right food for your dog, learn how to read those bags and cans. Dog food labeling is regulated by both the U.S. Food and Drug Administration (FDA) and the Association of American Feed Control Officials (AAFCO). By law, the ingredients on that package of dog food must be listed in order of their predominance by weight.

Protein percentages are important as well, ranging from around 28 percent for growing pups to 22 to 24 percent for adults to 17 or 18 percent for overweight or aging dogs. Fat percentages follow the same sort of pyramid—more for puppies, less as dogs grow from adults to senior citizens. Fiber content is highest for dogs on a low-calorie diet, as it makes them feel full. Also listed are stabilizers, artificial colors, and preservatives.

 Fact

"Artificial colors are not really necessary, except to please the pet owner's eye," states the FDA document on dog food labeling. "If used, they must be from approved sources, the same as for human foods."

As to package claims of "no preservatives," unless something is used to prevent fat in dog food from becoming rancid, it could be toxic to your pet.

No product can claim to be "complete," "balanced," or "100 percent nutritious" if it is inadequate as the sole food for your pet. Labels must also list the life stage for which a food is intended. Just because the food provides 100 percent complete nutrition for your adult dog does not imply it will do the same for your puppy.

AAFCO has a "95 percent rule" on ingredients like the meat, poultry, or fish. If the label reads "Beef for dogs," for example, the product must be at least 95 percent beef. If it says "Chicken and liver," the two must be present in equal amounts to make up 95 percent of the product.

The agency also has a "25 percent" or "dinner" rule. This states that in food described as "Beef Dinner for Dogs," beef should comprise at least 25 percent and less than 95 of the ingredients by weight. Similarly, if more than one ingredient is listed in a dinner, such as "Chicken and Fish Dinner," that second ingredient must comprise at least 3 percent of the total 25 percent.

Alert!

To avoid stomach upset when changing your dog's diet, it's best to make a gradual change to the new food. Add it slowly over a five- to seven-day period, increasing the amount of new food daily so that the switch is completed by day seven.

Under the rule regarding use of the term *flavor*, a specific percentage is not required, but the food must contain "an amount sufficient to be able to be detected." Beef flavor doesn't even have to come from beef. It can be a beefy-tasting facsimile concocted in the lab instead.

Finally, check the expiration date on that bag of food, and don't store it longer than a month to ensure freshness and good taste. Dog food labels contain a wealth of information, but you have to know how to read them. Most companies provide a toll-free telephone number, so if you have any questions, don't hesitate to call the manufacturer.

Are Supplements Necessary?

Today's premium dog foods are light years ahead of the bargain brands. They also purport to be 100 percent nutritionally complete. But dogs are individuals, just like the people who care for them. Some have special nutritional needs and conditions that make it necessary to supplement their diet. Supplements are needed only when the dog's diet fails to supply the optimal levels of a needed nutrient.

For dogs with immune deficiencies, a high-potency multivitamin and mineral supplement will help correct such deficiencies, building strength and vitality. Older dogs with arthritis, degenerative disc disease, or hip and joint problems benefit from supplements containing glucosamine, chondroitin sulfate, and MSM (methylsulfonylmethane, a naturally occurring sulfur from grapeseed that reduces inflammation and provides pain relief). Shark cartilage is also used to support joint and connective tissue functions in dogs.

For dogs with skin problems, supplements containing essential fatty acids (omega-3, omega-6, and omega-9), and oils from fish, flaxseed, borage seed, primrose, and sunflower help revitalize dull coats and flaky skin.

The nutritional needs of breeding bitches call for a high-calorie growth and/or lactation diet. Lactating females need approximately three times their normal maintenance requirement. In addition to their higher calorie needs, some small-breed dams need calcium supplements to prevent eclampsia, a dangerous drop in the production of calcium. This condition is common with large litters, which places too great a demand on the dam's calcium reserves and it can be a life-threatening event. Upping her calcium intake without medical supervision could do more harm than good, so this is a call that must be made by your vet.

Dimethylglycine (DMG) is a supplement used to improve athletic ability and stamina by boosting the dog's ability to utilize oxygen and improve respiratory function. It also increases recovery time and supports the immune system, cardiovascular health, and liver function. It is used primarily for dogs involved in athletic competition.

The popularity of raw food diets for dogs has spotlighted supplements and whetted the public's desire to learn more about them. Most such diets are formulated on a 90/10 ratio (90-percent animal and animal-related ingredients, 10-percent foragable plants) plus other biologically necessary ingredients for enzymes and proper digestion. Raw-food proponents also rely on herbs to bridge the gap between what the dog needs to function properly and what it requires for extra support.

Wild carnivores obtained many essential nutrients when they ate all parts of an animal's body. Often, their prey were herbivores like deer and rabbit, so that meat was rich in these substances as well. But animals used as protein sources in commercial dog food are fed grain, and they are often given hormones and antibiotics in large doses.

Raw-fooders also endorse the probiotic acidophilus, the so-called good bacteria that aids in the digestive process. Found in many yogurts, acidophilus helps alleviate gas, bloating, and diarrhea.

 Fact

Plain canned pumpkin (not pumpkin pie filling, with all its sugar, spice, and creamy fat) is another favored remedy for both diarrhea and constipation, used widely by those who serve raw foods.

Mixtures of greens are also used, sometimes with such added ingredients as kelp, spirulina (blue-green algae), garlic, pumpkin seed, flax, and burdock. Available in liquid, capsule, and powdered form, dietary supplements should be used carefully and under the supervision of your vet.

What about Treats?

Dogs are crazy about treats, so much so that they are a huge aid in training as well as a great way just to show your love. Dogs relish biscuits, freeze-dried liver, preserved tendons, jerky treats, gristle, pig ears, hooves, and a host of animal body parts that make some of us feel squeamish. They also love nylon bones, dental bones treated with chlorophyll for clean teeth and fresh breath, rawhide, and real bones—fresh, frozen, or preserved. Like chew toys, these provide good chewing activity, strengthening jaw muscles and cleaning the teeth in the process. Still, some may be too big or too hard for small dogs, causing tooth fractures.

When it comes to cookies and biscuits, the smaller the better. Dogs don't know the difference, and they don't need the extra calories. As you would with dog food, look for healthy ingredients. Cookies should not be high in sugar or fat, and their ingredients should complement the good food you feed your tiny dog. Some contain meat and cheese, while natural varieties offer peanuts, yogurt, apples, bananas, fish, and sweet potatoes plus omega-3 and omega-6 fatty acids. Some are simply a premium dog food in cookie form.

Look for whole-grain sources and good proteins. If yours is an older dog, offer treats with glucosamine and chondroitin to relieve arthritis and joint pain. If you have a chubby canine, go for the low-calorie biscuits.

Alert!

Don't let your dog fill up on treats before meals. If you use treats for training, cut back on meal portions after the training session so you won't overstuff your little dog.

Rawhide and bones, real or processed, present a potential choking hazard, so dogs should be supervised while enjoying these treats. If they break off a piece and ingest it, they can choke. If it lodges in their digestive tract, dogs can suffer an intestinal blockage that can be fatal. Pups with tiny teeth or dogs that are extremely powerful chewers should not be given real bones. They can chew too hard and fracture their teeth or splinter the bones. Hard rubber toys with healthy treats stuffed inside are safer for them. Don't be afraid to sparingly offer raw carrots, apples, bananas, or a bit of cheese instead of store-bought goodies. Avoid raw white potatoes, especially if they have sprouted or have green skins. Milk and cream can cause diarrhea but yogurt and cottage cheese are fine.

Finally, remember that human snacks are often dangerous to dogs. Treats are a great way to show affection to your little dog but your time, attention, kind words, and hands-on pats are also a great way to show your love.

Chapter 9

Health and Preventive Care

The veterinarian you choose for your small dog will be your partner and best resource in caring for your dog's health. Take as much care choosing this medical professional as you would in finding your own physician. You want a person who will take the time to explain a treatment plan, whether it's a regular routine of preventive medicine or an illness or injury that calls for surgery or other medical intervention. Not all veterinarians work well with toy breeds. Your breeder or local breed club should be able to recommend one who knows and appreciates a dog like yours.

Visiting a Veterinarian

Your small dog is a member of your family. Your vet should treat your dog with tender loving care and understand that when it comes to handling, a papillon is not a Labrador retriever. The best vets for small dogs understand their special needs. Some high-strung small dogs find a trip to the vet highly stressful. Some are so strongly bonded to their owners that they become fearful in the hands of another person. This calls for a vet with a gentle, kind approach and a soothing manner.

You can usually sense whether a vet likes your breed and your dog in particular. Not surprisingly, so can your little dog. Dogs are amazingly adept at reading our body language and emotions through our tone and touch. It may take awhile for your dog to trust this important new person in its life, but if you find the right vet, eventually you and your dog will find that all-important rapport that makes for a good doctor-patient relationship.

Small dogs can be just as difficult for the vet to handle as big dogs, especially if they are used to being coddled and getting their own way. Any dog that feels fearful and anxious is likely to nip in self-defense. Even if it doesn't bite, it can panic and struggle, staging a dramatic performance worthy of Hollywood and making the examination very difficult for all concerned. Achieving a good relationship with your vet is not all up to the vet. You have an important part to play in this equation as well.

Preparing for Your First Visit

You can prepare your little dog for its vet visit and lower its anxiety level by initiating your own handling sessions at home. First, socialize it within the family circle by letting everybody hold it and pet it. Although we all like to think we are the center of our dog's universe, life will be far easier for all concerned if that pup learns to trust other people, too.

Get your dog used to being handled. Touch its feet; rub its ears and look inside; open its mouth; check its teeth. This will help desensitize your dog so that it does not panic when the vet does the same thing.

Train your dog to stand for examination. Placing your dog on a table or counter with its leash on, teach it the "Stand" command. Place one hand under its tummy and gently pull the leash toward you while saying "Stand." Reward your pup with a treat or lavish praise when it complies.

 Fact

By visiting the vet early and regularly, congenital diseases may be detected and often can be managed or corrected.

What to Expect

Once you've accustomed your dog to being handled all over its body, the first step in its preventive medicine routine is a physical exam by your vet. When you enter the waiting room, keep your dog on a short leash, in your lap, or in its carrier. Letting it approach animals it does not know in the vet's waiting room can be dangerous. Keeping your small dog calm and quiet will make you feel less anxious as well.

The vet will begin your dog's basic series of "core" vaccinations, typically given at eight, ten, and twelve weeks of age, followed by a rabies vaccination at fourteen weeks. If your pup has not been dewormed, bring along a stool sample. In addition to its core vaccinations, the vet will also recommend vaccinating against other illnesses if your puppy's risk of exposure calls for such protection.

If your new dog is an adult that is up-to-date on its shots, an introductory checkup is still a good idea. This visit will provide the perfect opportunity for you, your dog, and the vet to get to know each other. Adult dogs require an annual physical examination, vaccinations, heartworm tests, and intestinal parasite checks. Your vet will check your dog all over, including eyes, ears, teeth, gums, heart, and lungs, and will observe its movement and determine if it is underweight or overweight. The dog's skin will be examined for parasites, lumps, sores, and signs of allergies, and the vet will answer any questions you may have about caring for this new family member. Blood tests may be performed on older dogs to check liver and kidney functions and blood sugar.

Vaccinations

The subject of canine vaccination is currently under scrutiny. It used to be unquestioned. Your puppy would undergo a rigorous series of shots to protect it from numerous diseases, usually bundled into one shot administered at two-week to three-week intervals beginning at eight weeks of age. Not anymore. Like all fields, veterinary science has evolved and changed, and numerous health problems in our dogs may indicate that we have taken all this vaccinating too far. Serious side effects have been linked to the number and types of vaccines administered, and in recent years, studies have shown that routine vaccinations are effective far longer than originally thought.

 **Fact**

Parvovirus is especially dangerous to puppies and is often fatal. It attacks their gastrointestinal system, causing bleeding, diarrhea, vomiting, and dehydration. It spreads through contact with infected dogs or their feces, food, or water. People who come in contact with infected dogs can carry the virus on their shoes and clothing.

So-called live viruses are weakened miniscule amounts of the virus itself, insufficient to give your dog the disease unless it has a weakened immune system. Killed vaccines are more stable, but they do not offer the same strong protection as the live variety and have to be given at more frequent intervals. It is now believed that the vaccines themselves, whether live or killed, and the practice of automatic yearly boosters, could harm a dog's immune system, triggering autoimmune diseases. Other serious side effects have been observed as well, among them anaphylactic shock, occurring most frequently among small dogs, as well as infections at the site where the vaccine has been injected.

Five years ago, bucking the knee-jerk practice of annual shots for our dogs, Dr. Ronald Schultz of the University of Wisconsin instead recommended an "every three- or more-year" vaccination schedule for cats and dogs. The Colorado State University Veterinary Teaching Hospital reinforced this change by announcing a new vaccination protocol. The American Animal Hospital Association (AAHA) followed suit, encouraging individual dog owners to work with their vet to devise the best program for their dog.

This trend was also reinforced by the American Veterinary Medical Association (AVMA), which agrees that "unnecessary stimulation of the immune system does not result in enhanced disease resistance and may increase the risk of adverse postvaccination events." The AVMA recommends that vets create "core" and "non-core" vaccination programs, and that schedules be customized to fit the needs of each individual animal. The core program of most vital shots would protect against rabies, parvovirus, adenovirus, hepatitis, and distemper. The non-core program targets diseases that are of limited risk in the region where you live or that pose less of a threat to the dog because of lifestyle.

Essential

Your small dog's vaccination schedule should be based upon its size, age, condition, and risk of exposure.

Note that none of these authorities recommends discontinuing vaccinations altogether. Vaccines remain our first line of defense against dread diseases that can be fatal to a dog. However, especially in the case of small- and toy-breed dogs, the practice of giving multiple vaccines in one shot and automatic yearly boosters is a matter of grave concern. These smaller canines have had more adverse reactions than their larger counterparts, and yet they are given the same dosage that Great Danes receive. Some breeders now advise against combination shots for small dogs, citing reactions ranging from fever, extreme exhaustion, and allergic reaction to anaphylactic shock. If you follow this dictum and ask your vet to rotate individual vaccines (rather than bundling them into one shot), be aware that this means more trips to the vet and increased out-of-pocket costs for you.

Many breeders now recommend that vets takes a titer, a blood test to determine a dog's immunity against a particular disease before administering the vaccination. This involves another expense as well. Your small dog's health is, of course, your first consideration—all the more reason why it's imperative to discuss the matter with your vet before choosing a course of action.

Denise Trapani, DVM, of The Animal Health Center in Walpole, Massachusetts, follows a core protocol for puppies. She administers three shots at eight, twelve, and sixteen weeks of age, from such diseases as parvovirus, adenovirus 2, parainfluenza, and distemper. "I don't automatically give the leptospirosis vaccine, especially to small dogs, because they tend to have more reactions to it," she says. "I will only do it if they are at risk."

Not all experts feel the same, as reflected in the view of Dr. Leanne Bertani. Writing on vaccines for *Cavaliers Online,* the newsletter for fanciers of the cavalier King Charles spaniel, Dr. Bertani states, "Leptospirosis is an important disease because it can be transmitted to man and some other animals, and can cause severe kidney disease." She adds that "it is one of the vaccines most likely to cause a fatal anaphylaxis in puppies." Similarly, she recommends vaccinations against coronavirus, bordetella, giardia, and Lyme disease only on a case-by-case basis. Again, as a small dog owner, you need to assess your own pet's risk when you plan its vaccination program.

Rabies is a different matter. Rabies is a viral disease affecting the central nervous system, transmitted by contact with the saliva of an infected animal. Once the symptoms appear, it is almost always fatal. This is why you should not let your dog come in contact with wildlife. Your dog's outdoor play should always be supervised. Any sightings of wild animals acting unusually aggressive or moving with a staggering gait should immediately be reported to your local animal control officer.

Rabies is on the rise among wildlife in the United States and is transmittable to humans as well. Vaccinated dogs and cats serve as buffers between us and infected wild animals. Raccoon, skunks, coyotes, foxes, woodchucks, bats, and some farm animals are most susceptible to getting rabies. Each state requires rabies vaccination, but the schedule varies from state to state. The first rabies shot is usually given at sixteen weeks of age.

Regular Checkups

Routinely, when our dogs went to the vet for yearly booster shots, they received an annual physical as well. Getting those shots was a built-in guarantee that they would see the vet at least once a year. With today's changing vaccination protocols, the emphasis has switched to preventive care.

Alert!

Just like us, our dogs need an annual physical. It's a good opportunity for the vet to keep tabs on their overall health and to uncover any problems that may have cropped up since the last visit.

Dogs change as they age. Small dogs in particular are noted for their longevity, living well into their teens. As your dog's primary caretaker, you are the expert on its day-to-day well-being. When you take it for its annual visit, report any changes you have noticed to the vet. Before you go, you may want to jot down a list of questions or topics you wish to discuss so you can make the most use of your time together. Keep a file on your dog's health records from day one. In case of an emergency, this information may be vital to your dog's treatment and recovery.

Spaying and Neutering

The main reason for spaying and neutering is to avoid unplanned pregnancies, but the procedures have many other health benefits for our dogs as well. For female dogs, spaying prevents breast, ovarian, and uterine cancer and a potentially fatal uterine disease called pyometra. Since spaying involves the removal of the ovaries and uterus, reproductive problems associated with heat cycles, pregnancy, and aging will also be prevented.

Spaying your dog will make your life easier too. You won't have to deal with the bloody discharge with its staining and odor every eight months or so, when your female comes into heat, or the gathering of lusty canine suitors on your front porch. Current research advocates spaying and neutering as early as sixteen to twenty-four weeks of age. The spaying procedure, known as ovariohysterectomy, is typically recommended before the female dog has had her first estrus, or heat.

Such early spaying may not be advantageous for small breeds, however. In the case of toy breeds, some vets prefer to wait until the dog is five and a half to six months of age before spaying and neutering. Because small female dogs mature much faster than their larger-breed counterparts, they may come into heat as early as six months of age, so to be on the safe side, the spaying may need to wait until after that first estrus. Make sure your vet takes your small dog's special needs into account before you schedule spaying or neutering surgery.

 **Fact**

Dogs that have been spayed or neutered live longer and healthier lives than those that have not.

Most vets will keep your dog overnight after it is spayed, and the at-home recuperation period lasts for about two weeks. The female's activity for the first week should be restricted. If she is determined to chew or lick at her sutures, get a plastic Elizabethan collar from the vet to prevent her from opening her incision. Spaying does decrease the metabolic rate in dogs, so be careful not to overfeed your little female, causing undesirable weight gain.

Some dog owners often balk at the suggestion that their male dogs should be neutered. Medically, this procedure is called orchidectomy, but its more common name is castration, so it's easy to understand why some male owners might have an emotional reaction. However, it is a safe and easy operation with many benefits for your dog. Because it involves removal of the testicles, testicular cancer will be prevented, as will prostate problems common to unneutered male dogs as they age.

In addition, neutering also has behavioral implications, decreasing aggression, territorial urine marking, mounting of other dogs, and the tendency to wander off in search of females. On most dogs, it is usually performed when the male is twelve weeks of age, but the procedure can be done as early as eight weeks. Once again, you need to ask the vet about risks involved with early surgery on small- and toy-breed dogs under six months of age. Once home, your little fellow should be kept quiet for a week or so, and the Elizabethan collar may also be used on him too to prevent licking the incision.

According to the Humane Society of the United States (HSUS), spaying and neutering are beneficial for your dog because the procedures help dogs live longer and healthier lives, eliminate health problems, and make them more affectionate companions. The HSUS also points to many ways in which spaying and neutering dogs benefits the community, including the following:

- Communities spend millions of dollars to control unwanted animals.
- Irresponsible breeding contributes to the problem of dog bites and attacks.
- Animal shelters are overburdened with surplus animals.
- Stray pets and homeless animals get into trash containers, defecate in public areas or on private lawns, and frighten or anger people who have no understanding of their misery or needs.
- Some stray animals also scare away or kill birds and wildlife.

Your little dog is highly unlikely to become a stray, but as a dog lover, neutering it is a positive step toward curbing the euthanasia of thousands of healthy pets that end up in shelters every year.

Flea Control

Fleas are small in size, but they cause untold misery to our pets. Each year we spend billions to get rid of them. At one millimeter in length, fleas are hard-shelled six-legged insects with powerful jaws and sucking mouths that must feed on blood to survive. They are wingless, but since they possess the uncanny ability to leap seven feet high and thirteen feet across a room, it's a snap for them to hop aboard a passing dog.

 Fact

A flea can jump as high as seven feet and as long as thirteen feet with the G-force of a rocket being launched.

Fleas thrive year-round in warm Southern climates and come out with the first flowers of spring everywhere else. In the Northeast, they peak in

August and September. No matter where you live or how harsh the winters, they can live in your house year-round.

The flea completes its life cycle in about a month, from egg to larva to pupa to adult. Once they have had a blood meal, they reproduce at an alarming rate, sometimes laying thousands of eggs. Though the adult fleas can live happily on your dog, the eggs they lay fall into the carpet, the yard, your dog's bed, or wherever the dog travels.

Besides causing the incessant itching and scratching that drives dogs and their owners crazy, fleas can make your dog sick. When they bite, the saliva they inject into the dog can cause an allergic reaction, ranging in severity from hair loss and sores to illness and disability. Some dogs lick and bite at themselves to the point of causing lick granulomas. These wounds become infected, are stubborn to heal, and can cause permanent damage. In extreme cases, infections can lead to thickened hairless skin, permanent sores, and limb amputations. Although each flea bite takes only a tiny bit of blood, a lot of bites can cause anemia. Very young and very old dogs are most at risk for this. Fleas also carry tapeworms, transmitted when the dog ingests the fleas while licking itself. To add insult to injury, fleas like to bite humans, too.

Alert!

The adult fleas you see on your pet are only the tip of the iceberg. In a serious infestation, the eggs, larvae, and pupae in your home and yard account for the 95 percent you don't see.

Here are some surefire ways to determine whether your itchy dog has fleas:

- Push the hair by its tail against the grain and look at the skin. You may not see the fleas themselves, but if you see what looks like salt and pepper, that is a combination of flea eggs and feces.
- Look at the dog's belly and groin. Hair is sparse in those areas, so it's easier to spot fleas.
- Run a fine-toothed flea comb through the coat. If you come up with the pesky pests on the comb, drop them into rubbing alcohol, soapy water, or flea spray to kill them.

- Place your dog on a white towel or sheet, and comb or brush the coat. Fleas or their feces, tiny black specks, will drop off and be visible on the light-colored surface.

If you discover the tiny terrors, your work has just begun. Flea control is not a one-shot deal. It takes persistence and vigilance to keep these little bloodsuckers at bay.

You need to get rid of fleas on the dog as well as those in its environment. You can book the dog at the groomer's for a flea bath, and schedule a professional exterminator to come while the dog is away from home. You can also buy products to use on the yard and home yourself (not advisable if you are pregnant). If you choose to be your own exterminator, begin by washing the dog's bedding, with dry bleach added to the wash. Next, vacuum thoroughly, then throw the vacuum bag, tightly sealed within another plastic bag, into the outdoor trash barrel or dumpster. Now use premise-control spray under the beds and on upholstered furniture, pulling off cushions and pillows to do a thorough job. Be sure to spray the interior of your car as well.

Place all foodstuffs in closed cabinets, and put the dog's dishes in the dishwasher. Then release one flea fogger (also known as a flea bomb) per room and leave the house immediately for three hours. To make sure you have gotten all the little hatchlings, you'll need to fog again in two weeks.

Outdoors, use a lawn-and-kennel spray, concentrating on areas frequented by your dog. Make sure to treat dark damp areas behind the garage or shed, the woodpile, or under the porch while you're at it. During flea season, it's best to spray the outdoor area every week. Together, these options give you a myriad of products to tackle the job of protecting your dog.

Long-acting residual flea products have drastically changed the way we fight fleas. Gone are the days when powders, sprays, and flea collars were our only defenses. Today's flea fighters for our dogs fall into three categories: topical products, oral treatments, and flea collars.

Topical Products

Applied once a month to one spot on your small dog's neck or to a spot between its shoulder blades, these flea-killing substances travel all over its body through the coat oils within twelve to seventy-two hours, wrapping the dog in a protective shield against fleas. Products that kill both fleas and ticks include Frontline and Advantage, both of which interfere with the flea's nerve transmissions. Advantage washes off if a dog goes swimming or gets a bath, while Frontline is waterproof.

Revolution, a wide-spectrum product, also paralyzes fleas and prevents ticks, mange, and mites. These products are available only from your vet, but Biospot, also applied monthly, is sold at pet supply shops and groomers.

Oral Treatments

Program is a pill that is given once a month and acts as flea birth control. It uses a man-made protein that prevents flea eggs and larvae from developing into adult fleas. Because it does not kill adult fleas on the dog, Program must be used in conjunction with a flea shampoo.

Alert!

One disadvantage to Program is that the flea must bite the dog to ingest its dose of flea birth control, preventing future generations of hatchlings. For dogs with allergies to flea saliva, even a few bites can trigger an allergic reaction—severe itching and self-inflicted skin damage caused by scratching.

Like Program, Sentinel also uses a manmade protein but combines it with a broad-spectrum parasite fighter called Interceptor, not only sterilizing the fleas but preventing heartworm, whipworm, hookworm, and roundworm as well. Because it doesn't kill adult fleas on the dog, you'll need to use a good flea shampoo with this product too.

A newer product, Capstar, offers no long-term residual effect but knocks out the live flea population on your dog within thirty minutes. It safe for puppies weighing two pounds or more as well as pregnant or nursing dogs and can be used as often as needed with no harmful effects.

Spot-on and pill flea-control products each have their own advantages and disadvantages. For pills to work, the flea must bite the dog. If a dog is highly allergic to flea saliva, a spot-on product would be a better choice.

However, some owners don't like the topical products because they can leave a greasy spot on the dog's back.

Flea Collars

The old standby in the war against fleas, flea collars offer mixed results. They are more effective on smaller dogs than their larger counterparts because the small dog has less of an area to cover and protect.

Ticks

Of the 850 species of ticks worldwide, the one posing the biggest threat to our dogs and us is the deer or black-legged tick. It carries Lyme disease as well as ehrlichiosis and babesiosis and is suspected of transmitting the virus that causes encephalitis in dogs.

Unlike fleas, ticks are not insects. They are members of the arachnid family. Like fleas, however, they are parasites that need blood meals from their host to survive. The female tick lays her eggs on the ground in the early spring. By late spring, they hatch and larvae emerge. These attach to small animals like mice for a blood meal.

Once the larvae have eaten their fill, they drop off and molt, shedding their hard exoskeletons and morphing into their nymph phase. The nymph is dormant over the winter but it wakes up hungry in the spring. The nymph's most common host is the white-tailed deer, but if it gets the chance, it will attach itself to humans and pets as well.

Ticks do not jump like fleas. They crawl onto their host, usually from a hiding place in tall grass. They respond to body heat, carbon dioxide, and the vibrations created by footsteps and they like warm hairy places. To transmit a disease, they have to be dug into their host for twenty-four hours.

On unvaccinated dogs, Lyme disease shows up about four weeks after the tick has bitten them. The symptoms are lameness, fever, lethargy, swollen joints, depression, and loss of appetite. If not treated immediately with a regimen of antibiotics, joint damage will progress and lesions will form on the kidneys, possibly leading to kidney failure. Other devastating effects are neurological and heart problems. Lyme disease is often hard to diagnose, so if you live in an area where ticks are prevalent and your dog spends a lot of time out-of-doors, it should receive the Lyme vaccination.

Alert!

The Center for Disease Control in Atlanta has confirmed that Lyme disease poses a serious threat for the entire northeastern region of the United States as far south as Maryland as well as the states of Minnesota, Wisconsin, and Michigan.

Ticks thrive in wooded areas, so cut back brushy areas on your property, get rid of wood and rock piles, and keep the lawn mowed. If you and your dog go walking in the woods, spray your dog with Permethrin or have it wear a tick collar containing Amitraz. Preventic and Tick Arrest are two such collars. They offer protection against ticks only, not fleas. Topical products such as Frontline, Advantage, Revolution, K9 Advantix, and Biospot will also kill ticks. However, on all such products, it is vitally important that you buy only the formulas labeled for use on small dogs.

If you find a tick on your dog, don't pull it off with your bare hands. Use a tissue, latex gloves, tweezers, or a tick remover (available at pet supply stores) to pull it off, making sure to remove its mouthparts in the process. Don't squish it or flush it down the toilet. Instead, drop it into a container of alcohol or flea and tick spray to kill it. If the resulting bite on your dog looks red and swollen, wash with hydrogen peroxide and apply an antibacterial ointment.

Observe your dog closely after applying any flea and tick products. If you suspect an adverse reaction, bathe immediately with a mild dog shampoo and rinse thoroughly. If the dog appears lethargic, is losing its balance, or shows signs of seizure or vomiting, take it to your vet right away. You should also report the incident to the product manufacturer and to the U.S. Environmental Protection Agency (EPA).

Today, we are fortunate to have such an arsenal of products to protect our dogs from fleas and ticks, but they must be used wisely. Combining such products willy-nilly without reading labels could cause more problems than the pests you are trying to prevent.

Chapter 10

Illness and Disease

Your little dog can't talk, but if you pay attention, it has other ways of letting you know how it feels. You know the signs of good health in your dog: bright clear eyes, a shiny coat without sores or bald patches, nice pink gums, and a healthy clean smell. It's upsetting to think of your small dog becoming sick or injured, but even with the best food, sufficient exercise, regular veterinary care, and lots of affection, there are bound to be times when your dog is under the weather and in need of medical attention. How will you know?

Recognizing Signs of Illness or Injury

You're already the expert on your dog's behavior. You know its personality, energy level, likes, and dislikes, so you have a big advantage when it comes to recognizing that something is amiss. Changes in your dog's appearance or behavior could indicate that all is not well. Pay particular attention to the following:

- **Loss of appetite:** Maybe Spunky is just fed up with the same old dog food. But if your little dog refuses to eat and a diet change doesn't do the trick, it may be a sign of illness.
- **Drinking habits:** If your small dog drinks water as if it can't quench its thirst or stops drinking it altogether, this could also signal a problem.
- **Elimination:** Diarrhea is always a concern. Pint-size dogs dehydrate more quickly. The problem may be something your dog ate, but it could also indicate a virus or a worm infestation. Note the color and consistency of your dog's normal stool so you'll be aware of changes. Evidence of parasites, blood, a dog that strains or cries when it tries to eliminate, a marked change in the frequency of needed potty calls, or increased accidents indoors should alert you to a possible medical problem.
- **Vomiting:** Dogs can be notoriously indiscreet about the things they eat and drink, so occasionally they will get an upset tummy. Withhold food and water for one feeding. If your dog keeps its next meal down, you don't need to run to the vet. Repeated stomach upsets and vomit containing blood or parts of ingested foreign objects indicate an emergency situation. Gagging might also indicate that the dog is trying to expel something it swallowed.
- **Coughing, wheezing, and sneezing:** These can indicate a respiratory infection as well as heart, lung, or tracheal problems, so they call for prompt checking by the vet.
- **Seizures:** In young dogs, these are not usually life-threatening and are commonly short in duration, but they need to be brought to the vet's attention, especially if they last more than five minutes or recur. When having a seizure, your dog may appear dazed and confused

and may shake, pant, or lose its balance. Seizures are often hereditary and are usually controllable with medication.

- **Weight changes:** If your little dog appears to be rapidly losing or
gaining weight or has a bloated belly, it needs to see the vet.

- **Discharge:** Runny eyes; a drippy nose; and brown, black, or yellow
discharge from the ears are all signs of illness or infection.

- **Eye problems:** A closed, swollen, or squinting eye could indicate an
ulcerated cornea or the presence of foreign matter. Flush gently with
eyewash and see the vet.

- **Growths:** If lumps and bumps pop up overnight, they need immediate checking. Lumps that emerge more slowly could range in severity from harmless fatty tumors to cancerous growths. Insect bites,
especially from bees and wasps, often have a serious effect on small
dogs, so monitor your little dog very closely after such an event.

- **Fatigue:** Panting, heavy breathing, lethargy, a lack of interest in normal activities, or a dramatic change in sleeping patterns should be
brought to the vet's attention.

- **Odor:** A foul smell from the mouth, ears, or skin could indicate illness or infection. Tooth decay, ear discharge, anal gland problems,
cancerous tumors, and mange all produce odors that are markedly
different from the normal smell of a healthy dog.

- **Coat and skin changes:** Redness; inflammation; rashes; crusty
lesions; hair loss; excessive dander; and constant scratching, licking, and biting can all indicate the presence of parasites, allergies,
or an underlying disease.

- **Abnormal behavior:** If your dog is just not its normal happy self, suddenly snapping, whining, depressed, anxious, or lethargic, it's time
to see the vet.

- **Impaired movement:** Limping, not being able to climb stairs if they
usually present no problem, crying when you pick it up, trembling,
falling, and dragging its back legs—these are signs of injury or disease in a dog.

Having a small dog is not much different than having a small child.
Sooner or later, you'll be faced with a trip to the doctor or the emergency
room for an illness or injury. Try not to panic. Whether it's a minor mishap

or a serious illness, your vet is your best resource in all such situations. With today's amazing advances in veterinary medicine, our dogs have never been in better hands.

 **Alert!**

If you are in doubt about the seriousness of symptoms, by all means call your vet. If the situation is potentially serious, waiting could make it worse.

Causes of Common Illnesses

Diseases in dogs have many causes. They can be genetic or caused by parasites, bacteria, viruses, fungi, or simply the result of old age. There are hundreds of canine diseases and conditions that are classified as heritable, many specific to particular breeds. If you obtained a purebred pup from a reputable breeder, your dog and its parents were probably screened to weed out such problems. If you did your homework before purchasing your pup, you should already be familiar with genetic abnormalities prevalent within that breed.

Genetic Diseases

Just as we are, dogs are plagued with a great number of inherited health problems. Some are prevalent in specific breeds: cancer in Bernese mountain dogs and golden retrievers; heart disease in boxers; bleeding disorders in Doberman pinschers; eye problems in pugs and Irish setters. Each year, veterinary science develops more genetic tests to provide greater information on these diseases.

Among small dogs, inherited maladies include the following:

- **Atopic dermatitis:** This is an allergic skin condition seen in short-haired breeds and poodles.
- **Dental problems:** These can include gingivitis, periodontal disease, and tooth loss, common in all small breeds, and malocclusion (overbite or underbite), common in short-muzzled breeds like the Pekingese, shih tzu, and Lhasa apso.
- **Cleft palate:** This condition is prevalent in short-nosed dogs including pugs, Boston terriers, and the shih tzu. It can sometimes be corrected by a skilled microsurgeon.
- **Diabetes mellitus:** Like humans, overweight dogs are more at risk for this disease, which is caused by insufficient insulin production. It is a genetic problem for most small dog breeds.
- **Heart and circulatory diseases:** These include mitral valve defect, pulmonic stenosis, and congestive heart failure. All are treatable through medication and surgery, but the smaller the dog, the more difficult the operation. Early diagnosis is key.
- **Elbow dysplasia:** This degenerative disease of the elbow causes pain and lameness and is usually correctable by surgery.
- **Epilepsy (seizures):** The dog's brain literally seizes up as nerve cells (neurons) react uncontrollably. Although hereditary, it can also be caused by brain injury. Seizures often become more severe and frequent as a dog ages and are sometimes controllable by medication.
- **Demodectic mange:** The demodectic mange mite is present on most dogs but usually lies dormant. Dogs with this form of mange may have immune deficiencies, making them unable to keep the mites at bay. The localized form usually occurs in pups and is characterized by hair loss on the face, head, and forelegs. It is treatable with medicated shampoos, antibiotics, and immune-boosting supplements. A more serious generalized form spreads over the dog's body, causing hair loss and skin breakdown. Treatment can be prolonged, and the condition is not always curable. Small breeds with a tendency to develop this include the West Highland white terrier, Scottish terrier, Boston terrier, and pug.
- **Hypothyroidism:** The thyroid glands regulate many body functions, stabilizing metabolic rate and affecting hair growth and energy levels. When this function is impaired, dogs become overweight and

lazy, frequently showing hair loss as well. Although it is not curable, this condition is controllable through medication.

- **Degenerative disc disease:** Disc problems are experienced more often by short-legged, long-backed small breeds like the dachshund and Lhasa apso. The condition develops when the disc is displaced from its normal position, protruding into the spinal canal. The resulting inflammation causes pain and partial paralysis. It can be precipitated by something as ordinary as jumping or twisting while the dog is at play. With rapid diagnosis and treatment, the odds of recovery improve. It is usually treated by anti-inflammatory drugs and surgery.

- **Patellar luxation:** Common among several small breeds including the poodle, Chihuahua, and bichon frise, this is a condition in which the kneecap pops out and causes pain and difficulty in walking. Anti-inflammatory drugs are sometimes prescribed, but the condition is only repairable through surgery.

- **Legg-Calve-Perthes disease:** This condition causes degeneration of the upper portion of a dog's thighbone, known as the femoral head. It usually starts in puppyhood, causing lameness with no apparent injury. Very common among small dogs, it may be completely or partially repaired through surgery.

- **Eye Diseases**
  - Keratitis, also known as dry eye, is caused by an impaired secretion of tears. Treatment involves the use of artificial tears, antibiotics, steroids, and flushing out the tear ducts.
  - Progressive retinal atrophy (PRA) involves the deterioration of the retina and eventual partial vision loss. Careful breeders prevent it in their line through Canine Eye Registration Foundation (CERF) vision screening prior to breeding dogs that have a high incidence of this malady. Schnauzers and Lhasa apsos are prone to this problem.
  - The opposite of PRA, epiphora causes excessive production of tears. It is caused by blocked nasalacrimal ducts, passages that usually allow the tears to drain inside the nasal cavity. These tears cause staining under the eyes, and the constant wetness often leads to infection. The ducts can be flushed and drops

prescribed to relieve the condition. Short-muzzled dogs like the Pekingese and shih tzu are likely victims.

- Glaucoma develops from the buildup of pressure in the vitreous fluids of the eyeball. It is caused by injury and old age as well as by heredity and leads to the loss of vision. The dog's eyeball will become enlarged, sometimes appearing cloudy. The pain and pressure of this condition can be relieved with drugs and occasionally through surgery.

- Distichiasis is caused by a double row of eyelashes that irritate the cornea, causing inflammation and tearing. It can be corrected through surgery.

- Another eyelash problem, trichiasis, occurs in small longhaired breeds with abnormally positioned lashes growing from the upper lid that need to be removed.

- Cataracts occur when the lens of the eye becomes opaque and is sometimes an inherited condition. It causes loss of vision. Corrective surgery is far more difficult and not as successful in dogs as in humans. It is prevalent in pugs.

- Entropion: This genetic fault exists in the skin surrounding the eyes of small dogs, often those with wrinkly faces. It involves the inversion of the eyelid itself and causes chronic irritation. The earlier it is diagnosed and surgically corrected, the better. The papillon, pug, Pekingese, and shih tzu all have a high incidence of this condition.

- **Tracheal collapse:** When its cartilage weakens, the trachea begins to collapse, and the amount of air that can get through to the lungs is restricted. Heat, humidity, and excitement exacerbate the problem. A dog with this condition has trouble breathing and may cough or gag to try to clear its airway. The condition can usually be managed with medication and restricted activity. A surgical procedure using stents to widen the trachea is available, but this is risky and only done as a last resort. Small breeds at highest risk are Chihuahuas, Italian greyhounds, Pomeranians, Maltese, toy poodles, and Yorkshire terriers.

Alert!

If your small dog has tracheal problems, use a harness rather than a collar to put less pressure on the neck and throat. Make sure the groomer does not use a noose while your dog is on the table or in the tub, and bring your dog home as quickly as possible to cut down on the stress factor.

Parasitic Diseases

Fleas and ticks are not the only parasites that plague our small dogs. These external bloodsuckers can sometimes pass along internal parasites, like worms or protozoa. Fleas carry tapeworm; ticks carry protozoal diseases, such as giardia; and mosquitoes carry heartworm, all of which are injected into the dog when these bugs take a bite. If you live in an area where mosquitoes are present, you should use a monthly heartworm medication, such as Heartguard, or regularly apply a wide-spectrum topical product like Revolution.

Viruses, Bacterial, and Fungal Infections

Viruses are another bugaboo for small dogs. These microscopic disease agents multiply inside their hosts and cause such illnesses as distemper, parvovirus, hepatitis, rabies, bordetella (kennel cough), adenovirus, and parainfluenza. A rabies vaccination is required in most states, and dogs may be vaccinated against the other viruses according to their risk factor.

Bacteria are a mixed bag. Not all bacteria are bad. Others cause diseases, the most common in dogs being leptospirosis, campylobacteriosis, and thrombocytopenia, as well as streptococcal and staphylococcal (strep and staph) infections, tetanus, brucellosis, and such tickborne infections as Lyme disease, ehrlichiosis, and Rocky Mountain spotted fever. Some are preventable through vaccination.

Fungi, plants that propagate by releasing spores, also cause disease. When inhaled by dogs, these spores can cause a wide array of infections, including blastomycosis, ringworm, and others. Some are indigenous to certain regions, thriving along riverbanks. Some propagate in areas where bird or bat feces have accumulated, inside animal dens, or in rotting vegetation where dogs like to dig. They cause a wide variety of maladies, from respiratory to central nervous system problems to skin sores. Fungal infections are hard to diagnose and resistant to cures. They are best prevented by being careful about where you take your dog, not letting it run free in places where they may thrive.

Lifestyle-Related Diseases

Some diseases may be lifestyle related. Pancreatitis is one, caused by a malfunction in the production of enzymes our dogs need to digest fats, proteins, and carbohydrates. Although these enzymes are biologically programmed not to work until they have been released into the small intestine, the disease strikes when they misfire and actually start digesting the pancreas itself. It occurs most often in dogs that are overweight and inactive. Feeding fatty foods, especially table scraps, is a known cause.

Alert!

Dogs fed fatty leftovers like roasted turkey skin or fatty meats are at risk for pancreatitis, a potentially fatal disease, as are dogs that regularly feed on garbage.

Chubby dogs are also at risk for diabetes mellitus, another disorder of the pancreas involving the production of insulin and glucagon, necessary to control levels of blood sugar. Signs include excessive thirst and frequent urination. It can be controlled by diet and insulin injections.

Aging

Old age itself is a cause of disease, taking a toll on the dog's body and internal organs. Regular veterinary care for your small dog is always important, but it becomes even more important as your dog ages. When caught early, many diseases, including cancer, are curable.

Kidney disease is common in older dogs. The dog's kidneys maintain the balance of certain chemicals within its blood while filtering out the body's wastes as urine. The kidneys also help regulate blood pressure and the production of calcium and red blood cells. In older dogs, chronic kidney failure is an irreversible loss of function that occurs gradually over months or years. The kidneys can no longer adequately filter toxins, including urea and creatnine, from the blood, resulting in abnormally high levels of wastes products in the dog's system. Other blood components normally regulated by the kidneys, including phosphorus, calcium, sodium, potassium, and chloride, may rise or fall abnormally as kidney function wanes. Early diagnosis is a key factor in treating this problem. Some dogs do well on a special diet.

Another age-related malady is arthritis. Signs include difficulty in rising or climbing stairs, falling on slippery floors, and trouble getting comfortable. Today, your vet can prescribe a wide range of anti-inflammatory medications to improve your dog's comfort, and you can also give supplements such as glucosamine and chondroitin to relieve joint pain.

Essential

Regular veterinary care for your small dog is always important, but it becomes even more vital as your dog ages, so that you may both make the most of the life you share.

Cushing's disease (hyperadrenocorticism), usually caused by the overproduction of cortisol from the adrenal glands, is also more prevalent in senior dogs. It produces a wide variety of symptoms ranging from skin problems to sore swollen paws and bloated bellies. It can also cause hair loss and color changes in skin and coat, high blood pressure, and disorders of the nervous system. The disease can also be caused by a tumor on the adrenal or pituitary gland.

Another endocrine disorder called hypothyroidism is caused by an underactive thyroid gland, which also affects the health of your dog. It occurs when the thyroid gland in the dog's neck secretes insufficient thyroid hormones, critical to maintaining normal metabolism. This causes a number of changes, among them weight gain, loss of energy, and hair loss. Proper treatment for both of these disorders may dramatically improve your dog's attitude, strength, and well-being.

As our dogs live longer, we also see a higher incidence of cancer. Just like us, dogs are susceptible to many different types of this dread disease. But because of the great strides in veterinary medicine, a cancer diagnosis is no longer a death sentence. Caught early, many cancers are curable through chemotherapy, surgery, and radiation. In more advanced cases, palliative care provides comfort and prolongs life.

Heart disease is also age-related. For senior dogs, the most common form is chronic valvular heart disease. The heart valves may thicken and develop abnormalities, leading to a lessened blood flow within the heart chambers and eventually to heart enlargement and failure. Early intervention and proper medication may slow the progression of this disease.

Liver diseases, including cirrhosis, become more common in older dogs. Anemia may also develop as a secondary problem to other conditions like cancer or kidney disease. Other age-related maladies are bladder stones, urinary incontinence, prostate problems, behavioral changes, and declining cognitive functions.

Chapter 11

Medical Emergencies

You don't want to push the panic button and run to the vet every time your dog's behavior is out of the ordinary, but you need to know when immediate medical care is called for. You should be aware of your vet's availability in emergency situations and have a phone number handy for round-the-clock emergency vets in your area.

What Is an Emergency?

Not every sign of illness indicates a medical emergency, but the following situations call for immediate veterinary attention:

- Being hit by a car (even if the dog shows no signs of injury)
- Difficulty in breathing
- Paralysis or limping
- Straining when defecating or urinating
- Blood in the stool or urine, or bleeding from body orifice (nose, eyes, mouth, anus, or genitals)
- Lacerations or bleeding from any part of the body that is not stopped when you apply pressure
- Broken bones
- Choking or trying unsuccessfully to vomit
- Vomiting or diarrhea that lasts longer than twenty-four hours
- Swollen joints
- Bloated belly
- Snakebite
- Allergic reaction to insect bite
- Eyes that look swollen or excessive rubbing of the eyes
- Temperature over 104 or under 100 degrees
- Swallowing a foreign object, such as a child's toy
- Suspected medication overdose
- Fall from a window or balcony
- Near drowning
- Any kind of puncture wound
- Fight with any wild animal or getting stuck by porcupine quills
- Loss of motor control such as staggering, walking in circles, a head tilt, or other odd gait
- Burn or shock from chewing an electric cord
- Prolapsed rectum or swollen genitals (both males and females)

Hyperthermia (Overheating)

Rapid action must be taken if your small dog gets overheated. Small dogs, especially short-muzzled breeds like the Pekingese, pug, and Boston terrier, are more at risk for this life-threatening event. Heatstroke causes brain damage and kills dogs. Its signs are rapid panting, drooling, dizziness, trembling, and a rise in body temperature to over 105 degrees. Fainting, seizures, convulsions, coma, brain damage, and death can follow. If possible, cool the overheated dog immediately with the hose, wet towels, and cold compresses before transporting it to the vet.

Alert!

Never leave any dog in a car in warm weather, even with the windows partially open and even for a short period of time. At home, never leave it outside without adequate shade and water (in a bowl that can't be tipped over).

Hypothermia

In cold climates, warm coats and sweaters for smooth and short-haired dogs are not simply fashion statements. Small dogs lose their body heat very rapidly if they get too cold. Hypothermia, an abnormal lowering of body temperature, is a serious condition that can lead to unconsciousness, shock, and death. Signs include a lowered body temperature, shivering, and vasoconstricting (the body's survival response to cold, in which the blood supply flows to the core of the body to warm the organs and the extremities get very cold). At this point, little dogs would be in danger of frostbite, which can result in the loss of limbs, toes, and ear tips. Use a hair dryer (not too hot!), a heating pad wrapped in a towel, heated towels from the clothes dryer, or a heat lamp, and seek veterinary care at once.

Household Dangers

Like toddlers, dogs put everything in their mouths. Your home needs to be puppy-proofed even if your dog is no longer a pup. It is unrealistic to assume that your dog's activities will always be visible to you or someone else in your household. Whether it's bored or just curious, it only takes a few seconds for a dog to get hold of something that could pose a danger to it.

Medicines

Our own medications can pose a great danger to dogs. For example, the amount of acetaminophen contained in many over-the-counter painkillers is a lethal dose for a dog. All medications for humans and dogs should be kept in cupboards the dog cannot reach or in a locked cabinet. In addition, never give your dog any medicine unless told to do so by your vet. Alcoholic beverages, tobacco, and illegal substances such as marijuana or cocaine can also poison a dog.

Alert!

When it comes to toxicity, size does matter. The smaller the dog, the less of any substance ingested—food, medication, cleaning products, or insecticides—is necessary to threaten its life.

People Food

Many of the foods we eat can be poisonous to a dog, sometimes in very small amounts. Carefully monitor your dog around food, especially during holidays and family celebrations when you might be distracted. Children must be taught not to share their food with the dog.

Caffeine, found in coffee, tea, chocolate, colas, and some stimulants, can be deadly. It affects dogs in the same way as people, increasing the heart rate and sometimes causing heartbeat irregularity. Theobromine, found in chocolate, is deadly at dosages of 52 mg per pound of body weight, caffeine at 63 mg per pound.

Question?

Is chocolate really dangerous for dogs?
Chocolate, especially the baker's chocolate used in cooking, contains theobromine, which is highly toxic to dogs. It is also present in milk chocolate, cocoa beans, cocoa powder, and baked goods containing chocolate.

Other toxic foods for dogs include those containing citrus oil, fat trimmings, grapes and raisins, persimmons, macadamia nuts, mushrooms, onions, garlic, and yeast dough. Foods that are not lethal but could still make a dog sick include baby food, liver in large amounts, raw fish, raw eggs, milk and other dairy products containing lactose, salt, sugary foods, and fruits with stones—such as peaches—that could obstruct the digestive tract. Rotten food and garbage can be extremely hazardous to small dogs as well.

Insecticides, rodenticides (rat and mouse poisons), mothballs, and other pesticides used around the house can also be lethal, so store them safely out of reach. Lawn chemicals also pose a danger. If your little dog walks on grass treated with such chemicals and licks its pads, it can become gravely ill. Even plant food can be deadly to a nosy pup. Always read and carefully follow directions before using any such product.

Household Products

Many household products can also be toxic to your little dog. Again, proper storage is a must. Commonly used cleaning products like soap, laundry detergent, shampoo, dishwashing liquid and powder, fabric softener, sanitizers, disinfectants, and bleach pose a great danger. Since even the smell of pine oil can make a dog ill, choose cleaners that do not contain this substance.

Even in small amounts, antifreeze can kill your dog. Its toxic ingredient is highly concentrated ethylene glycol, an extremely dangerous toxin that is lethal to dogs at 2 to 3 milliliters per pound of body weight. Two tablespoons could kill a fifteen-pound dog, and smaller amounts could make it critically ill. Its sweet taste attracts dogs. Ingesting batteries of any size can also be fatal to a dog.

Dangerous Plants

Because dogs often chew on plants indoors and out, greenery poses a threat as well. The following are among the house and garden plants poisonous to dogs: amaryllis, avocado, azalea, boxwood, caladium, castor bean, cherry pits, daffodil, delphinium, dieffenbachia, elephant ear, English ivy, foxglove, holly, hyacinth, iris, jasmine, larkspur, marigold, mistletoe, narcissus, oleander, philodendron, poinsettia, rhododendron, and tulips.

If you suspect your dog has been poisoned, contact your vet or one of the following animal poison hotlines:

- ASPCA National Animal Poison Control Center at (900) 443-0000. A charge of $50 per case will be billed directly to your phone.
- (888) 4-ANI-HELP (888-426-4435), also $50 per case, will be billed to your credit card.
- Animal Poison Hotline, a joint service provided by North Shore Animal League America (NSAL) and PROSAR International Animal Poison Center (IAPC) at (888) 232-8870. A charge of $35 per case will be billed to your credit card.

All such hotlines are staffed twenty-four hours a day, seven days a week.

Alert!

Protect your dog from poisoning by knowing which foods, household items, and plants pose a danger to its safety.

According to the Massachusetts Society for the Prevention of Cruelty to Animals (MSPCA), symptoms of poisoning include "swelling, cramps, abdominal pain, vomiting, diarrhea, effects on breathing and circulation, weakness, drooling, and sneezing. Any abnormal odor on your dog's breath or body could be a sign that your dog was exposed to a potential poison."

If you think that your dog may have been poisoned, keep it warm and dry. Give it any antidote that appears on the label of the item ingested. Then call your veterinarian immediately to let them know you are bringing your dog in. If known, take a sample of the suspected poison with you.

Allergic Reactions

Allergies can also warrant a visit to the vet. Among small breeds, they are especially common in the Scottish, West Highland white, cairn, and wire-haired fox terriers, as well as the Lhasa apso and bichon frise. Here are some of the ways you can tell if a dog has allergies:

- Chewing their feet
- Scratching their body
- Rubbing their face on the rug or furniture
- Chronic ear infections
- Hair loss
- Red, raw skin
- Rashes and hives

Skin lesions often result from all that chewing and scratching. Such mutilation can lead to secondary infections that need to be treated with antibiotics. Skin problems and itching are the most common signs of allergies in dogs.

Allergens that cause reactions in our dogs include the following:

- Plants such as grass, weeds, and trees, as well as their pollen
- Household fabrics like wool or nylon
- Rubber and plastics
- Foods, including dog food
- Dust and dust mites
- Flea saliva
- Insect bites

In small dogs, the stings of bees, wasps, and ants can cause a severe allergic reaction, including anaphylactic shock. This is the most urgent allergic reaction a dog can face and requires immediate veterinary intervention. Stings and bites can quickly swell up and the dog may experience trouble breathing. Other allergic reactions include pale gums, a weak pulse, increased heart rate, fever, cold extremities, trembling, vomiting, diarrhea, wheezing, and collapse.

Accidents and injuries often call for an emergency vet visit. If your little dog is hurt, be careful when approaching it. An animal in pain will bite the hand that tries to help it, even that of its beloved caretaker. You may need to use a muzzle for your dog's safety as well as for your own. If the dog is not moving, something could be fractured, so it is best to slide it onto a rigid board to transport it to the vet. The most urgent situations—bleeding, difficulty in breathing, inability to stand or walk, or loss of consciousness—call for rapid intervention. Monitor your dog's demeanor following any accident or injury, no matter how insignificant it may seem at the time. When in doubt about your dog's condition, it's always better to be safe than sorry.

What to Do in an Emergency

No matter how careful and responsible you are with your dog, emergencies will probably arise. It's a scary prospect, but you can decrease your stress level and make your dog safer by having a game plan. Most emergencies happen when we least expect them, so know where vet care is available twenty-four hours a day, seven days a week. Keep those telephone numbers handy, along with the poison-control hotline numbers.

It helps to know your dog's normal vital signs as well. Its temperature should be between 101 and 102 degrees, respiration rate fifteen to twenty breaths per minute, and heart rate eighty to 120 beats per minute. You should learn how to take your dog's temperature, too. This procedure is much easier if you have a helper to keep the dog standing while the thermometer is in place.

Using the same type of thermometer you would use on a person. Shake it down to 96 degrees and lubricate it with petroleum jelly. Holding up your dog's tail, place it inside the dog's anus. For a small dog, it should be inserted about an inch inside the anus. Hold it in place for one to two minutes. After removing it and reading the temperature, wipe the thermometer with alcohol and store it in a safe place. Do not use this thermometer for any other purpose.

When your dog is ill, knowing such information can help the vet make a diagnosis. You should also note when the symptoms first appeared and how often they have occurred. As a responsible dog owner, having a basic knowledge of pet first aid is most helpful. Many excellent books and videos are available on this topic in stores and online.

 Essential

Keep your dog's health records handy. In an emergency, the vet caring for your dog may need to have immunization records and other health data when coming up with a diagnosis and treatment plan.

In any emergency, remain calm. Call your vet or the emergency clinic to inform them of the problem. They may tell you to come right in or offer advice on handling the situation at home. Of course, getting your dog to the hospital is up to you. It is enormously helpful to have a friend or family member accompany you. If your dog cannot be placed in a crate, put it on a blanket for the ride. For your dog's sake, remain calm and drive safely.

At the hospital, you will probably not be allowed to accompany the dog into the treatment area. Just as you would at a human hospital, you'll remain in the waiting room for word on your dog's condition while emergency care is administered. Be prepared to pay for the emergency services at the time of the visit.

Keeping a First Aid Kit

Just like children, animals can get sick or injured and require immediate care any time and any place, often when the doctor is unavailable. If you learn the basics of pet first aid, the chances of a happy outcome will increase significantly. The American Animal Hospital Association (AAHA) suggests the following supplies for your dog's first aid kit:

- Your veterinarian's phone number
- Gauze to wrap wounds or muzzle animal
- Adhesive tape for bandages
- Nonstick bandages to protect wounds or control bleeding
- Towels or other clean cloth
- Hydrogen peroxide (3%)
- Milk of magnesia or activated charcoal
- Large syringe without needle or eyedropper (for oral treatments)
- Muzzle (soft cloth, rope, necktie, or nylon stocking may be used) or a towel to cover a small animal's head. Do not use in case of vomiting.
- Stretcher (a door, board, blanket, or floor mat)

The AAHA recommends that you contact your veterinarian immediately if your dog is injured or ill. It notes on its Web site, *www.healthypet.com*, that first aid and the recommended first aid kit are not a substitute for veterinary treatment. However, having the proper supplies on hand and knowing basic first aid procedures could help save your dog's life.

Caring for a Sick Dog

When your dog is recuperating at home from illness or surgery, your care will have a profound effect upon its recovery. First and foremost, follow your vet's instructions regarding medication, diet, and activity level. After surgery and during illness, this means confining your dog to its crate. Unless they are gravely ill, dogs generally don't take it upon themselves to convalesce, and trying to walk, jump, or climb stairs could set back the recovery process. Make sure the crate is comfortably lined with a soft pad, and have at least one spare on hand so that you can keep them freshly laundered. Crate pads come in a wide variety of comfy materials—imitation lamb's wool, fleece, faux fur, and puffy quilted cotton. Egg-crate foam mattresses with removable zippered covers are highly therapeutic for postsurgical, arthritic, and elderly dogs as well.

Just like us, dogs can get stiff lying in one position for an extended period. If your little dog is unable to move around, gently turn it over now and then to make it comfortable. This also prevents hair loss or callused skin caused by lying on the same area of the body too long. Your dog loves the sound of your voice and your touch, so be sure to speak soothingly, using its name often, and giving gentle pats in areas that will not cause any pain.

Think of the environment you would like if you were the patient and try to create it for your dog. It's a time for quiet rest, so keep noise levels to a minimum (no music blasting from the radio or loud television). Small children should not be allowed to race in and out of the room or bother the dog while it rests, and visitors should be kept to a minimum. Keep the light dim, drawing the blinds during the daytime and turning lights off at night.

Because your dog's sense of smell is at least 100 times stronger than your own, go easy on any scents in the area where it is recovering. Candles, perfume, room deodorizers, and household cleaners can be especially noxious during recuperation.

Keep the room temperature appropriate to the dog's condition—not too warm if your dog is running a fever, not too cold for a postsurgical or elderly small dog, as they are more prone to chilling and hypothermia.

Offer plenty of water, and be patient with feedings. It's wise to keep an eye on your little dog, but try to monitor its condition without interfering with its rest. There will be lots of opportunities to give one-on-one attention when you feed, clean up, or change bedding or surgical dressings.

Stay with your dog while it eats and be understanding if it makes a mess or has accidents. Illness or medication can cause diarrhea, and some dogs feel ashamed when they soil their own space. Since sick or recuperating dogs can't clean themselves, use soap and warm water or a waterless shampoo to clean your little friend if it makes a mess.

After illness or surgery, some small dogs spring back faster than others. If your dog is not ready to get back to its normal activities, don't rush it. Stay in contact with your vet throughout the recovery process in case any changes in treatment need to be made.

Keep in mind that your dog cannot tell you whether something in its environment is disturbing, so try to anticipate its needs. Mindful, loving care and a restful environment will give your little patient the support it needs to make a full recovery.

Chapter 12

Looking Good

Undoubtedly one of the reasons you were drawn to your small dog was because of its adorable looks. Maybe you were captivated by the comical mug of a pug or the enchanting elegance of an Italian greyhound. Perhaps you fell for a silky-smooth miniature pinscher or a fetchingly fluffy bichon frise. Whatever the breed or mix, your dog's appearance probably played a big part in its appeal. Whether your dog is a wash-and-wear smoothie or a bouffant beauty, the responsibility for keeping it well groomed is now yours.

Why Grooming Is Healthy

Grooming is about more than good looks. It is also essential for healthy skin and coat. Just like us, dogs like to feel clean and beautiful. Even dogs with short, smooth coats require regular rubdowns with a rubber curry brush to keep their coats healthy and shiny. Dogs with medium to long coats need brushing and combing to keep mats from forming.

Mats are caused by moisture, shedding hair, dirt, debris, rough-and-tumble play, and even your loving tickles behind Bowser's ears. They can pull painfully on a dog's skin, impede its movement, and lead to irritated skin, including hot spots, or infected weeping sores. Bugs, twigs, grit, and fungal infections can be hidden inside a matted coat as well. When those awful clumps reach a critical mass, brushing them out is no longer an option. The dog must be shaved right down to the skin and the coat regrown. This can be a difficult procedure for both groomer and dog because the skin underneath those mats may be inflamed before the groomer even touches it with the clippers.

Some double-coated dogs shed their coats twice a year, usually in the spring and fall. Their undercoat starts emerging in tufts until they look as if they are molting. Groomers call this built-up hair cushion packing, and like matting, it needs to be brushed from the coat.

 Essential

Home grooming gives you an opportunity to check your dog from head to tail, uncovering any potential problems. Along with brushing its coat, examine your dog's ears, feet, teeth, and skin, checking for sores, discharges, lumps, rashes, cuts, brambles, twigs, fleas, and ticks in the process.

Even if your dog is a fluffy little beauty that requires professional styling to look the way it's supposed to, you will still need to do some brushing and combing at home. Your efforts will save money, too. Professional groomers have to charge more to split and comb out a matted coat than to prep a well-maintained coat.

Home grooming sessions also help socialize your dog and build the bond you share. Getting a puppy used to the grooming ritual is also a good chance for you to establish your leadership, setting limits that lead to a better owner/dog relationship. Just like good food, exercise, and training, grooming should become part of your small dog's routine.

It's All about the Coat

Nature and heredity provide dogs with coats in a kaleidoscope of colors, textures, lengths, and layers. When some people hear the word "grooming," they visualize poodles being primped and beribboned, but all dogs need to be groomed. Grooming is as much about health and hygiene as it is about beauty. The type of coat your little dog sports and the lifestyle you share will determine how much and how often it needs to be groomed.

Ideally, you familiarized yourself with your dog's grooming requirements before you brought it home. Never choose a canine companion without any idea of how much fur it will sprout or the amount of care and expense involved in keeping it looking spiffy. Most adult dog coats have two layers, an outer coat, made up of glossy guard hairs, and a soft downy undercoat, their built-in insulation against wetness and weather. But double coats don't start out that way.

Most puppies are born with a single layer of soft woolly hair. This puppy coat sometimes bears little resemblance to what it will look like when the pup grows up. Whatever their breed, most puppy coats change texture as they grow, with hair turning coarser and longer by the time the adult coat comes in at around six to eight months. A poodle puppy's cotton-candy fuzz will morph into curly ringlets by the time it's grown.

Some coats change color as well as texture. The black fluffy part of a Yorkie pup's coat will turn silky and silvery as it matures. Each breed, and each individual within that breed, has a different rate of coat growth. Factors such as diet, hormones, the amount of daylight, and the weather all play a part in coat development. Because most small dogs live indoors under artificial lighting, their coats don't take many cues from Mother Nature. Therefore, most dogs tend to shed year-round. (Dogs that are outdoors a lot will shed seasonally, their coats changing to adapt to the weather.) Some indoor dogs leave their telltale fuzz on the floor and furniture, while others retain the shedded hair within the coat itself.

Dog coats come in six main types: long, silky, smooth, nonshedding, curly, and wiry. For the allergy-prone, the nonshedding coat of the poodle, bichon frise, Maltese, Coton de Tulear, and Havanese are a big plus, but those little beauties require frequent grooming. The flowing coats of the Lhasa apso and shih tzu and the Yorkshire, silky, and Skye terriers form mats easily. Groomers can lessen your homework by performing short pet trims called puppy cuts or teddy bear trims on just about any long or full-coated breed, which look adorable and greatly reduce coat maintenance between salon visits.

Some wiry coats, such as those of the West Highland white, Scottish, cairn and wire fox terriers as well as the wirehaired dachshund, may be hand-stripped every eight to twelve weeks to preserve the coarse texture of their outer coat.

 **Fact**

In their days of charging through the brush and digging into burrows in pursuit of prey, wire-coated dogs needed that harsh body armor to protect them. Purists still consider it a hallmark of their beauty.

Today, clippered cuts for pet dogs (rather than show prospects) of these terrier breeds are quite popular. After they get haircuts, their coats do tend to grow back with a softer texture. Clippered terriers usually need grooming every six to eight weeks.

Smooth-coated breeds like the min-pin, toy fox terrier, smooth fox terrier, Italian greyhound, Boston terrier, smooth dachshund, Manchester terrier, and short-haired version of the Chihuahua are wash-and-wear dogs, a snap to groom with a rubber curry. The bottom line on your dog's grooming needs is this: The more hair it has, the more brushing and combing it will require.

Some high-maintenance dandies of the small dog world should be brushed and combed several times a week, if not daily. These include the Lhasa apso, Maltese, shih tzu, Pekingese, Havanese, Coton de Tulear, Bolognese, the powderpuff Chinese crested, and the Yorkshire, silky, Skye, and Australian terriers. Most owners have them professionally groomed every four to six weeks. Breeds that require brushing about three times a week are the Pomeranian, bichon frise, Japanese Chin, wire fox and Lakeland terriers, American Eskimo, schipperke, and poodle (along with the doodle dog breeds) if they are kept in full coated styles. Breeds in this group that need haircuts—the bichon, wire fox terrier, Lakeland terrier, and doodle dogs—should see the groomer every four to six weeks, while schedules for the others vary widely according to your home care.

A thorough brushing twice a week will suffice for most small dogs, including the affenpinscher, Brussels griffon, English toy spaniel, cavalier King Charles spaniel, Tibetan spaniel, papillon, West Highland white, Scottish terrier, cairn terrier, Dandie Dinmont terrier, Sealyham terrier, Norfolk terrier, Norwich terrier, Welsh terrier, miniature schnauzer, longhaired dachshund, longhaired Chihuahua, and the pug, which sheds profusely despite its short coat. Their grooming visits will depend upon whether they get trimmed and how much brushing you do in between visits.

The lowest-maintenance small dogs need home grooming only once a week. These include the Border terrier, Parson Russell terrier, Boston terrier, Manchester terrier, smooth and toy fox terrier, miniature pinscher, shorthaired Chihuahua, smooth and wirehaired dachshund, Italian greyhound, and the hairless Chinese crested. All these breeds benefit from a professional grooming now and then, but the frequency is up to you.

Basic Grooming for Small Dogs

The amount of upkeep necessary to keep your small dog looking fabulous depends upon its coat type. To do the job right, you need the right equipment. For most coated breeds, a wire slicker brush works best. They are available in a gentle straight-bristled style and the professional groomer's favorite, the curve-bristled variety. Their wire bristles are embedded in a rubber backing and are available in different sizes to suit the size of your hand and your dog.

Using a slicker correctly takes a little practice. You want to brush deeply enough so that you penetrate the coat all the way to the skin, but you don't want to scratch your dog in the process. You will also need a double-sided stainless steel comb, essential for checking the coat after brushing to ensure that you have eliminated all the tangles. If you do encounter such snarls, go at them slowly and patiently. Use the end of your comb in a knifelike motion, separating the tangles a little at a time. Yanking the dog's hair feels about the same as having someone pull your own hair—it hurts.

Mat splitters are groomers' tools with removable razor blades that slice through mats so they can be brushed out, which are also available to the public. However, improperly using these devices can be extremely dangerous to you and your dog, so have a groomer demonstrate their proper use. (Pull with a gentle sawing motion in the direction the hair grows and never use near ears, skin folds, leg tendons, or genitals.)

Alert!

Using a slicker brush with too heavy a hand can produce what is known as slicker burn, a painful skin irritation that may require veterinary attention. Because of their sensitive skin, white-coated dogs like the Maltese, Westie, and bichon frise are especially prone to this type of injury.

For flowing coats and the dense double coats of Northern breeds, an undercoat rake and a pin brush will help complete your chores. A fine-toothed flea comb, preferably stainless steel, is useful for more than trapping pesky parasites within its teeth. It also works well at removing a fuzzy undercoat from short-coated breeds like the pug. For smooth coats, the rubber curry brush or grooming mitt is great for removing dead hair and giving the coat a healthy sheen.

Your grooming kit should also include cotton balls, ear wash, a small set of nail clippers and styptic powder (an anticoagulant to instantly stop bleeding if you accidentally nick a nail), and a doggie toothbrush and toothpaste.

On white and light-colored dogs with facial hair, tear-stain remover may also be needed. Such products come in liquid and paste form. Excessive tearing in small dogs can lead to a yeast infection, one form of which is called red yeast, causing an unsightly reddish brown stain under the eyes. Excessive tearing can also lead to a bacterial infection. A visit to the vet to check for blocked tear ducts may be called for to get to the root of this problem.

The best way to brush a dog is to start at one spot and work your way around the body. This way, you won't skip any area. To properly brush the legs of a long-coated dog, start at the paw and work your way up the leg, lifting the coat up and brushing the hair down to make sure you get all the way through. After brushing, check your work with the comb, following the same pattern. When grooming the face, be careful not to injure or irritate the eyes. Clean the facial wrinkles on breeds like pugs, Boston terriers, and Pekingese with cotton balls moistened with warm water or special eye wipes, available at pet supply stores.

On smooth-coated dogs, use the rubber curry in the direction the hair grows. Following up with a spray of coat dressing, another useful product to have in your kit, will impart a shine to the coat as well. On long-coated breeds, lightly misting the coat with this product as you brush will cut down on static as well. Basic grooming on all dogs also involves cleaning the ears, cutting the toenails, and brushing the teeth. Dog colognes are also available in a great variety of fragrances.

Ears

Using a cotton ball or soft tissue, swab out the ear to remove wax and dirt with a cleanser made specifically for this purpose. A little honey-colored wax is normal, but a yellow substance could indicate an infection, while a darker discharge may indicate ear mites. Have your vet check ears that look inflamed or that have an unpleasant odor. Your dog may let you know its ears are bothering it by digging at them, shaking its head, or wincing in pain when you handle them.

 Essential

Regularly cleaning your dog's ears gives you a chance to detect any minor problems before they develop into serious ear infections.

Hair sprouts inside the ear canal on many breeds, especially bichons, poodles, and schnauzers. This can lead to infection and loss of air circulation. Groomers either shave this hair with clippers or pluck it, using their fingers, tweezers, or hemostats, after first applying a drying powder to make it easier to grasp. This product is available where pet products are sold. If you do this at home, pull only a few hairs at a time so you won't injure your dog. Once you are done plucking, use ear wash to wipe excess powder from the ear canal.

Nails

Because overgrown nails can ruin a dog's appearance, deform its feet, and make walking difficult, they must be trimmed frequently. Left untrimmed, toenails can curl around and perforate the footpad, a situation that requires the vet's attention. For most dogs, a once-a-month pedicure will fit the bill. Nail trimmers come in various sizes and types; for your little dog, small is best. The easiest to use are the pliers type, which operate like pruning shears with two inwardly curving blades. A guillotine style is also available, featuring a replaceable blade. Have styptic powder on hand in case you should nick the quick, the vein inside the nail that looks pink on white nails. The quick is invisible in black nails, so pare off only a little off at a time.

The nail is solid as it emerges from the paw, but at the tip it looks hollow, like a shell. This hollow portion is the part you want to trim. Clip a little bit at a time. If the cut edge starts to look moist, you've gone far enough. If you should nick the quick, a dab of the powder will stop bleeding immediately. If you don't have this product available, rub the nicked nail with a soft bar of soap or dab it with flour or cornstarch to control the bleeding.

The easiest way to trim nails is to stand your dog on a table. Grooming tables are available for about $100, and they are well worth having. If your little dog is very squirmy, enlist the aid of a friend to do this job. Begin with a rear paw, your back to the dog as you lift its feet only as high as necessary so you won't overextend the legs. It's like shoeing a horse; you trim each nail with the paw turned up toward you. Moving to the front paws, bend over the dog and lift its paw so that you are looking down on it, then follow the same procedure. Don't forget to trim the dewclaws as well, those little thumblike nails on the inside of the front legs and occasionally on the back legs.

Nails should be cut once a month, but every time you groom your dog, examine the underside of its paws. Dirt, road salt, pebbles, sticks, burrs, and debris can get stuck between the pads, causing irritation. In the winter, ice and snow between the pads should be melted with either warm water or your own handheld hair dryer, on the warm setting only. If the pads appear to be red and sore, a little Bag Balm or other soothing ointment will help them heal.

Always praise your dog for its cooperation when you trim its nails. Some breeds object to this procedure more strenuously than others—notably the Scottie, pug, min-pin, dachshund, and Lhasa apso. If your little friend proves too hard to handle despite your best efforts, the groomer or the vet can perform its pedicure.

Teeth

Dogs don't suffer from cavities as we do, but they still require dental care. They lose teeth from gingivitis and periodontal disease brought on by tartar buildup on their teeth. More than 85 percent of dogs over the age of six develop periodontal disease, a gum infection that leads to the loss of underlying bone and teeth. Gum infections don't stop in the mouth. Bacteria can also spread to other organs as well, resulting in heart, kidney, and liver damage.

Periodontal disease is caused by plaque, a mixture of bacteria, food debris, and cell mucus that forms a light-colored film on the teeth and gums. As plaque gets under the gumline, bacteria eat away at the bone that holds the teeth in place. The problem is more common in small dogs because this underlying bone is thinner and their teeth are closer together.

Gum disease and tooth loss are not inevitable. If you brush your dog's teeth regularly from puppyhood on, you can prevent periodontal disease. Having nice clean teeth will make your dog's breath smell sweeter too, making it nicer to be near them.

 **Essential**

For adult dogs, it's best to start with a professional cleaning before you begin oral care at home. The vet will do a thorough cleaning and scraping with the dog under anesthesia.

If your small dog is a puppy, buy a dog toothbrush and start brushing! Toothbrushes for dogs are soft-bristled and long-handled, enabling you to reach deep into the dog's mouth. Use the special toothpaste made for dogs. Ours is too sudsy and can make them sick. (Unlike us, they don't spit it out—they swallow it).

The best thing you can do for your dog's oral health is to brush its teeth every day. Start getting your pup used to it early, letting it lick or chew the brush. After you do this a few times, the pup won't be leery of the brushing process. Initially, brush just a few teeth, gradually building up to a full treatment as the dog gets accustomed to it. Spend about thirty seconds per group of three or four teeth, and be sure to massage the gumline as well. While you are brushing the teeth, look them over to make sure none are loose or broken. If you notice such fractures, or if your dog paws at its mouth or winces in pain when you touch it, you need to see the vet.

Safe chew toys will also help keep your dog's teeth clean and free of tartar. Hard rubber toys, nylon bones, rope bones, and small raw bones soft enough to be chewed without breaking the teeth work well, as do special dental bones infused with chlorophyll to sweeten breath. Hard biscuits and dry food also help keep teeth clean. In addition, you can purchase sprays that help eliminate bacteria and heal gum tissue.

Grooming Puppies

Just as you prepared your little dog for the vet by getting it accustomed to standing and being touched, the same type of desensitization and socialization will get it ready to visit the groomer. All dogs benefit from a professional grooming periodically, even those that don't require precision trimming. Since you will be performing a lot of its upkeep at home, having a dog that's used to being groomed will make your job easier, too.

Most puppies go to their new owners at eight to twelve weeks of age, the perfect time to accustom them to being handled. Like petting and playing, grooming is a physical interaction that you share with your dog. If it doesn't get used to being handled at this stage of life, a puppy can grow into a shy and mistrustful adult.

Your early grooming preparation won't even require a comb or brush. Pat the pup, tickle its tummy, look in its ears, and handle its paws and tail. Puppies are mouthy little creatures, so don't be alarmed if your little pal gets nippy. Now is the time to begin teaching the dog that this behavior is a no-no. Gently holding its mouth closed, make firm eye contact and give a firm "No!"

Since positive reinforcement is always the best motivator in training a pup, offer lots of praise and affection when your pup cooperates. Using an excited happy tone, speak your dog's name and ask, "Do you want to get brushed?" Your puppy may actually begin to believe that grooming is a fun activity, like playing fetch or going for a walk.

Once your little friend gets used to being handled, the next step is to practice the "Stand" command. With the leash and collar on and the pup on a table, gently pull it toward you, lifting from under its belly, also known as the tuck-up area, as you say "Stand." Offer lavish praise or a tasty treat as a reward for its cooperation.

 Alert!

Never leave a dog unattended on a grooming table. A fall or jump could cause severe injury.

Now it's time to acquaint your dog with the brush and comb. Brush your way around its body, starting at the same spot each time. Brush the coat in small sections, getting all the way through to the skin. Have your small dog stand up on its back feet facing face you while you hold its front paws so you can brush the inside of the back legs, tummy, and chest, taking care not to brush these tender areas too hard.

After mastering the rudiments of grooming, set aside ten minutes or so each day for a grooming session, gradually increasing the time as the pup gets used to the process. Schedule these sessions after a walk or playtime when the pup's energy level is a bit lower.

Bath Time

Because puppies get into everything, they often get dirty. Food, fecal matter, newsprint, and mud have a way of attaching themselves to these little sprites. Don't panic. Getting a small dog used to having a bath is much easier if you begin when it's just a pup. Whether their coats are short or long, all dogs need a bath now and then. If you use a quality shampoo made just for dogs and you rinse well, you can bathe your dog as often as necessary without worrying about drying out the coat.

To make bath time easier, organization is key. Have on hand a tearless puppy shampoo, conditioner, or crème rinse if your dog has a lot of coat, as well as a brush, comb, cotton balls, ear cleaner, nail trimmers, styptic powder, fluffy towels, and pet cologne if you like. Brush and comb long coats thoroughly before bathing. Once wet, any mats or tangles left in the coat will get bigger and multiply. Clean the pup's ears with cotton balls and ear cleaner, and trim the nails if needed.

Place a rubber mat on the bottom of the kitchen or laundry sink and add a few inches of warm water (a temperature that would be comfortable to a baby). No hose-downs in the driveway, please—you wouldn't enjoy such an ice-cold bath, and neither will your little dog.

Speak lovingly as your puppy gets used to the water. Wet it down from the back end so you won't startle it with water squirted in its face. Placing cotton balls inside the ears will prevent water from getting into the ear canals. For a regular bath, use a hypoallergenic tearless shampoo. It your little one has dry, flaky skin, use an oatmeal shampoo, leaving the lather on for at least ten minutes before rising. This is also advisable when using a flea shampoo. It needs time to kill those pesky pests before you rinse. Then, rinse thoroughly—any shampoo left in the coat will cause dry skin and itching.

No matter what shampoo you use, don't get it in the dog's eyes. If you are following up with a conditioning rinse, make sure it is diluted according to directions so it won't leave the coat greasy. Once rinsed, towel-dry the dog and use your handheld dryer to complete the process. Make sure the setting is not too hot and don't aim it at one area too long. Afterward, don't let the dog outdoors until it is completely dry. A damp dog will roll in whatever it finds out there, undoing all your work.

Once your dog is dry, give it another brush-through. If you wish, apply a little pet cologne or coat dressing to make it smell great and look shiny. Keep in mind that bathing a small dog is much easier than bathing a large one, another reason to congratulate yourself for choosing a small dog. Offer a treat to make it a happy experience, and have a human treat yourself for being such a great caretaker!

Hiring a Groomer

Your puppy's first visit to a professional groomer is like a toddler's first haircut. Understandably, you may feel some trepidation leaving it in someone else's care, so you need to find a groomer who makes you feel comfortable, a professional you can trust with your baby. Before you make that first appointment, you should have already done your homework, visiting a few salons to determine which one might be best.

Beyond the basic issue of safety is the question of expertise. If yours is a breed that requires skilled grooming to make it look like it should—a poodle, bichon frise, or one of the terriers—you may have sought a recommendation from your breeder or seen examples of the groomer's work.

A reputable groomer should welcome your exploratory visit, answer your questions courteously, and assure you that the pup won't need to be kept at the salon all day long for its first visit. To accommodate dogs with special needs, caring groomers will try to get very young dogs, canine senior citizens, and dogs with health issues in and out as quickly as possible. The shop should look and smell clean, and you should be able to observe the personnel caring for their canine clients in a kind and respectful way as they are being bathed and groomed.

To make your groomer's job easier, be a good customer and observe the following guidelines:

- Don't telephone repeatedly to check on the dog or ask whether it can be done any sooner than the time you were given when you dropped it off.
- Don't bring in a badly matted dog, expecting the groomer to brush it out and leave it full. Some matted coats are simply not brushable. Groomers are skilled artists, but they are not miracle workers.
- Don't call out to your dog if you arrive while it is still on the grooming table. The groomer is working with sharp clippers. If your dog gets excited by your presence, it could easily be injured, and so could the groomer.
- Inform the groomer of any special health problems, such as seizures, a heart condition, aggressive behavior toward people or other dogs, back problems, arthritis, or hip problems that make it difficult for your dog to stand.

Pet Grooming versus Show Grooming

Those canine champions you see parading around the show ring on television are the superstars of the canine world. They are as highly trained and physically conditioned as professional human athletes, meticulously preparing for this role every day of their life. As they progress through the different levels of competition, they are judged by how close they come to their breed standard, the ideal of perfection written by the national breed club and accepted by the AKC. This standard defines a particular breed's coat quality and color, teeth, gait, temperament, and even its jaw or the color of its nose. Many show dogs live in kennels, and even when they are beloved family pets, they spend much of the year on the show circuit with professional handlers. In other words, while they are competing in conformation—being judged for their physical structure and beauty—show dogs and pet dogs live in two different worlds, and they are groomed differently as well.

Show coats on most breeds are treated with a vast array of products, including hot oil treatments and conditioners, to keep them in tip-top shape. The coats of Yorkshire terrier and shih tzu champions are wrapped in rice paper with elastic bands to keep the hair from breaking and tangling between shows, while the coarse coats of some terrier-breed show dogs are hardened with chalk as they are prepared for competition.

Like those who groom for show, pet groomers also work hard to make dogs look their best, but their goal is to please the pet owner, not the show judge. The groomer's expertise stems from a wide-ranging knowledge of dog breeds and their standards and the skill level to interpret these styles on individual pet dogs. The velvety smooth perfection they achieve with their scissors on a poodle or bichon coat takes years of practice, as does the dashing sharply styled precision you see on a well-groomed terrier. Like show groomers, pet groomers sometimes use their grooming skills to camouflage a particular dog's faults—for example, taking a dog that is too long in the body or short in the leg and making it appear well-proportioned.

Can you groom your own dog yourself? Yes and no. You can certainly keep its coat mat-free. If it is a coated breed that calls for very little in the way of trimming, you can learn to do it yourself. A set of electric clippers will be needed for ear-shaving on the Yorkie and silky terriers and should be used to clean out the feet on breeds that grow copious hair between their pads. For sanitary reasons, clippers may also be used to keep the area around the anus and genitals neat and tidy.

 **Fact**

Low-maintenance breeds include the following: cavalier King Charles spaniel, English toy spaniel, Japanese Chin, Pomeranian, papillon, Brussels griffon, affenpinscher, long-haired Chihuahua, schipperke, American Eskimo, longhaired dachshund, Tibetan spaniel, Chinese crested, Parson Russell terrier, Pekingese, silky terrier, Yorkie, and Skye terrier.

If you learn how and when to hand-strip, you can groom your Border, Australian, Norwich or Norfolk terrier as well as your Brussels griffon or affenpinscher. If you keep its hair long and brush religiously, you can also groom your Lhasa apso, Pekingese, Coton de Tulear, Havanese, and Bolognese. The same holds true for the shih tzu and Maltese, but you will need to learn how to tie up their topknots. For long-coated breeds, a good set of grooming shears, preferably with curved blades, will be needed to trim the feet round but never short enough to see the toenails. A good set of thinning shears will help you keep hair out of the eye corners and thin out excess feathering on many breeds. You'll need time, knowledge of the proper styling, and skill to properly groom a long-coated dog.

Most people can learn to shave a dog down with clippers, a style that groomers call a strip, but fuller scissored haircuts on any breed are best left to the professional groomer. It's not that different from getting your own haircut. You could do it yourself, but it looks far more attractive when done by a trained professional.

Breeds that require the expert touch of a professional groomer are the poodle, bichon, West Highland white, Scottish terrier, Sealyham terrier, wire fox terrier, Lakeland terrier, Welsh terrier, Dandie Dinmont terrier, and miniature schnauzer. Short and smooth-coated small dogs are the easy keepers in the bunch. If you bathe and brush them regularly and master the job of cutting their nails, you'll have yourself a do-it-yourself pet.

Chapter 13

Housetraining

When it comes to being the proud owner of a new puppy, housetraining will probably be the biggest challenge you face. It is time-consuming and sometimes frustrating, but patience, a positive attitude, and good organization from day one will ensure a successful outcome for you and your four-legged baby. Housetraining is part of being a responsible dog owner, and it should begin before that little newcomer sets paw inside your house.

Day One

Before you leave the breeder or the pet store, you should give your puppy its first potty-training lesson. Of course, it will be on a leash, and you'll give the nosy little critter plenty of time to sniff around for the perfect spot. Offer praise lovingly if the pup accomplishes its mission. Adopt this practice every time your dog goes potty in the right place to reinforce the behavior.

Once you've arrived home, take it to a potty area you have already selected. It should be close enough to the door so you can whisk your little friend in and out swiftly, and it should not be filled with interesting distractions like street traffic, passersby, or other animals. Puppies are extremely distractible, and getting them to focus on the job at hand is crucial to the housetraining process. Small dogs also tend to feel vulnerable because of their size. Your puppy needs to feel safe to comfortably use its outdoor bathroom.

If the little one succeeds on this potty call, praise it lovingly once more, but don't go crazy with your voice or gestures. A cheerful encouraging attitude works best—if you get too carried away, you might scare or confuse the pup. This is not playtime, and your little friend needs to focus on the job at hand.

Crate Training

Having its own crate gives your small dog a safe haven from the chaos of the household, as well as a room of its own where it can spend the night and take frequent naps. Because yours is a small dog, it's easy to move this portable crate from room to room or put it in the car when you are traveling. (Most hotels and motels that allow dogs require them to be crated in your room to prevent damage.) The crate is not an instrument of punishment. When the pup gets too rambunctious, the crate is the perfect place for a time-out. It should always be treated as a positive environment, never used in an angry or punitive manner.

Dogs are dependent upon humans, but they are not little humans. In all their infinite variety, from the tiny toy poodle to the giant Great Dane, they are descendents of the wolf. Finding solace and comfort within a den is imprinted in their DNA; for a puppy, a crate serves this purpose perfectly. For your dog, the crate will become a room of its own, where it goes to get away from the hustle and bustle of the household and spend some needed downtime. It is also a boon when you are housebreaking your furry baby. And when you need to leave Fido alone, crating him with a comfy blanket and a few well-loved toys will prevent him from chewing the furniture and soiling the carpet.

Question?

Isn't it cruel to crate my dog?
Many dog owners view the crate as solitary confinement, and what could be a more punitive concept than that to a human? But like a wolf pup, a young dog finds its own personal den a place of safety and sanctuary. As long as you don't use the crate as a punishment and help your dog get used to it with a lot of positive reinforcement, it will become your dog's cozy retreat.

Some small dogs, especially the toy breeds, are notoriously hard to housetrain. Maybe it's because we dote on them so much that we tend to overlook their slips. After all, their messes are much smaller and easier to clean up than those of a Lab or German shepherd. Unless you commit yourself to the housetraining process, sooner or later your little dog will make a mess you cannot shrug off, and you will feel upset and resentful. You'll also quickly tire of having your house smell like a kennel that needs to be cleaned.

Sometimes your own inconsistency can be part of the problem. You can't overlook Fifi's accident in the kitchen corner because you waited too long to take her out and then stage an angry outburst when you step in something nasty in the middle of the night. Mixed messages lead to one confused puppy and lots of household tension.

Most dog owners want their dog to defecate and urinate in a designated area outside, but you may opt to use litter or a newspaper indoors, especially if you are a city dweller in a high-rise. Whatever its bathroom of choice, when it comes to housetraining, your dog's crate will be your best friend. In its early days with its mother and littermates, one of the first lessons your pup learned was not to soil its sleeping quarters. Taking advantage of this predisposition will help you crate train your little dog.

Choosing a Crate

What size and type crate will you need? It depends on your dog's size. A small crate or cage will do for dogs up to twenty pounds, while a medium one is better for those from twenty to twenty-five pounds. If the crate is too big, the puppy will have plenty of room to wander to the far end to do its business without feeling that it is fouling the nest. Most crates cost between $25 and $50, and they are worth every penny when it comes to protecting your home from accidents (and having your dress shoes turned into chew toys).

The fiberglass type is easy to assemble and gives your dog a sense of privacy. It is lightweight and easy to tote from place to place. Wire mesh cages are collapsible, folding up like a suitcase, and most have a removable tray in the bottom, making them easy to clean. To make a cage like this more private, especially at night for sleeping, you may cover the sides and back with a blanket.

 Alert!

If you don't have air-conditioning, you should not crate your dog in hot weather. Short-muzzled dogs like Pekes, Boston terriers, and pugs, as well as full-coated breeds like the spaniels, shih tzu, Lhasa apso, and American Eskimo, are prone to heat prostration when the temperature reaches uncomfortable levels, indoors or out.

Equip the crate with a comfy washable pad or blanket. Keep a few spares on hand, as they will probably need frequent washing. A stainless-steel water dish that attaches to the crate door and a couple of well-loved toys will make your dog feel at home. Make sure the toys are safe—no tiny pieces, cotton ropes, or rawhide to choke on or swallow. It's best not to leave a collar on your little dog in the crate as the buckle could catch on the mesh sides or door and cause choking. Instead, hang the collar and leash nearby so you can grab them when needed.

Acclimating Your Puppy

On its first day home, get the puppy used to the crate in small doses. Encourage its use by first letting the dog go in and out with the door left open, offering a tasty treat and words of praise when it does. The puppy may protest when you first confine it. If it has been fed and you know it doesn't need to relieve itself, don't give in and let it out of the crate. That response will teach it that when it cries, you'll come running. Ignore any barking and whining and tell it "No" in a firm voice, then go about your business, in and out of the room where the crate is. This is lesson one in establishing your leadership. At night, it's best to place the crate next to your bed. This will be a comforting presence for the new arrival and will help build the bond between you.

Paper or Litter Box Training

Small dogs have small bladders so they need to go more often than their larger cousins. If you find it impossible to run in and out every couple of hours with your puppy, training it to use litter or newspaper instead of the great outdoors may be your best solution. Litter or paper training does not have to be a permanent solution, however. Some puppies can be trained later to go outside, and some can get used to both methods.

First, decide on a designated area, one with a tile or linoleum floor that can be washed frequently. Place the puppy's crate in that room with the litter box or papered area nearby. You may also use an exercise pen with the dog crate and potty area both inside it to limit the dog's access to the entire room. These foldable wire pens, called x-pens for short, come in a wide variety of sizes and are reasonably priced.

Dog litter comes in a variety of sizes and is dust-free and nontracking. Some litter-training enthusiasts prefer compressed wood pellets like those used in wood-burning stoves. At less than $3 for a forty-pound bag, they're a lot less expensive than packaged litter. Dog litter pans are also available that are lower and easier for little canines to get in and out of than large cat litter boxes.

 Essential

When you are feeling frustrated by your pup's accidents during housetraining, remember that your little friend needs your help in mastering the potty process. Be realistic. The muscles that help your puppy control elimination do not begin to develop until it is at least four months old.

Litter-training proponents are quick to point out that this is the perfect solution for small-breed owners who live in a high-rise buildings or don't have a yard or for frequent travelers who stay in hotels with small dogs. Since many small dogs hate going outside in bad weather, they would probably like this solution as well.

Those who opt to paper-train often use disposable housebreaking pads along with the newspaper layers or by themselves, some made to fit inside their own plastic trays. These are highly absorbent and treated with pheromones or artificial scents that attract puppies to do their business. As the dogs get used to going on paper, some owners make the potty area smaller and smaller. Some devise their own litterbox solutions, such as placing layers of newspapers inside the removable tray from a large dog crate.

How to Housetrain Your Puppy

Your puppy is not the one in charge of its potty schedule—you are! As in all areas of training, you will set the rules as to what is expected of your little dog—and whether your new dog is a pup or an adult, you are also in charge of the housetraining process.

Your goal should be to prevent accidents, not to continually catch the dog in the act. To do this successfully, you need to know how often your furry friend will need to take care of business. Puppies under three months of age have very little bladder control. They usually let you know it's time to go by circling and sniffing the floor. Their powerful little noses are seeking a familiar smell that tells them the area has been used before so it's okay to use it again. You need to be tuned in to such signals. You'll often catch the pup in the nick of time and make a mad dash for the door, but it's better to anticipate the need and carry your dog outside or to the potty area before it starts signaling its intentions, usually twenty to thirty minutes after it eats and every two hours when you first bring it home.

 Fact

No dog should have the run of the house until it has earned the privilege by mastering the housetraining process.

If you obtained your puppy from a breeder, its housetraining may have begun before you brought it home, but if it came from a pet store, house-training is as unfamiliar as space travel to the little dog. Unfortunately, pet-store puppies get used to soiling their cages or pens. Although dogs naturally prefer to live in a clean environment that does not smell like feces, they get used to the odor when they have no choice. Undoing this behavior will take time and patience.

Some experts recommend feeding the pup in its crate to keep matters more controlled while you are housetraining. But pups are not very neat diners, so this means more work for you keeping the crate clean. Most people prefer the feeding area in the kitchen, preferably with a baby gate in place to keep the pup from going into other rooms. After mealtime, remember that you have approximately twenty-five minutes before your puppy needs to relieve itself. Carry the dog outside to the potty area, and let it take all the time it needs to do its business. Keeping it on a leash outside may help it to focus on the job at hand, rather than following its nose all over the yard.

Your daily routine will go like this. When you wake up in the morning, carry the pup out before you even have your coffee. Carrying it is important—once those little feet hit the floor, it will want to relieve itself. Let it get used to feeling the grass under its feet and associating that with going potty. Use consistent verbal cues as well, such as "Go potty" or "Do your business" every time you go out. After the pup relieves itself, reward it with a treat and let it play inside in a safe area where you can keep an eye on it for about an hour. Feed the pup, confine it for twenty to thirty minutes, and then once again, out you go! During its first month with you, your pup will probably eat four meals a day, so that's a lot of feeding, waiting, and hustling in and out for potty trips. Plan accordingly.

Fact

Puppies need to go potty when they wake up in the morning, twenty to thirty minutes after each meal, after each nap, and before going to bed for the night.

Keeping your pup on a predictable routine and not offering water after 4:00 or 5:00 P.M. will also help. Your little sprite will soon get the message and be able to last longer between potty calls. By then, you'll be getting good at picking up the signals, but you'll still have to move fast when it's time to go!

Some owners train their dogs to ring a bell when they need to go out. It sounds far-fetched, but it's not that hard to do. Hang a wind chime or bell on a string off the doorknob, just at your dog's nose level. Ring it every time you go out to potty, using a verbal cue as well, like "Want to go potty?" or "Want to go out?" Reinforce it by going outside the door yourself with a favorite treat or toy, closing the door all or part way, and calling to your dog, using the same words. When it noses the bell, let it out and give it the treat or toy and lots of praise. Every time you ask the dog that same question, and when it runs to the door and rings the bell, reward it with praise and a treat. Dogs live to please, and positive reinforcement is a powerful motivator.

Hold off on major redecorating projects for six months or so after the pup's arrival. There may still be an occasional accident, but once it has achieved that wonderful state of being housetrained, you'll hardly remember these busy days when you had to keep reminding yourself that "This too shall pass."

How to Housetrain Your Adult Dog

You should also use the crate-training method to housetrain an older dog. Just like a puppy, it should be put on a schedule though adults can wait longer between potty calls. Again, get outside first thing in the morning without fanfare, with no petting or playing until the mission is accomplished. During training, take your dog out every three to four hours. Don't offer water after 4:00 p.m., and don't give it the run of the house yet. Shelter dogs or dogs that have lived in a kennel may be a challenge to housetrain because no one has insisted that they go only in a designated area. They can be taught to let you know when they need to go out, and just like pups, they respond to praise and rewards.

Rescue dogs often have a troubled past involving abuse or neglect. Once they get used to the safety and security of their new home, they will want nothing more than to please you, so be patient through the training process and seek the help of a trainer or behaviorist if necessary.

Common Housetraining Problems

If your little dog goes out, sniffs every blade of grass in the yard without going potty, and then sneaks behind the furniture to do its business after you take it back inside, you have a confusion problem on your hands. Your own reaction when you catch it in the middle of such an episode may help solve the mystery behind this behavior.

You are only human, but if you yell and scream when little Max is caught in the act, he might think it's because of *what* he is doing, not *where* he is doing it. In other words, he's probably afraid to go potty in front of you, even out-of-doors. Small dogs can be very sensitive and easily shamed when they do something wrong. In such situations, it's best to give a firm "No, Max" and carry him outside or to the designated potty area—again and again until he gets the message. When he does go in the right place, give loving feedback and a treat every time. If you find an old accident, take him the scene of the crime, point to the evidence, and firmly say "No, Max!" and then take the little offender outside to go.

Alert!

Never scream angrily at your dog or hit it with your hand or a newspaper if it has an accident. Rubbing its nose in it doesn't work either. The dog will become afraid and confused, and it will learn to distrust you as well. It may also react defensively by growling or biting.

Dominance Marking

Sometimes housetraining problems are not really about housetraining at all. Some male dogs attempt to establish their dominance by urinating on anything they perceive to be their domain. (We all know how male dogs like to stop at every fire hydrant when they are out for a walk.) A male dog will let you know when he's entering canine adolescence by lifting his leg to pee, usually between four and nine months of age, a sure sign that your baby is reaching sexual maturity.

Urine marking is not about the dog's need to empty its bladder. It is primitive territorial, sexual, and social behavior. Your dog's ancestors in the wild laid down their boundary markers with urine, a practice that enforced the pack system that was crucial to their safety and survival as a species. On a walk, it's your dog's way of reporting, "I was here." On your table leg, it's his way of saying, "Everything here belongs to me."

When your male dog marks in your house, he may be asserting his dominance over his pack or the humans and other dogs in your household, or he may be sexually aroused by a female dog within smelling distance. Neutering often solves the problem, but if it persists, the dog must be taught that *you* are the top dog in the house and he is a subordinate member of the pack. You may need to call upon a professional trainer or behaviorist for assistance. Obedience training itself may help, making your dog feel more confident and less inclined to mark territory. Male dogs also lift their legs indoors when they feel stressed or anxious about a change in their environment, such as a new baby, strangers working at your house, or a visiting dog. If you are single, your dog may become jealous of a new roommate or romantic partner.

Besides seeking professional help, you can crate the dog when you leave the house. When you're at home and see the dog nosing around for a spot to mark, be vigilant about swiftly getting him outdoors, using a firm "No! Outside!" as you catch him in the act. Of course, you should also offer lots of praise when he goes where he should.

Submissive Marking

Submissive urination is another common housetraining problem, more prevalent among female dogs. It also has its roots in pack behavior. When she urinates as you greet her upon returning home from work, little Ginger is telling you, "I am your love slave. I am just an insignificant underling, but you are the boss of all bosses." It is an act of obeisance, like bowing and scraping to curry favor. Sometimes these insecure little dogs will first roll over and present their bellies, another submissive gesture that says, "Do with me what you will!"

An angry outburst from you will only make matters worse. The dog will try even harder to express her submission to you, the pack leader. Your best bet is to ignore this behavioral display and greet your dog in a quiet, calm manner. To get her out of the submissive mode, offer an obedience command, such as "Sit." Then take her to the potty area. Don't make a big deal of cleaning up the puddle either. Again, building your dog's ego through obedience training will help teach her that this behavior is not necessary. If ignoring and redirecting the behavior does not stop it completely, use washable rugs by the front door and keep your emotions under control. Knowing that submission urination is a dog's way of saying "I worship you" might help.

Physical or Emotional Distress

If your little dog suddenly forgets its housebreaking manners, there may be a medical explanation. A urinary tract infection, bladder stones, kidney problems caused by diabetes, or the side effects of some medications could be the culprit. Imagine how bad you would feel if you realized those accidents happened because your poor little dog couldn't control its bodily functions. Visiting the vet will help get to the root of this lapse in acceptable behavior.

If the vet uncovers no physical cause, it might be an emotional problem. Has something changed in the dog's environment? Have there been family problems? A recent move? A change in your lifestyle? Are you too busy these days to pay attention to your dog?

Like a small child who acts out to get attention, your dog may be making a mess to get noticed. In its mind, negative attention is better than no attention at all. Try spending more time with your dog, whether walking, training, playing, or just sitting on the sofa together. After all, one of the reasons you wanted this little dog in the first place was for companionship.

 Fact

Your dog craves your companionship as much as good food and a warm place to sleep.

Stool Eating

Another problem related to elimination is coprophagia, otherwise known as stool eating. It's disgusting to humans, but it is common behavior in dogs. Many small-breed pups try eating their stools as they explore their world by putting everything in their mouths. Beyond puppy curiosity, this behavior might be caused by a dietary deficiency, allergies, or food intolerance.

Crated puppies that get bored may have accidents and eat their own feces. If your puppy cannot be taken out of his crate to go potty during the day, it would be better to confine it to a gated-off room with the crate door open. Paper or litter training might also be good solutions in a case like this.

Some believe that dog foods containing corn, wheat, or soy, not easily digested by dogs, can lead to this problem. Human food could also be a culprit. Try switching your dog's food to a high-quality brand with more varied and digestible ingredients. Cut down on treats. Adding a digestive enzyme supplement may help as well. There are also products on the market in pill or powder form to alleviate this problem, making your little dog kissable once more.

If you want to curb such behavior, you need to catch the dog in the act. Say "No" like you really mean it! Making a scary noise with a can of rocks or a loud whistle when you observe the behavior is another way to curtail this. Of course, the best way to make sure it doesn't happen is to be vigilant about cleaning up any poop before the dog has a chance to eat it.

Cleaning Up

All dogs occasionally have an accident indoors, but the way you clean it up can determine whether your little dog does it again. Even if the spot looks clean to you, your dog's powerful smelling ability will enable it to find its own scent there and lead it to use the same place again. When your dog makes a mess indoors, use an enzymatic cleaner to wipe it up. Such products contain bacteria and enzymes that actually digest the proteins in the waste, neutralizing the odors rather than just masking them. Using homemade solutions or store-bought products containing ammonia will make matters worse. Urine itself contains ammonia, so rather than deterring the dog, this smell calls it back to the same spot. Using a steam cleaner to remove urine is not a good idea either—the heat from the machine can permanently set the stain in your carpet.

Soak the area with the enzyme cleaner for about ten minutes before blotting it up with paper towels or a soft cloth, and then allow it to dry naturally. Stubborn stains may need to be treated more than once. If the dog dirties scatter rugs, blankets, or other bedding material, use baking powder or dry bleach along with your regular detergent when you launder these items to ensure that you eliminate the odor completely. Stool stains on the carpet may be removed with a solution of liquid dish detergent, warm water, and vinegar.

Outdoor cleanup is also vitally important. If your little dog has been snacking on its own stool, regular cleanup will remove the temptation. Keeping your dog on a leash when you take it out will also help. Pooper-scoopers and doggie bags are readily available where pet supplies are sold to make this job more manageable.

Alert!

Poop bags have come a long way. They are now available in biodegradable materials that won't sit around the landfill for twenty years like plastic grocery bags do. Some can even be flushed down the toilet. Picking up after your dog is a given, but now you can do it in a more earth-friendly manner.

In addition to keeping your yard clean, it's a good idea to get into the habit of picking up after your dog because you'll need to do it everywhere you go with your dog. It's part of being a responsible dog owner. Not picking up the poop when you and your dog go walking can lead to major problems with your neighbors. You may also be violating the law. Some municipalities fine owners who neglect to pick up after their dogs.

In heavily populated areas, the runoff from dog waste can pollute lakes and streams. In addition to soil and water contamination, it causes foul odors and attracts disease-carrying insects and rodents. In outdoor areas, including your own backyard, dog feces may be infested with microscopic organisms that spread diseases to humans. Salmonella is the most common bacterial infection present in dog excrement, causing fever, muscle aches, headaches, vomiting, and diarrhea. Hookworms found in dog stool are transmittable to children who run barefoot or handle dirt in such contaminated areas. Roundworm is another danger, capable of causing damage to the lungs, liver, and eyes of humans exposed to dog waste.

 Obedience Begins at Home

Raising a pup is a lot like raising a child. When it comes to acceptable behavior, every family has its own rules and regulations. Teaching your dog to conform to your rules is the secret to happy dog ownership. Although it takes a lot of time and attention, your dog needs to live in a world beyond your home, so the training you provide now will prepare your dog to behave properly in any circumstance.

When to Begin

Ideally, you will think about your own house rules before you acquire that little bundle of love. Although owners of small dogs tend to think of them as babies, they are in fact dogs, and sometimes their doggy behavior can cause problems to the people in their lives. It's up to you to raise a canine companion you can be proud of, and the teaching process will take place everyday. It can and should be a labor of love.

Your puppy will start learning good manners the first day you bring it home. Before that memorable day, your household members should discuss the rules for good puppyhood. Inconsistency from its human caretakers will lead to one confused and naughty little pup. How can Buddy learn to conform with the house rules if they keep changing?

To raise a puppy properly, you need to be patient and consistent. One person within the family, probably you, will be doing the lion's share of training. But since all household members will enjoy the little tyke, you all need to agree to the same rules and methods of correction. Discuss the terms you will use as commands and what is acceptable and unacceptable behavior for this new little family member.

Question?

Do small dogs really need training?
A dog of any size needs to be trained so that you can take it with you anywhere. All dogs should be under their owners' control or removed from situations that they cannot handle. A dog that poses a threat to other pets or people is a liability, no matter what its size.

Make sure no one thinks it's okay to hit the young dog. Obviously, no one should allow nipping or games that encourage aggression. To ensure your dog's good health, make sure family members don't feed him from their plates. And until he is fully housetrained, the little guy should not have the run of the house.

Most owners of small dogs don't mind them on the furniture. They are lap dogs, after all, and they won't grow up to be ninety-pound dynamos that take up the whole couch. Nonetheless, teach your dog to wait to join you until it is invited. You might be eating, sewing, or reading and not want a ten-pound missile landing in your lap. You teach this by both verbal and nonverbal signals, such as tapping your thigh and saying "Up!" when you want canine company, then rewarding the pup's compliance with praise and a treat. Establishing your leadership is done in subtle ways like this. If you don't want the little imp to share the sofa, make sure you have a comfy little bed or mat nearby instead.

As far as sharing your own bed with a pup, this practice can lead to problems. A small pup could jump off the bed, causing severe injury. It could also wet the bed, not a pleasant way for you to awaken in the middle of the night. If yours is a dominant pup, it may get possessive about the bed, guarding it against other family members. Again, it boils down to a leadership issue. The puppy is not your equal. Your family is now its pack, and you are the pack leader. For everyone's sake, including its own, it needs to accept this subordinate role. When it's time to go to sleep for the night, your pup will be far better off in its own crate, next to your bed.

Socialization

Small dogs need to live in a big world, and sometimes it can be scary. Small dogs that are frightened react in numerous ways—by staging an aggressive display of growling, grimacing and biting, by retreating and hiding, or simply by freezing in place like scared little rabbits, their way of trying to become invisible. These responses are hard-wired into dogs as survival techniques. You can help your little dog by safely exposing it to different situations. If you were fortunate enough to get your dog from a reputable breeder, this socialization process may have been jump-started before it left its littermates.

At Home

Socialization begins at home. Introduce your pup to new sounds, sights, and smells within your household. Building your dog's confidence will prepare it for unfamiliar situations in the big wide world beyond your doors.

The first way you will socialize the pup is through your touch. Lovingly handle it all over, from head to tail. Play with its paws and tickle its tummy. If it balks at being touched on one particular area, go back to its comfort zone and gradually work your way back to the touchy spot. Repetition and a soothing tone of voice helps underscore your trust-building activity. Desensitization through touch is also a great way to acclimate a dog to the grooming process as you introduce the brush and comb in these brief nonthreatening sessions.

Alert!

The first sixteen weeks of a puppy's life are a crucial time, sometimes referred to as the fear imprint period. If it does not learn to trust humans and accept their touch during this time, it could develop a fear response that stays with it throughout its life.

Let the puppy get used to all kinds of background noises in your home. Unless your puppy has been raised underfoot in a family setting, vacuum cleaners, hair dryers, and dishwashers may be new and startling. Having someone hold the puppy when it hears these sounds will make them less frightening. If a particular noise is too loud and the puppy reacts with fear, move further away or lower the decibel level. It may take several such encounters to make a puppy feel less anxious. These exercises in desensitization are all about building confidence.

You need to adapt the socialization process to the individual pup. A little rascal may want to kill the vacuum cleaner, while a more timid tyke may be overcome with fright. You don't want to push a pup beyond its limits, so expose it to new situations in small doses, always offering comfort, reassurance, and tangible rewards like treats as the tolerance level increases. Positive reinforcement is the key to effective training. If your puppy accepts a treat as part of the exercise, that's a good sign. If it wants no part of the tidbit, it's too scared to enjoy a tasty morsel at the moment.

Rapid movements may also frighten your little dog. Big arm motions, dancing, exercising, running, or walking fast across the room may cause it to retreat to a safe place. Calm things down a bit, and tell other family members to be aware of how their movements affect the pup. Take it slowly, increasing such high-motion activities in small doses, and keeping your distance from the pup as it gets used to this kind of normal everyday activity.

Objects like tricycles, strollers, umbrellas, recliner chairs, or even big boxes can spook a puppy too. If your dog has a meltdown when it sees an umbrella, how will you be able to walk in the rain? If there are children in the house, bikes and strollers are there to stay. Again, let the puppy get used to them from a distance, and don't force them upon the four-legged baby until it feels less threatened. Never force your dog any closer to a scary object. It takes lots of time and patience to move beyond a small pup's fears, but if you do so successfully, you will prevent a lifetime of phobias.

Essential

Your puppy's genetic inheritance plays a big part in its temperament. Socialization to alleviate its fears and a variety of friendly encounters with diverse people, places, and things will help your dog develop a confident attitude so that it can enjoy a full and happy life.

Sometimes, the best thing you can do is put your puppy in its crate when you know a fear-inducing situation cannot be avoided. This is another instance in which crate-training can be helpful. For example, some dogs are terrified of thunder, so being in their safe little haven may help them cope with it. You can also sit nearby and talk soothingly while it takes refuge in the crate. Turning up the volume on the radio or television or putting on a fan or air conditioner will help lessen the noise of the storm.

Away from Home

Your little dog needs to be socialized to the big wide world outside as well. Puppies that are always kept at home may find it extremely hard to cope with new places. This will make your life difficult as well because your little friend needs to venture out to go to the vet, the groomer, or training classes, or to accompany you on vacations. Exposing your pup to other places and other people is just as important as getting it used to objects and situations at home.

Because pups don't tend to catch infections from humans, there are places you can safely take your dog to meet people even before it can be exposed to other dogs. Until it has had its second round of vaccinations, avoid places where dogs congregate. Even if their waste has been cleaned up, harmful germs may still be present on the ground.

In order to grow up to be a dog that is comfortable anywhere, your puppy needs to meet people of every size and shape. In the first six months of its life, the wider the variety of humans your pup is exposed to, the less fearful it will be of those who are different. In a busy family setting with lots of visitors coming and going, your job is made easier. But you still need to make an effort to accustom the pup to strangers.

The pup should meet people of different races, men with facial hair and without, short people, tall people, and all those in between. People also wear different styles of clothing, such as uniforms, hats, costumes, flowing dresses, and all kinds of footwear. Dogs need to accept these sartorial differences, no matter how odd they may appear. Just like their owners, dogs notice differences in people, and they pick up on your reactions. If you act apprehensive around someone, you reinforce that reaction in your dog.

Let the dog also meet people in wheelchairs or on walkers, crutches, or canes. Pups need to witness the variety of ways in which people move about—walking, skipping, riding bikes, and roller-blading or carrying bags and other objects. Not all human voices sound alike either. Expose your dog to a variety of voices—foreign accents, laughing, whispering, yelling, singing, and so on.

Sometimes people will remark that their dog does not like men. Such a fear may not come from a bad experience with an abusive male but simply from a lack of interaction with males of the human species. If you don't have a man in the house, get the dog used to male friends or relatives. Since they make up half the world's population, this is a good idea!

Interacting with Children

With a small dog, socialization with small children may require special handling. Some small dogs naturally fear children who have not been taught to act appropriately around dogs. It's not that they are mean or that they hate kids. They have a legitimate reason to be scared. Children are capable of unintentionally injuring them. Preschoolers may not have learned how to empathize with animals. Older kids can also have problems dealing with dogs, especially if they have not been taught the consequences of startling, teasing, or provoking an animal. Unfortunately, this makes them prime candidates for dog bites, and the dog usually gets blamed.

Alert!

Supervision is of the utmost importance when introducing your puppy to young children. No screaming or rowdy play, and no holding the pup, either. An accidental dropping could be fatal. Because of its size, your dog will always need supervision around children.

The good news is that children can be taught to be gentle and nonthreatening to a small dog. Introduce your dog to them slowly, one at a time, so that it won't feel crowded or overwhelmed. Tell youngsters to talk softly and to touch the pup gently only if it does not appear to be afraid. With the proper training and socialization, kids and dogs can benefit tremendously from their relationships, forming bonds that instill love, kindness, and responsibility in children and creating lifelong memories as well.

Appropriate Outings for Puppies

Most of us lead active, busy lives, and there is no reason to leave your little buddy at home when you need to run an errand or meet a friend for coffee. Here are some places you can take your pup to socialize, either in your arms or on a leash:

- The mall or shopping center
- The beach
- An outdoor café
- A local youth sporting event, such as a soccer match
- A flea market or street fair

Bring along a bag of treats. When you introduce your dog to new people, they can give it a tasty morsel for positive reinforcement. This early exposure will accustom your dog to the presence of new people, which will benefit both of you as novel situations arise.

Once your dog is fully vaccinated, you may also visit the vet's office or grooming salon, just to say hello. Try to schedule such visits when these professionals are not too busy. A pleasant interaction and a tasty treat will make your dog less fearful when it needs to go back for grooming or medical care.

Pups tire easily, so keep these outings short until the puppy matures. Before the pup has had its second series of shots, carry it to avoid exposure to areas where other dogs may have relieved themselves. Once it gets that immunization, it can mingle with compatible dogs of its own size as long as their meetings are well supervised.

If your best efforts at socialization just don't seem to alleviate your dog's fears of specific things, people, or situations, seek the help of a veterinary behaviorist. Early intervention can work wonders, since the longer you wait, the more ingrained fear will become. In some cases, your vet may recommend prescription drugs to reduce a fearful dog's anxiety level.

Getting Started

Combining tasty treats with loving praise is the best way to train your dog. When it comes to treating a small dog, a little goes a long way. Intersperse those tidbits with loving pats and verbal appreciation. Don't forget that you are dealing with a tiny tummy. Once it is filled up with treats, the incentive they should provide will be greatly diminished—and you could end up with a little friend that looks like Porky Pig!

Positive reinforcement helps your little dog know that it is safe and loved. It is up to you to teach it to be a loving companion and family member, a dog that both receives and gives joy.

Just as you make time for feeding, grooming, and play, set aside daily time to work on obedience lessons. Keep the sessions brief at first, only ten or fifteen minutes, and work your way up to longer lessons as your dog masters each command. Don't overload the puppy with too many things at once, confusing it and postponing its progress. Beyond learning where to go potty and where not to, small-breed and toy dogs need to learn some basic obedience commands to make your life easier and their lives safer.

Question?

At what age should training begin?

Before the pup is three months old, you should begin teaching the behaviors needed for its own safety and your peace of mind. Although they can always learn new things, dogs are most trainable in the first six months of life.

Sit

Every puppy should learn how to sit on command. Before you give Buster a treat, make him sit. This establishes your leadership by making him earn every privilege he receives. Before going out for a walk, feeding, or playing, make him sit again. In your pup's eyes, you are like a god, the source of everything good in the world. Teaching your dog to sit before you dole out all those goodies makes him aware that first he must submit to you.

Teach the "Sit" command by treat training and verbal praise. Offer a small tidbit, holding it at the pup's nose level. As he moves toward the food, pull it back slightly and raise it above the pup's head. As he stretches to reach it, repeat the word "Sit!" and keep moving it back over his rear end. As soon as he sits, give him the treat and praise him. If you raise the treat too high over its head, the pup may stand up on his back legs. You may need to exert some gentle pressure on his hindquarters as you speak the command to get the message across.

Continue these training sessions until your puppy's hind end automatically hits the floor at the word "Sit." Every family member should make the puppy sit for his privileges.

Walking on a Leash

Leash training should begin before the age of three months. When you first put on the leash and collar, little Daisy will have no clue, and she probably won't like it one bit. She will either stage a sit-down strike or try to pull away. Don't get mad—get playful! Try getting her to follow you as you make a game of it. Be patient, and never drag your small dog. If she protests by nipping at the leash or your clothing, distract her with a treat and continue. Because yours is a small-breed puppy, use a narrow-width lightweight nylon leash for training.

Come

This one is fairly easy to teach. It's the basic reward setup. You call Buffy in a happy excited voice, and when she comes running, you ask her to sit and then give her a goody. Since you are the source of both food and entertainment, she will learn this one fast. Play hide-and-seek with her too, calling her name and rewarding her when she finds you. Fun and games aside, in a dangerous situation, this command could save her life.

Stay

This one may take a little longer. First, put little Petey in a sit. Place your opened palm in front of his nose and say "Stay!" in a firm voice, using strong eye contact as well. Now back up a few paces, then say "Petey! Come!" Expect the puppy to break the stay several times before he gets it.

Wait

Opening the door can be dangerous when you have a fifteen-pound dynamo poised and ready to bolt. For her own safety, little Princess needs to learn to wait while you get the mail, welcome a friend, or put out the trash. This is taught by using a leash to restrain the eager beaver from running outside when she shouldn't. When you do release her, you can say "Go!" It will take lots of repetition and rewarding but it is vitally important for your small dog's safety. Practice the "Wait!" command indoors to reinforce it.

Off

Many obedience trainers feel that this command is as important for protecting people as it is for your dog. The "Off" command is most needed when you open your door to an unfamiliar person who might be put off by having your dog jump up on them in a yapping frenzy. Teach this command with the help of a friend or family member. With the dog on a leash, pull your dog off the person it is jumping up on while stating "Off!" Reward if for compliance. Persistent attempts to jump up on people can be corrected by saying "Off!" and redirecting the dog's behavior by walking it around in a circle, putting it in a sit, and then giving a reward.

Essential

If you open the door with your small dog in your arms, hold the dog so that it faces away from the other person, with its head on your shoulder, to defuse a potential confrontation.

Leave It and Give It

Back in the litter, when another puppy tried to take his toy away, little Gus would growl and make fierce faces, warning his sibling to back off. If your child tries to take his toy or food and Gus does the same thing, he is asserting his rank over the child. Around three months of age, the dog learns what's his and what isn't. He's also still inclined to play with and chew on things he shouldn't. Teaching the "Leave it" command will protect family members from nippings and enable you to take back forbidden objects. The dog should release the object when you say "Leave it!" and allow you to take it when you say "Give it!" Keep the leash on for this lesson and repeat it several times until he masters it.

One way to ward off a protective attitude about food is to hand-feed your small dog. Eating in isolation makes dogs more protective of their food, so avoid feeding Muffy in her crate or in an isolated kitchen corner. Instead, put the dog's dish right in the center of the kitchen, close to other family members and activity.

No

This little word should be part of your dog's vocabulary. As he progresses through puppyhood, you'll be using it often. On the list of things a dog must learn, not biting is at the top. If Sparky is nipping youngsters when they try to take his toy or treat, you are being remiss in your supervision. Had you been watching, you would have noticed that the pup was issuing warnings by growling and raising its hackles, and you could have corrected the behavior before the biting occurred. In any case, steady eye contact and a firm "No" will teach him that it's not okay to bite.

Nipping is also common in play and should be corrected and redirected then as well. Such play biting can be avoided if you give the pup its own chew toys and bones and do not encourage aggressive games. If the pup gets too excited and out of control, there is always the crate for a needed time-out to calm down.

Many trainers recommend the alpha roll technique to control a dominant aggressive dog. This involves rolling the dog over on its back into a submissive position to demonstrate that you are the alpha dog. You should start with a soft version in early puppyhood, rather than wait until a more forceful alternative is needed. Gently put your puppy in a submissive position, rolled over on its back. Let it up when it breaks eye contact, which is your dog's way of acknowledging that you are in charge. For the safety of both pups and children, reserve this exercise for adult family members only.

How Your Small Dog Thinks

Dogs learn how to be dogs from each other, a process that begins with their mother and littermates. Within the litter, personality differences emerge— the pushiest one at feeding time, the one that always came out on top in a puppy wrestling match, the submissive one that the others pushed around, or the lazy one that would rather nap than play. Its mother and littermates formed the puppy's first pack, and now it needs to learn how to act in your human pack.

If yours was a dominant pup with its littermates, it may be just as pushy with you. If it was shy and submissive, it may initially act that way in your house too. The little newcomer will be experimenting and testing to figure out just where it fits into this new pack. It's all about rank, and your actions and reactions will teach the pup where it stands in the pecking order.

When you give your dog a firm correction, you are establishing your higher rank. Over time, similar incidents are likely to occur with every member of its new human pack. The response of each family member to the puppy's actions will determine its ultimate ranking. To understand how your pup thinks, it helps if you learn to think like it does.

Within the litter, the mother dog set the limits. When her demanding pups want to nurse on demand, she rebuffs their efforts if she isn't ready. Nipping and biting are also curtailed by Mom, and the siblings too. Her way of admonishing is to scruff the misbehaving offspring and remove it from the fray, while a littermate might howl in pain and withdraw from the play fighting, calling a halt to the fun. Such checks and balances help teach a pup what is acceptable behavior and what is not. Similarly, when your mouthy little pup gives you a nip, give a forceful "No!" and curtail the activity at once.

Alert!

Hitting a pup to curtail biting behavior is not only inhumane, it often has the opposite effect. Your hand becomes a target, encouraging the dog to grab hold and play rough, just like it did with its littermates. Habitually hitting a dog will also cause it to bite to defend itself.

Dogs have an innate desire to please their pack leader. They also take any kind of attention as a reward, so put a stop to objectionable behavior and remove the dog from the situation. Waving your arms, yelling, and pushing it away might be interpreted as an invitation to continue this fun game. The only way to train your pup is to understand that it is an animal and to think like an animal yourself, setting limits and establishing your role as its undisputed leader.

The Importance of Consistency

To get your message across, the puppy's action should always be met with the same reaction from you and other household members, whether it is behavior you want to encourage or behavior you want to correct. It can't be okay to stick its nose in the kitty litter box one day and forbidden the next. For your little dog, consistency is paramount when it comes to training. This means always using the same command for a particular behavior. You should also give the command itself, without extraneous conversation. It's "Off, Suzy" not "I told you get off—now don't jump on me, Suzy!" And you say it once. If you keep repeating it, your dog will think she has several chances to obey, so what's the hurry?

Use a firm voice for correcting unwanted behavior and a cheerful upbeat tone for encouraging the desired behavior. Be generous and loving in your praise when your puppy does something right. Again, never hit the dog with your hand or a newspaper. This is counterproductive to positive training and if you lose your temper, you could seriously injure your small dog. Never discipline it for something unless you catch it in the act. Dogs don't understand why you are all worked up about a mess they made hours ago or a recent report you just heard on their past bad behavior. They connect the disciplinary action only with what they are doing the moment when it occurs.

Repetition and reinforcement are the keys to effective training. If you slack off, your dog will forget the rules, and you will have to break it of its bad habits all over again.

Make It Positive

Remember to be generous and loving in your praise when your dog does the right thing. Make training part of everyday life, incorporating teaching opportunities and exercises into playtime. This way, your dog will associate training with having fun.

You know what your dog likes best—praise, love pats, treats, playing games with you, and enjoying its favorite toys. You also know its least favorite things—being ignored and incurring your harsh disapproval. It's all about the carrot-and-stick approach when it comes to training your small dog (minus the stick, of course).

Chapter 15

Obedience 101: Off to School

Regardless of your dog's size, formal obedience training should be part of its life. Your dog's mastery of the rudimentary commands will give you a common language in which you can let your small companion know what you expect. As you work and learn together, you'll strengthen your mutual bond and build your pup's confidence in the process. It's also a fun way to open a whole new world of friendship for you and your dog.

What Is Obedience Training?

Obedience training means much more than "Do what I say." It covers a wide range of behaviors, including house manners, tricks, and the correct way to move in the show ring. It also hones inborn skills that are part of a breed's nature, such as hunting, herding, and tracking. Taken to a higher level, obedience training prepares dogs to go to work. Service dogs for the handicapped, bomb-sniffing dogs, search-and-rescue dogs, and sled dogs all undergo intensive obedience training. Your pint-size pooch will probably never get a job with the police department, but you can take its training as far as you want.

Choosing a Professional Trainer

If you can't get a recommendation from friends, ask your breeder, breed club, vet, humane society, or groomer for the name of a good trainer. Finding the right trainer may take some time and effort on your part. Of course, you want a seasoned professional, but more than that, you want a trainer with experience in working safely and successfully with small dogs like yours. When searching for the right trainer, here are some points to consider:

- **Breadth of knowledge:** Although you want a trainer skilled at working with small and toy breeds, you also want someone with a wide knowledge of all dogs. A trainer who really knows dogs won't jeopardize the safety of your nosy little papillon by seating it next to a ninety-five-pound rottweiler. A good trainer puts safety first and knows that dogs with serious aggression issues need intensive private training before they can be allowed into a group setting.
- **Demeanor:** The trainer should exude confidence without being arrogant, a down-to-earth person you can approach with your questions, even when they seem foolish to you.
- **Kindness:** This quality is essential, both toward canines and their human handlers. No harsh techniques or screaming at dogs should be acceptable, and no yanking, hanging, or hitting. Of course, you

should see no prejudice against the littlest members of the class or their inexperienced owners either.

- **Fun:** The best trainers enjoy their calling. They incorporate games into the class and show affection for their pupils. They are nonjudgmental to people and dogs alike, able to be tickled by a dog's silly antics without putting it down in the process. You can tell that they delight in dogs, whether that means their pupils or their own cherished dogs. Besides teaching the basic commands that every dog needs, they might throw in a few pet tricks, too.

- **Reality:** Professional trainers are training both you and your dog. They know that in order to be successful, you will have to put in lots of practice time between formal sessions. They can't promise to put an obedience title on little Peaches if you are inconsistent in your dedication and lacking in your leadership.

- **Individual attention:** Some dogs are more hardheaded than others. They may need a no-nonsense approach to get the message across. Others may collapse in a puddle if you raise your voice. Some little terriers have short attention spans, and if they get bored in class, they won't learn. And just like humans, canines vary in intelligence. Some are very bright, and some take longer to learn. Good trainers vary their techniques to ensure success with each student.

- **Success:** Most accomplished trainers began by training their own dogs. They know firsthand what it's like to earn an obedience title. They have increased their knowledge by attending school, taking courses, and going to conferences and camps, and they belong to national training organizations. They should be able to provide you with references and the assurance that they never stop growing and learning about dogs.

Puppy Kindergarten

Formal obedience training begins early. Because small dogs won't grow up to be furry bulldozers that can topple Grandma and yank you into oncoming traffic, they are not seen as often as larger canines in puppy kindergarten classes. Their doting and indulgent owners tend to overlook behavioral issues until they greatly interfere with their lives. But puppy kindergarten will provide an important learning experience for your little dog.

Some kindergarten classes, held for very young dogs from two to four months of age, could be considered puppy preschool. They stress socializing your pup while they teach you about leadership. They also introduce basic commands like "Sit," "Stay," and "Come"; familiarize the pup with walking on a leash; and show you how to curb naughty puppy behaviors like biting, digging, stealing, chewing, and jumping up on people. Sure, you could do all this at home, but it's more fun in a group setting. Also, the built-in structure means that you will participate regularly, guaranteeing the consistency stressed in the preceding chapter.

Most puppy kindergarten classes are for dogs three to five months of age. If your trainer offers a preliminary course for very young puppies, puppy kindergarten might be considered graduate school for your pup. Here you will sharpen the basic skills you and your pup learned at the introductory level. If this is your dog's first obedience course, it will be your formal introduction to the basic commands.

 Question?

Is training a puppy with treats a good idea?
While treat-based training helps enormously in gaining your small dog's attention from way down there on the floor, most instructors will later switch to a combination of verbal praising and treat rewards. After all, you might not always have a pocket full of goodies when you want your dog to obey a command.

Beyond its obvious benefit of making life easier with your new dog, kindergarten is important because pups are most receptive to learning at three to four months of age. After this, small dogs reach adolescence. They rebel, test their owners left and right, and try to establish their independence. In other words, they act like human teenagers! By ten months or so, they will outgrow this stage, but without a solid foundation of "the rules," it can be tough to live with a puppy that has suddenly turned into a pushy little rebel.

Only positive reinforcement techniques should be used for your little dog. That means no harsh jerking. If choke chains (more correctly known as chain collars or training collars) are used, it should be used with limited pressure. Forceful leash corrections can injure small dogs. Their necks don't have the thick musculature of the larger breeds, and they can suffer tracheal damage or serious neck injury if yanked too hard.

It takes only a light pressure on that collar, accompanied by a verbal command, to get your message across. Nylon training collars are also available, but you need the kind with a solid nylon core. Plain braided or woven ones could choke your dog because they are too limp and don't release properly.

Before you sign up, sit in on some puppy classes. Because safety is your first consideration in choosing a kindergarten class, make sure the trainer is used to working with small dogs. Does the trainer seem knowledgeable and use humane teaching methods? Is the trainer good at communicating with both dogs and people? There are some extremely authoritarian types in this field who may intimidate you as well. You and your dog can't learn if you're afraid of making mistakes. "If what you see goes against the grain, it's the wrong place for you and your dog," says veteran trainer Caryl Crouse.

 Essential

Small dogs mature much more quickly than big dogs do, so they catch on pretty fast. After all, they will be reaching young adulthood around six months of age. However, their small size means they are also more fragile, so your trainer must not let them mix and mingle with larger classmates.

After formal lessons, instructors often schedule playtime for the puppies, but your dog should only be allowed to play with friends its own size. Puppy kindergarten usually lasts for six or seven weeks. Once your dog has graduated from puppy kindergarten, you may wish to continue its training.

The Canine Good Citizen Test

Started by the AKC in 1989, the Canine Good Citizen (CGC) test is a certification program in obedience that emphasizes good manners rather than precision, skill, or speed in following commands. Most trainers and local AKC clubs now offer courses to prepare for this ten-step test. Within our increasingly litigious society, and with more restrictions on places where dogs are welcomed, the CGC is a wonderful idea for dogs and those who cherish them. Its goal is to train and recognize canine companions as respected members of the community.

In addition to promoting responsible dog ownership, the CGC is a great prerequisite to further training in obedience, agility, tracking, and performance events, as well as for future therapy dogs.

Fact

The CGC is open to all dogs over six months of age. If testing is offered at an AKC show and yours is a mixed-breed dog, check to make sure it can participate with the purebreds.

The test involves having the dog allow the examiner to brush and handle the dog, having it accept a friendly stranger's approach, sitting politely for petting, and standing for a perfunctory exam. Showing aggression, fearfulness, or even excessive friendliness could be grounds for failure. The examiner will check the dog's self-control by having you play with it and then calming it down.

The dog must walk on a leash without pulling, and you'll need to walk it through a group of people doing various everyday activities without having it show fear or aggression. It must sit, lie down, and come on command and remain in a down-stay for three minutes when you leave its sight.

The CGC is growing in popularity worldwide at home and abroad. Some 4-H groups are using it as a beginning dog-training program for children. State legislatures have also begun recognizing the program as a means of promoting responsible dog ownership, with seventeen states so far passing resolutions recognizing its merit.

Obedience Classes and Titles

There are two types of basic obedience courses: competitive and noncompetitive. The competitive courses are for those who intend to enter their dog in AKC-sanctioned obedience competitions, earning titles as they progress. Most people who take a beginner's course in obedience training do not plan to participate in AKC competition. Right now, putting an obedience title on little Pebbles might be the furthest thing from your mind.

Noncompetitive Classes

Informal noncompetitive obedience classes are often sponsored by the local humane society, 4-H clubs, and pet superstores like Petco and PetSmart. They will improve your dog's ability to walk on a leash, sharpen its responses to basic commands, and strengthen your leadership. Children are often welcome in such classes so training little Teddy can become a family affair.

For those who would like their dog to earn an obedience title as a Companion Dog (CD), you would begin basic obedience at either the novice or prenovice level, depending upon how much your dog has already learned and your own experience. A recognized obedience trainer who teaches classes for competition would be your best bet for this type of training.

Obedience titles are earned in a series of sanctioned matches. Your dog will need to demonstrate his ability to heel, walking closely at different speeds as if attached to your ankle. He will also need to come when called and to stay, remaining in a sit without being distracted by his canine classmates. When you call his name, Bowser must make a beeline for you, sit sharply in front of you, and then finish by circling your feet and sitting close by your left side. He must also stand on command for a simple examination by the judge.

Competitive Classes

Of course, it takes a good deal of class time and practice before you and your dog are ready to go into the obedience ring at an AKC show or trial. As you prepare, you can enter some matches, informal shows where you and your canine prodigy can check your skills in a practice competition. You won't be scored or win any prizes, but you will get a taste of being in the ring.

Once you enter an official AKC obedience trial, your dog will be scored on each prescribed exercise. There are three levels at which your dog can earn a title. Each level is more difficult than the one before. If you find this kind of intensive training lights your fire, a kennel club or breed club may be the best source of training. You need a trainer who specializes in preparing dogs for advanced competition. Most such trainers aim for a high score in the ring, not just a passing grade. As you pursue your goals, you will need this person's guidance and expertise every step of the way so you want someone who has the time and patience to give you and your dog the individual attention that you need.

Essential

Look upon the trainer as your partner in helping you shape the behavior of your dog so it can be happily integrated into your life. The dog is not the only one being trained—you must also learn your part in the human-animal equation!

Training Terms and Credentials

To help you distinguish between the many types of instruction and teachers out there, here are some terms, titles, and organizations that describe trainers and where they get their training:

- **Dog trainer:** By itself, this title requires no formal credentials. Anyone can call themselves a dog trainer. Narrowly interpreted, a dog trainer teaches the dog the commands and then teaches the dog owner how to use them.

- **Obedience instructor:** These people teach obedience classes, sometimes in groups and sometimes in private lessons. They will teach your dog to heel, sit, and come when called while helping you understand your dog's instinctual drives and motivations. Some offer classes for those who wish to compete for obedience titles. At the highest level, they train other trainers.

- **Animal behaviorists:** These academically trained specialists have usually completed graduate work in psychology, neurology, biology, or zoology, with an emphasis on canine behavior. They usually work in conjunction with a veterinary school or hospital and have a background in observing and understanding dog behavior and correcting problems.

- **NADOI:** Founded in 1965, the National Association of Dog Obedience Instructors (NADOI) offers certification to trainers at different levels of expertise and experience. With members worldwide, its stated mission is "to endorse dog obedience instructors of the highest caliber; to provide continuing education and learning resources to those instructors; and to continue to promote humane, effective training methods and competent instructors." You can find a member near you at *www.nadoi.org.*

- **APDT:** Founded in 1993 by renowned training expert and veterinarian Ian Dunbar, this 5,000-member organization was established as the voice of professional trainers, promoting their image and professionalism. Primarily an educational organization, it hosts conferences and encourages its members to "make use of training methods that use reinforcement and rewards, not punishment, to achieve desired behavior." Although it does not endorse or certify members, it offers a directory to those who visit its web page, *www.apdt.com.*

- **The National K-9 Dog Training School:** Located in Columbus, Ohio, this school was opened in 1975. It trains obedience trainers, most of whom complete its six-week course to become a Master Trainer. You can find it online at *www.nk9.com.*

Many great trainers are also self-educated people whose natural skills in training became evident with family and friends first and who went on to increase their knowledge by attending courses and seminars. For some, this work has an underlying spiritual component. Within the realm of those who work with animals, there is room for the intangible—an innate ability to understand and connect with our four-legged friends.

Training Styles and Techniques

Early dog-training methods were based mainly upon the work of William Koehler, a renowned trainer for the military and the movie industry who advocated aversion training. In other words, if a dog did not perform an exercise correctly, it would receive a sharp jerk and be snapped back into the right position. While this wake-up call method was effective, some trainers took it to inhumane extremes. One technique used to curb a dog's aggression was to hang it by the choke chain, its feet dangling in the air, until it got the message. Then there were those who would "helicopter" a dog, swinging the airborne canine around in circles. Such methods could injure a dog of any size but would obviously have the worst possible consequences for the smallest of the species. Thankfully, the harsh training methods of the past have been replaced by more humane methods.

Within the past fifteen years, the pendulum has swung the other way. Most trainers now rely on motivational training, which is based upon shaping their behavior through rewards and praise. This approach is based upon the behavior modification techniques of B. F. Skinner, who termed his method *operand conditioning*. (This technique is also used for training the dolphins you see performing in aquatic shows.) Clicker training and treat training are based upon this method. Initially, the clicker sound is followed by a treat each time the dog obeys a command. Skinner's basic tenets were simple:

1. An animal will not learn if its response is not rewarded.
2. A behavior will be learned more rapidly if it is reinforced.
3. Once a behavior is learned, it will be more likely to be repeated if it is rewarded occasionally, rather than every time.

Because there are thousands of trainers out there with many different approaches, some still handle dogs roughly and teach through intimidation. You want to avoid these trainers like the plague. Before you choose a trainer, sit in on a class to observe how he or she handles the dogs. Refer to the section titled "Choosing a Professional Trainer" in this chapter for specific things to look for in a trainer.

Alert!

On your exploratory visits to various trainers, if you like what you observe and decide to sign up, make sure your little dog is thoroughly immunized before it goes off to school.

More Competitions and Activities

If competition and dog sports really thrill you, an increasing number of activities are available to you and your dog. Agility and tracking are two AKC activities you and your dog can enjoy together. Any purebred dog over six months of age can compete in tracking tests and field trials, although the most proficient are those with the keenest noses. For small dogs, these are dachshunds and the terrier breeds. Fly ball, freestyle, and other sports will also strengthen the bond between you and your dog.

Agility

Any dog over the age of one year may compete in agility. This active dog sport requires having your unleashed dog negotiate an obstacle course, climbing over an A-frame or elevated dog walk, leaping over hurdles, and zigzagging through weave poles like a tiny slalom skier, all within an allotted time.

The AKC offers two types of agility classes. The Standard Class includes such obstacles as the dog walk, the A-frame, and seesaw (all involving climbing skills), while Jumpers with Weaves has hurdles, tunnels, and weave poles. Both offer increasing levels of difficulty as you and your dog go after its

Novice, Open, Excellent, and Master titles. After earning both an Excellent Standard and Excellent Jumpers title, dog and handler can go on to compete for the Master Agility Champion title (MACH), a highly appropriate acronym, as these swift-moving canines seem to move faster than the speed of sound!

One of the best things about agility is that any dog can compete. From the most petite Pomeranian to the gargantuan Irish wolfhound, everyone can play! The newest division, termed the *Preferred Class*, features modifications with lower jumps to accommodate all breeds as well as older canine participants. This would be the best place to start with your small dog. Preferred Classes offer titles in Novice, Open, and Excellent levels in both Standard and Jumper divisions.

Safety of the dogs is a primary concern. The height of the jumps is set according to the dog's height so your little dog won't be expected to perform like a German shepherd. Because every trial presents a different course, communication between the team's human and canine members is of the utmost importance. The three basic titles to be earned here are Novice Agility Dog, Open Agility Dog, and Excellent Agility Dog. With safety in mind, look for a small-dog agility class where your dog will have more fun and be less intimidated among other small fry.

Tracking

This age-old dog activity allows dogs to demonstrate their inborn ability to follow a human scent. Unlike obedience and agility events that require your dog to qualify three times on its way to a title, your dog need only complete one event successfully to earn a tracking title. According to AKC rules, a dog earns that coveted TD (Tracking Dog) distinction by following a track 440 to 500 yards long with three to five changes of direction as it searches for a scented article. With a long leash attached, the owner follows behind. Further titles, Tracking Dog Excellent (TDX) and Variable Surface Tracking (VST) increase the difficulty factor. A Champion Tracker (CT) is a dog that has successfully captured all three titles.

Earthdog Trials

Another fun outdoor activity for dogs led around by their noses can be found in Earthdog trials. In these events, the dog must enter a simulated burrow, following a scented trail to find two caged rats. The tunnels vary in length, depending on the participants' skill levels, with titles to be earned divided into Junior Earthdog (JE), Senior Earthdog (SE), or Master Earthdog (ME). It's a great way to get your little terrier or Doxie in touch with its ancestral heritage and have some fun outdoors. Dachshunds, Border terriers, and Parson Russells led the pack with the most Earthdog titles in 2003.

Flyball

An additional activity just for the fun of it that can lead to championship titles is flyball, in which a team of four dogs participate in a relay race, clearing four jumps as they race. At the end of the hurdles, the runner must press a trigger, releasing a tennis ball. The dog must catch the ball, then clear the jumps again on its return leg. Your little flyballer will also collect certificates, pins, and plaques along the way for participating in this fast-paced dog sport and may earn the title Flyball Dog Champion (FDCH). If you have a little ball-crazy dog that plays well with others, ask your trainer or local club about this kind of competition, or check the North American Flyball Association Web site at *www.flyballdogs.com.*

Freestyle

A newer dog-and-owner activity is called freestyle. Basically, it's dancing with dogs. An offshoot of obedience training in which people and dogs perform choreographed routines to music, freestyle incorporates standard obedience moves but features plenty of improvisation too. Its artistry and creativity highlights the amazing bond between handler and dog. It's all about showing off and having fun while challenging your dog in the process. To see this amazing activity, ask your trainer where classes and demonstrations are held or check out the Canine Freestyle Federation Web page at *www.canine-freestyle.org.*

Chapter 16

Common Behavior Problems

Even the best dogs sometimes get in trouble. In puppyhood, it's to be expected. Puppy shenanigans like potty slip-ups, biting, barking, mouthing, running away, digging up the flowerbeds, or gnawing on the table leg go with the territory. Adult dogs get in trouble, too, most often for behaviors that should have been corrected in puppyhood. Aggression, territorial behavior, and separation anxiety are problems that need to be addressed and corrected. Prevention is still the best way to avoid problems, but sometimes you need to consult a professional for intensive one-on-one help.

Preventing Problems

Although far fewer dogs are now euthanized at shelters, behavior problems are still the main reason for the sad decision to give up ownership of a dog. Last year, more than 2 million dogs lost their lives because they were not safe and suitable pets. Most were larger canines, but when a small dog's unacceptable behavior goes uncorrected, its owner will often throw in the towel as well. Genetic makeup is rarely the source of temperament troubles. Most behavior problems result from a dog's lack of training and an owner's lack of leadership.

 Essential

Don't switch trainers while you are trying to teach your dog something or trying to break a bad habit. If one method isn't working, try another.

You've already learned the importance of early socialization and training. To underscore your leadership role, you need to make your little dog earn every privilege, whether it's the run of the house after housetraining or dinner, which it eats with your permission. Obedience has a much larger meaning for the pup than simply doing what it is told. It's your way of letting that pup know who is in charge.

Alpha Dog Exercises

Most behavior problems can be prevented if a dog accepts the leadership of its human caretakers. Dogs' ancestral wolf genes make them need and want a leader to direct them. Knowing what is expected gives them a sense of security. If you don't provide that leadership, the dog will jump right in to take that role upon itself.

Back in its early days with his mother, the puppy knew who was boss. Mother knew best, and she put him in his place by scruffing him by the neck to discourage unacceptable behavior. She also growled and made eye contact to communicate her disapproval. If your little dog is turning into a dictator, you need to reclaim your place as leader of the pack. To do that, you need to teach him that it is subordinate to you, just like his mother did. This is why making the pup obey commands before he gets any rewards or privileges is crucial in shaping desirable behavior.

To truly become the alpha dog in your little pack, you must gain the puppy's respect without breaking its spirit or losing its trust. Even if you initially feel silly doing them (or your family members chuckle), alpha dog exercises provide an effective method to get your message across. Since you are much bigger and stronger than your pup, you must be extremely careful not to be too forceful with any of these exercises—you could easily injure your dog. These activities are for adults only.

Try sitting on the floor and making your puppy stand up on its back legs as you hold it under its armpits, facing you. Lift the pup off the ground, making eye contact as you hold it for a few seconds. In the ancestral wolf pack, the alpha wolf used his penetrating stare to remind the pack members that he was in charge. You can also harness the power of eye contact in all kinds of training situations.

If the puppy squirms and struggles, make like a dog and give a low growl while you hold the little rascal aloft until he submits to your will. Back in the litter, the mother's growls meant whatever you're doing, stop it now; and right now, you're speaking her language.

 Fact

Direct eye contact is a big part of canine body language. It tells the pup that you mean business. In canine language, breaking eye contact by looking away is a sign of submission.

Again while sitting on the floor, cradle the pup in your arms like a human infant. This belly-up position is submissive, and the little upstart may protest. Keep on holding (and again growl if you must) and maintain eye contact as you keep the pup in this position until it relaxes, holding it for just a few seconds the first few times.

The most familiar alpha role-playing exercise involves rolling the pup over with you above it in a straddling position. Never rest your body weight on the pup when you do this! Holding the front forelegs, make eye contact, and growl if a struggle ensues. Again, hold the pup for just a few seconds initially.

It's great to be the alpha dog, but getting the respect you deserve from a dominant pup may require you to repeat these exercises several times, increasing the number of seconds you hold the pup each time.

Thinking Like a Dog

To understand your dog's annoying behaviors, it helps to think like a dog yourself. Understanding your dog's instinctual behavior can help you go with the flow in problem correction. Redirect that destructive chewing, turn barking into a command performance instead of forbidding it, channel the high energy of your dog into challenging activities, and desensitize it in situations that cause it to be fearful. Harnessing your dog's instincts and redirecting its behavior will make your life together more pleasurable.

People are prone to humanize the behavior of small dogs. You may consider little Muffin your furry baby, but she's still a dog. Once you understand why your dog engages in behavior that drives you up the wall, you can work on correcting them in a firm and positive manner.

Biting

Dog bites are a major health problem in this country. The most comprehensive Web site devoted to this topic is *www.dogbitelaw.com*, produced by California attorney Kenneth Phillips. A leading expert on the topic and a frequent guest on network and cable television on the topic, Phillips cites a survey by the Centers for Disease Control and Prevention in Atlanta (CDC) that concludes that nearly 2 percent of U.S. residents, or almost 5 million people a year, will be dog bite victims, 60 percent of them children. Countless more bites, especially from small dogs, go unreported.

Some 61 percent of dog bites happen at home or in a familiar place, and 77 percent of the biters belong to the victim's family or friend. While it is true that the majority of dogs that bite are the larger breeds, any dog is capable of biting.

🐕 Alert!

In a notorious California case in October 2000, a six-week-old baby girl was killed by her family's pet Pomeranian, a breed hardly thought of as dangerous. The baby's uncle had left the infant and the dog on a bed while he prepared her bottle, returning to find the child being mauled by the dog.

Dogbitelaw.com cites several factors that may cause a dog to bite:

- **Dominance aggression:** Aggressive behavior usually directed to family members who take something from the dog, pet it, hold it, pick it up, or disturb it while it is resting.
- **Defensive or fear aggression:** Directed at family or strangers who approach too quickly or too closely when the dog is afraid.
- **Protective/territorial aggression:** Directed at strangers to approach the owner or the home of the owner.
- **Predatory aggression:** Directed at small, quickly moving animals and children, especially where more than one dog is involved.
- **Pain-elicited aggression:** Directed at family or strangers who approach or touch when the dog is in pain or injured.
- **Punishment-elicited aggression:** Directed to family or strangers who hit, kick, or verbally assault the dog.
- **Redirected aggression:** Directed at family, strangers, and animals who approach or touch the dog when it is aggressive in another context.

When a child under four years of age is bitten, half the time the family dog is the attacker, and the attack nearly always happens at home. Sadly, it often occurs when a family gets the wrong breed of dog, when small children are not supervised with the dog, and when adults have not taught the child how to behave safely around dogs. A brochure coproduced by the American Veterinary Medical Association and State Farm Insurance Company offers some helpful tips on how to lessen your chances of being the owner of a dog that bites:

- **Carefully consider your pet selection:** Before and after selection, your veterinarian is the best source for information about behavior and suitability.
- **Socialize your dog as a young puppy:** Early socialization will help your dog feel at ease around other people and animals. Expose your puppy to a variety of situations a little at a time and under controlled circumstances, and continue that exposure on a regular basis as your dog gets older. If you're not sure how your dog will react to a large crowd or a busy street, be cautious. Don't put your dog in a position where it feels threatened or gets teased.
- **Train your dog:** The basic commands "Sit," "Stay," "No," and "Come" can be incorporated into fun activities that build a bond of obedience and trust between dogs and people. Don't play aggressive games like wrestling or tug-of-war with your dog.
- **Keep your dog healthy:** Have it vaccinated against rabies and preventable infectious diseases. Parasite control is important.
- **Neuter your male dog:** Neutered dogs are less likely to bite. Be a responsible pet owner. License your dog with the community as required, and obey leash laws. Dogs are social animals, and spending time with your dog is important. Dogs that are frequently left alone have a greater chance of developing behavior problems.
- **Be alert:** Know your dog. You would naturally be alert to signs of illness, but you must also watch for signs that your dog is uncomfortable or feeling aggressive.

Because children are the most frequent victims of dog bites, children must be taught not to approach strange dogs. They should also be taught to ask permission from a dog's owner before petting any dog. In addition, parents and caregivers should do the following:

- Never leave a baby or small child alone with a dog.
- Be on the lookout for potentially dangerous situations.
- Start teaching young children, including toddlers, to be careful around dogs.

If your dog bites someone for any reason, you should do the following:

- Restrain and confine the dog immediately.
- Check on the victim's condition. Wash wounds with soap and water. Professional medical advice should be sought to evaluate the risk of rabies or other infections. Call 911 if immediate help is required.
- Provide important information, including your name and address, and information about your dog's most recent rabies vaccination. If your dog does not have a current rabies vaccination, it may be necessary to quarantine it or even euthanize it for rabies testing. The person bitten may need to undergo rabies treatment.
- Report the incident to your local animal control officer.
- Report the bite to your insurance company.
- Consult your vet to help determine why the dog acted this way and to seek corrective professional help for the dog if needed.

Again, prevention is always the best medicine. Biting is to be expected in a pup, but as the dog matures, such behavior should be discouraged. Again, it helps to mimic dog behavior as a reaction to a painful nip from your pup. When your pup bit a littermate, the nipped sibling yelped and withdrew, abruptly ending the rough play. You can do the same thing. Yell "Ouch!" and stop playing. It also helps to redirect the behavior by providing lots of chew toys to the mouthy little munchkin as well.

Destructive Chewing

Chewing is part of teething behavior for your pup, and it's also a young dog's way of exploring the world. At around four weeks of age, a puppy starts getting its milk teeth: twenty-eight needle-sharp little baby teeth, with no molars. These remain until the puppy begins teething at four months of age, a process that can continue in small dogs until around seven months of age. Next come the adult teeth, forty-two of them, including molars. Stock up on those chew toys! When those permanent teeth arrive, your little dog will probably want to chew vigorously once more, just to break them in!

Fact

> Dogs chew for many reasons besides teething. They explore their world with all their senses, include their teeth and taste buds. Chewing also relieves stress and releases pent up energy.

Sometimes adult dogs chew because they are bored or anxious. To cut down on the damage this can inflict on your home and possessions, you should confine the chewer when you cannot keep an eye on him. While he is under house arrest, provide the usual fun chew toys and safe bones. Always offer praise when your dog chews acceptable objects. You may also apply a repellent product like Bitter Apple to furniture and baseboards so they won't taste so good to your little canine home-wrecker.

You can also use the repellent spray as a teaching tool. When the pup starts chewing on your shoe or a magazine, take the forbidden object away and spray him while giving a no-nonsense "No! Leave it!" Then grab a chew toy and dangle it before the dog in an inviting way. When the dog seeks the toy, give it to him and praise him lovingly. In seizing this teaching opportunity, your goal is to redirect the dog's attention to the appropriate toy, conveying the message that chewing is okay—just not on the forbidden object.

Aggression

Growling, snapping, and nipping can be just as scary as an actual bite, and they are just as inappropriate. Puppies that are confident and have been taught good manners are less likely to grow up to be aggressive dogs. But if such tendencies are not addressed by sufficient training in puppyhood, they will probably get worse as the dog gets more dominant or more fearful as it matures. Aggression may take several forms, depending on the dog's history and circumstances.

Toward the Owner

A dog that shows aggression to its owner definitely thinks it has the upper hand in the relationship. Nipping and snapping behavior that is not effectively corrected will lead to biting behavior and even though yours is a small dog, it can do plenty of damage. If it nips when you are trying to correct it or perform an activity like grooming or nail trimming and your response is to cease and desist, the puppy has learned that nipping works well as a strategy in getting its own way. Problem correction with a trainer will curb this behavior. Enforcing your leadership will also be necessary. You're back to square one in obedience—the dog needs to get your permission for everything good in its life, from eating to being petted. You'll be using the word "No" a lot, and you'll need lots of patience and restraint not to smack a dog that tries to bite the hand that feeds it. Not only is hitting a dog inhumane but in the case of a small dog, it usually makes matters worse.

Toward Children

Aggressive behavior is fairly common among small breeds. Dominant dogs look upon children as subordinate littermates, and they frequently inflict serious and disfiguring injuries to children, so you need a trainer's help to make life safer for all concerned. Other small dogs live in fear of kids because they perceive them as a threat to their safety.

You also need to manage the child as attentively as you do the dog. Aggressive activities like tug-of-war or teasing must not be permitted, and a child should never hug or squeeze the dog because such affection may be mistaken for physical dominance. Children are excitable, and when they run and scream, many small dogs get upset enough to bite them. Some small dogs learn to be loving housemates to children within their own family but not with strange children who visit. Simply put, managing a dog that is not trustworthy with children presents a lifelong challenge.

Toward Strangers

Small dogs are so darned cute that everyone wants to pick them up and cuddle them, but that is often a bad idea. You can be sued if your dog bites. More importantly, you do not want to be responsible for anyone getting injured, so you need to be careful about situations with strangers. You also need to begin a campaign of intense training and socialization, preferably working one-on-one with a trainer skilled in problem correction who will act the part of the stranger until your dog learns to be less fearful and defensive.

Toward Other Dogs

People tend to be amused by tiny dogs that think they are tough. It may seem comical when your Chihuahua threatens a German shepherd, but this behavior can get the little squirt in a lot of trouble. Owners who make a joke of such behavior are ignoring a real and serious danger. Laughing at such antics gives the little troublemaker positive reinforcement, actually encouraging such unacceptable behavior. Not all big dogs will take kindly to a pint-size upstart, and your little tyrant could be killed or injured if one of those big boys decided to retaliate.

Alert!

It is never safe to let your pint-size pet get in the face of a larger dog it does not know. One chomp from the jaws of a rottweiler or German shepherd can spell disaster to a feisty little Yorkie or Chihuahua. Whether in your neighborhood, the park, a puppy play group, or at doggie daycare, before dogs are allowed to play together, they should be closely observed and screened to make sure they make compatible companions.

Obedience training is the best way to address this problem. If you notice your little friend "getting tall," stiffly standing on tiptoes, it's time to quickly intervene, using the leash to pull the dog away while giving a firm "No!" It's imperative to act quickly, as one chomp from the big dog could kill your pet. Having the instructor teach you how to get the message across might someday save the life of your little Napoleon. Carefully monitoring your pint-size pet around bigger dogs will be a lifelong requirement.

Running Away

Obedience training—specifically, coming when called—is the best prevention for this problem. You should always walk your little escape artist on a leash and fence your yard as well. Invisible fencing is not a safe solution as it allows larger dogs to come onto your property, possibly harming your much smaller pet. Obedience classes provide the building blocks that will make your dog comply with your wishes. Teaching the "Wait" command and using it every single time you open a door will make your life easier and your dog safer.

Canine Houdinis that have proven they can dig or climb their way out of just about anywhere should never be allowed outside unsupervised. Tying a small dog out in the yard is also a bad idea. Tiny dogs can get tangled in the leash or tether or walk up the porch steps and fall off, hanging themselves in the process. Often they become aggressive to anyone who approaches. The solution to this problem is to keep your dog out of this kind of situation to begin with.

Digging

Digging is a hard problem to solve because like wagging the tail or hydrant-sniffing, it's normal canine behavior. Except for the more sedentary companion breeds, most small dogs were bred to hunt vermin, and those critters lived underground. When your little terrier unearths your tulip bulbs, he is probably hot on the trail of a chipmunk or field mouse. If your dog is digging to cool himself off in a nice comfy hole, it's too hot for him to be outside in the first place.

If you want to indulge your dog's compulsion to dig, you can always give him a dig-safe area in the yard where you can bury his stuff to keep him away from the garden. If you want his company while you're outside planting those flowers, you may need to confine him to an exercise pen with some chew toys to get your work done.

Hyperactivity

Some small terriers and toys have extremely high energy levels. They seem to require endless physical activity and toys galore, most of which they shred. Breeds and mixes with extra batteries include the terriers, especially the wire fox and Parson Russell, as well as the min-pins. Even in class, these dogs can get easily bored or distracted. Many trainers encourage attention training to keep them focused, promoting eye contact with the "Watch me" command and using clicker training helps get their attention. When these dogs learn to focus on their owners, they will learn faster and be less distracted by all the other dogs and people around them.

 **Fact**

Clicker training, the latest trend in obedience classes, was developed in training dolphins in aquarium shows. It is based on behavior shaping, the concept that training is a method of communicating between two individuals, not something that one forces upon the other. Dogs—and dolphins—both learn faster when the clicker sound is accompanied by a treat!

To keep their high energy from turning into destructive behavior or driving you crazy, find some other activities for your little dervish. Agility is a great way to burn off that endless energy, and Earthdog trials let your little dog hunt and sniff to its heart's content. Go for lots of walks and hikes; teach your dog to play fun games like fetch and Frisbee. If possible, find a little doggie pal or two and form your own small dog play-group. For the very active small dog, life is all about keeping busy and having fun.

Barking

Making noise is your little dog's favorite way of making himself heard. Because it usually gets a response, this behavior works. He barks when someone is at the door, and you come running. He barks again, and you whisk him outside for a potty call. If he barks when he's hungry, dinner is served. Some dogs feel it is their duty to alert you when the mailman comes or the landscapers start working. Some simply want your attention, asking you to drop those household chores and play with them. Dogs usually reserve a distinctive voice for telling their owners they want to come inside or warning of a perceived threat.

 **Question?**

Are little dogs naturally inclined to be yippy?
While it is true that some breeds are more inclined to bark—terriers like the wire fox, miniature schnauzer, or West Highland white (all Type A personalities), or little busybodies like the papillon—but it's usually for a reason. Small dogs are individuals, just like the people who own them.

It's absolutely true that the high-pitched bark of a bichon or a Yorkie can be even more annoying than the deep-voiced baying of a big dog. But no matter what its size, a dog's excessive barking can usually be eliminated through training and by modifying its environment. If your dog barks when you're not home, leave the radio or television on for background noise and slip out of its sight without fanfare, not making a big production of saying good-bye. Teach your dog the "Quiet" command, and reward good behavior with treats and praise. For the pesky attention-seeker, spend more time in vigorous play, then put the little loudmouth in its crate for a restful time-out.

Remember that barking is one of the dog's most effective forms of communication. Once you figure out why your dog is so vocal, you'll be on the right track for dealing with the problem.

The best way to get a handle on this behavior is to teach your dog to bark on command. Make him speak to get a treat. After a few barks, tell him "Enough!" and give him the biscuit. Tell him "Good dog!" and go on your merry way. Now you are harnessing the little yapper's behavior so you can stand to live with him. When the doorbell rings, praise his barking, then tell him "Enough!" and hand over that cookie. You are teaching him to bark when he is supposed to and to stop on command. Once he has mastered this command, you need to correct him when he ignores it (and he probably will). If he doesn't cease and desist, give him a sharp tug on his collar and a "No!" With patience and persistence, it will eventually sink in.

Alert!

If all else fails, get an anti-bark collar. They come in two types: electronic, which delivers a mild shock when the dog barks, or the herbal spray type, which uses a spurt of citronella to startle the dog with its pungent aroma. Although the so-called shock collars have proven effective in correcting this problem, the herbal collars are more advisable for use on a small dog.

A noisy little dog can also cause friction with your neighbors. For your dog's safety and to keep peace in the neighborhood, your dog should not be allowed outside unsupervised in the first place. Inside the house, in addition to the "Enough" command, you need to consider when and why the dog barks. Is it looking for attention? Are you making it a part of all aspects of your family life? Sometimes dogs bark because they have nothing better to do. They need plenty of companionship and the more you take them out with you, the happier they will be. If the dog barks in the car, keep it crated and take along a squirt bottle filled with water to give it a zap and a "No!" when it starts up.

Separation Anxiety

Dogs that suffer from this emotional reaction when left alone are sometimes accused of being destructive just for spite. Actually, they are more like people in the grip of a full-blown panic attack. Their fears of abandonment have gotten the best of them, and their destructive behavior demonstrates their lack of control. It's more understandable in puppies that have recently left their littermates behind. They are not used to being alone, so you need to build their tolerance in increments, getting them good and tired from training or exercise, then leaving them for increasingly longer periods.

Pups that engage in destructive behavior when you are not home need to be crated. Turn the radio on and provide lots of toys. Throw an unlaundered piece of your own clothing into the crate. Your scent will be reassuring. Above all, don't make a big production of saying goodbye.

Older dogs need to be left in areas where they won't dump the trash or eat the sofa. Sometimes, they will self-mutilate if left in the crate. Work with a trainer on how to get your fearful dog used to being left alone. Don't lose your temper if you come home to find a mess. Unless you catch the dog in the act of being destructive, it won't get the message. Another helpful solution might be doggie daycare or even adopting another dog to provide companionship while you're away.

Getting Help

Most dog-behavior problems are really management problems. In other words, you need to get Roscoe to stop nipping or chasing the cat. In the vast majority of such situations, dedicating yourself to obedience training for your dog and exerting your leadership will remedy the situation. For example, if the dog is acting destructive out of boredom, providing an activity or a stimulating setting like doggie daycare may provide the solution. Jumping on people or furniture, pulling the leash when walking, not coming when called, racing out the front door every time you open it—these are common problems calling for targeted training solutions.

When a dog becomes a danger to its owner, itself, or the community, however, it's time to seek one-on-one professional help. Start with a complete veterinary checkup to make sure there is not a medical cause for a dog's aggression, anxiety, or obsessive behavior. In addition to diseases that affect their temperament, dogs can suffer from fear, stress, and anxiety. Their symptoms can be relieved by some of the same medications we use, like Prozac.

If obedience training has not solved your problems with your dog, seek out a trainer who specializes in problem correction. "You don't wait," advises certified trainer Nancy Bradley of Bradley Canine Education in Norton, Massachusetts. "As soon as you hear a little growl, that's a dog's warning. If you don't handle it immediately, the dog learns it can control people with this sort of behavior." Ask your vet or groomer for the names of trainers in your area who offer private correction at home. Some veterinary hospitals offer referrals for such professionals. When you are afraid you'll have to give up your dog because of its bad behavior, a skilled trainer can often turn things around, making it possible for you to live peacefully and happily with your dog.

Fact

Canine compulsive disorder occurs in about 2 percent of all pet dogs. Such canines display compulsive behavior such as tail chasing, biting the air, licking excessively, and barking without letup. In small dogs, it often involves constant chewing of the paws and nails. The disorder is also caused by anxiety and may be an inherited characteristic. Drug therapy combined with behavior modification seems to work best in dealing with this problem.

An animal behaviorist is another option if your dog has phobias, fears, or anxiety, or if it demonstrates dangerous aggression. You know what normal bratty-dog behavior is—pushing the limits, doing everything it can get away with because no one has put it in its place. You also know what's abnormal—biting the hand that feeds it, a Jekyll-and-Hyde personality, or throwing violent temper tantrums. Such behaviors call for intensive behavioral therapy.

Chapter 17

To a Long and Healthy Life

Bette Davis once said, "Growing old is not for sissies!" That cheeky observation applies to dogs as well. With their shorter life spans, they age much more quickly than their owners do. Just like people, as they get older, they start to slow down and exhibit physical and emotional changes. By understanding both how your dog communicates with you and how it ages, you can ensure that it remains with you as long as possible and enjoys the highest quality of life along the way.

What Your Dog Wants You to Know

When you first acquire your dog, you are like a new parent. You have to ask the experts—in this case, the breeder, vet, and trainer—for advice in making sure you are doing a proper job of bringing up baby. Things became significantly easier as your dog matures, but at each stage of its life, you need to adapt to changes.

Puppyhood is the most demanding time, with its frequent feedings, housetraining, socialization, and teaching good manners as you learn the ropes of responsible ownership. Midlife is the frosting on the cake, as you enjoy a bright and active pal whose needs are predictable. Your dog now only need two meals a day, and you have the potty schedule down pat. In its senior years, more care is required. You need to adjust its diet and provide adequate exercise, enriching its environment to make these precious years enjoyable and challenging. In all your years together, you and your dog will both learn a lot.

One of the greatest things about sharing your life with a dog is the communication skills you accumulate on this journey. As your relationship progresses, you will better understand what your dog wants and needs, and your dog will know what pleases and displeases you as well.

 Fact

Your dog reads a lot into your body language, touch, and tone of voice. You'll be amazed at how it seems to know when you need its snuggling, comforting presence when you're feeling down in the dumps.

A dog communicates in two ways, through vocalization and body language. It can't talk like a person, but it produces quite a repertoire of sounds. You will learn to interpret your dog's different barks, from the sharp announcement that someone is at the door to the matter-of-fact way it lets you know when it's time to go potty. It also barks to get your attention when it wants a treat or some playtime. Snarling and growling can range from playing, "I'm the baddest dog on the block" to, "Consider this a warning. I feel threatened and I might bite." Whimpering can tell you it's in pain or feeling neglected. Howling signals heartbreak and distress. Some small dogs with short muzzles like the Peke and pug also have their own amazing variety of snorts, snuffles, grunts, and snores.

As your relationship with your dog evolves, you will become adept at reading its canine body language. Here are some universal ways in which dogs communicate physically:

- **Tail wagging:** Wagging, of course, is the most common expression of a happy dog. It says, "Boy, am I glad to see you!" The faster that tail wags, the happier your dog. A wagging tail is often accompanied by prancing around and an attempt to entice you to play. But not all tail wagging is happy behavior. Some dogs wag their tails when they are agitated, frightened, or not too sure what's going on. Their tails may wag slowly, from side to side, when they are tense.
- **Tail carriage:** A tail carried high as you go for a walk is a statement of confidence and contentment. A tail tucked between the legs tells you the dog is anxious or apprehensive. If its head is lowered as well, it may be feeling guilty or ashamed. The shorter the tail, the less it can convey, but there is nothing as endearing as the happy twitch of a stumpy little tail. Some dogs wag their entire hind end when they are feeling very happy.
- **Play bowing:** This pose, with the rear in the air and the front end bowed as your dog's bright eyes entice you, means "Let's play!" It is both submissive and aggressive, but it's all in fun. Healthy dogs remain playful throughout all stages of their lives. That's probably because humans react positively to their puppy-like behavior. Some dogs also raise a front paw to invite play.
- **Rolling over:** This is a submissive posture. When a dog wants to acknowledge another canine's dominance, this is its way of saying, "You're the boss." Sometimes a dog does this to tell you how happy and safe it feels. Sometimes it's just looking for a belly rub.
- **Ears up:** The dog is on alert. During training, a dog watching you attentively with its ears up is ready to learn.
- **Ears back:** This can be a sign of either submission or aggression. If the eyes are half-closed or blinking, the tail hanging low and

wagging slowly, and the dog's paw is raised, it is submissive. If the tail is down and tensed and the dog is in a crouched position with its hackles raised and teeth exposed, the signal is aggression and dominance.

- **In your face:** A dog standing stock-still as it faces another dog or person and making direct eye contact is asserting its dominance and may be getting ready to attack, especially if it "stands tall" on its tiptoes and has its hackles raised and tail bushed out. Growling and "grinning," lips curled and teeth bared, are also warning signals.

How Dogs Age

As dogs grow older, their hair color fades, their muzzles get gray, their eyes cloud up, they sleep more often and more deeply, they move more slowly and stiffly, and they become less adaptable to change. Some dogs get lumpy and bumpy with fatty tumors or warts popping up. They do not hear as well, and they have more dental problems. They are prone to weight changes, are easily startled, and may be less tolerant of children. Some lose their mental acuity, becoming confused and disoriented. It's a bittersweet time when they also grow more dependent upon their owners. Now more than ever, your dog will need all the love and support you can give.

 Essential

Just like their human caretakers, senior dogs begin to suffer from arthritis, hearing loss, vision problems, and organ failure. They have different nutritional needs and need to be watched more closely for age-related illnesses.

Life Expectancy of Small Dogs

The old rule of thumb that a year in your dog's life equals seven years in yours no longer holds sway. Instead, popular wisdom now dictates that in general, a six-year-old dog is equivalent in age to a forty-five-year-old person; a ten-year-old dog is like a person of sixty-five; and a fifteen-year-old canine is comparable to a person of ninety. The average dog life span is now twelve years of age, an increase of more than 70 percent since the 1930s; and the good news for small-dog owners is that on the whole, the smaller canines are usually the longest-lived of all.

In general, large dogs live shorter lives because their bodies must work harder, but there are some wild cards in the deck for small dogs too. The tinier they are, the more susceptible these dogs are to accidents and illnesses, and those bred down to teacup-size often have inbred genetic weaknesses affecting their health and longevity.

Of course, breed-specific health problems also skew life expectancy projections. The cavalier King Charles spaniel, for example, is prone to mitral valve disease, shortening its life expectancy to ten or eleven years of age. Von Willebrands disease in schnauzers and Scotties can also shorten their lives, but most still last into the double digits. English toy spaniels and Norfolk and Norwich terriers usually live until about eleven years of age. But the majority of toy and small dogs are expected to live from twelve to fifteen years. Smaller mixed breeds generally outlast their larger counterparts as well.

The life expectancy of the Maltese and miniature schnauzer, and shih tzu, as well as the Parson Russell, West Highland white, Sealyham, Lakeland, cairn, Boston, and Yorkshire terriers is from fourteen to sixteen years. Statistically, the longest-lived of all are the miniature dachshund, toy and miniature poodle, Chihuahua, and Lhasa apso, often living from fifteen to eighteen years.

No one can predict how long your dog will live, but the care you provide—including proper nutrition, weight control, exercise, and mental stimulation—will definitely put the odds for a long life in your favor. It's up to you to make the most of every year of your dog's life and to lovingly and realistically deal with the changes that old age brings.

Stages of a Dog's Life

After the perils and pleasures of early puppyhood, your small dog will hit adolescence at about four months of age. You'll know when your dog reaches this stage because he will become more independent and often disobedient just to test you. When you give your dog a command now, his new response will be the dog's equivalent of "Make me!" If you have neglected obedience training up until this point, you will now have a real challenge on your hands. By about six months of age, your pup will have grown into a young adult, and if you've done your job right, things will get easier. The dog will leave the "punk puppy" attitude behind and be as amenable to training as it was in the kindergarten stages, around three months of age. Maturity in a dog means two things: sexual maturity and physical maturity.

Sexual Maturity

Sexual maturity comes early to small dogs. The mounting behavior your little male might have displayed in early puppyhood may return at around five months of age, but now he has the sperm to go with it. This poses a conundrum for small-dog owners. Their dogs reach puberty by six months of age, often before it's advisable to spay or neuter them, so you must be vigilant to prevent unwanted pregnancies. Conversely, spaying and neutering before six months of age is favored by many vets who maintain that it leads to a longer life. You and your vet should discuss health and risk factors for your particular dog.

Alert!

Young small dogs metabolize drugs differently than their older and larger counterparts, making them more at risk for anesthesia overdose and adverse drug reactions. They have an immature ability to sustain normal body temperature, putting them at risk for hypothermia while under anesthesia. They are also more prone to hypoglycemia than larger and older dogs.

A tiny female dog's sexual maturity often occurs before her physical maturity and pregnancy could place a great stress on her system. Some small-breed males are able to sire a litter before they reach five months of age. Small-breed females tend to have their first heat at around five or six months of age, way ahead of giant breeds that do not come into heat until they are eighteen to twenty-four months old.

Physical Maturity

Small dogs reach physical maturity by eight to ten months of age. Now your dog is in its prime. With luck and good health on its side, it will remain in these peak years until it reaches middle age, around eight years of age for small dogs, the second stage of your dog's adulthood. Take heart—your little darling will still be an active adult at this stage, but now its body's systems will begin to slow down, with cells starting to deteriorate faster than its body can repair them.

Essential

The changes that take place now may be invisible to you, but this life stage is the forerunner to your dog's senior years. Proper nutrition becomes more vital than ever to maintain and repair your dog's cells, delaying the effects of aging and optimizing its quality of life.

This is a good time for a complete checkup by your vet. Detected early, most problems associated with the mature dog can be addressed through dietary or lifestyle changes. Keeping up with the dog's vaccination protection from rabies, distemper, hepatitis, leptospirosis, parvovirus, and bordetella, as well as having annual heartworm checks and Lyme disease protection, will help it stay healthy. Lastly, the rate at which your dog will age has much to do with its genetic history as well as with the care you provide. If its parents lived to a ripe old age, chances are your dog will too.

Keeping your mature dog's weight under control grows more important at this stage as its metabolism rate begins to lower.

If you are among those owners who show their love with food—either dog treats or people food—now is the time to cut down. Shower your affection in other ways, by playing, going for walks, or just spending more quality time with your dog. Responding to those imploring eyes every time you sit down to eat will make your dog fat and shorten its life. If you must offer a treat, try low-fat dog cookies, carrots, unbuttered popcorn, apple slices, or a piece of banana. And if you have been handing out the treats, always adjust your dog's meal portion accordingly.

 Alert!

Canine obesity is a serious medical problem, putting dogs at risk if they need surgery and placing more stress on the heart, lungs, joints, kidneys, and liver. Being overweight also makes dogs more injury-prone.

Exercise is also important to keep your aging dog in shape. That daily walk becomes more important than ever, and don't forget your little friend still loves to play with toys, by himself as well with you. Maintain good dental health by regularly brushing your dog's teeth to prevent gum disease, and don't neglect its grooming either. Your regular grooming sessions with the brush and comb will keep your dog looking its best and enable you to monitor its overall condition while you're at it.

Senior Citizens

As our dogs live longer, care of the aging dog has become one of the fastest-growing fields in veterinary medicine. Still, you probably won't give it much thought until it applies to your beloved dog. One day you'll notice that Lucy is slowing down. She sleeps a lot and seems less enthusiastic about participating in family activities. She needs to be coaxed to go for a walk or play with her toys. She moves more carefully, takes longer to get comfortable, and prefers a soft bed over the hard floor. She's stiff for a while after she wakes up from a nap.

Fact

The American Animal Hospital Association (AAHA) recommends that healthy senior dogs visit the veterinarian twice a year for complete exams and laboratory testing, allowing you to stay current with your aging dog's health status.

You joke that she has developed selective hearing, but the truth is she's experiencing hearing loss. Her eyesight has probably dimmed as well. It takes her a bit longer to recognize you and other people she knows coming through the door.

Lucy's lustrous coat may be thinning or growing dull. Her skin is dryer, as its oil-producing glands diminish their production. If she has dental problems, her breath may smell bad. In old age, organ function will lessen as well. The heart, liver, kidneys, and bladder will not be as efficient as they used to be. Lucy may need to urinate more frequently, or she may become incontinent. It's hard to witness these changes in our beloved dog, but here are some steps you can take to make your senior canine's life more comfortable and enjoyable:

- **Don't let her become a couch potato:** Take her out for exercise, some fresh air, or a ride in the car. A change of scenery is good for her head as well as her body.
- **Keep her mind sharp through training:** She may be too old for the agility course, but regular exercise will be beneficial and the mental challenge they provide will help keep her mind alert.
- **Pamper her with a nice soft bed:** Cushy quilted mats, faux lamb's wool, or plush velour over soft foam will comfort those tired little bones. Just make sure the bed is washable or has a removable cover for easy laundering.
- **Feed her properly:** Place her on a premium senior diet, lower in calories and protein for weight control and to lessen the workload on her kidneys. Look for a quality food containing omega-3 and omega-6 fatty acids, great for the skin and anti-inflammatory as well as glucosamine and chondroitin sulfate to increase mobility and relieve joint pain.
- **Attend to her hygiene:** Keep Lucy looking pretty and smelling good. Old age is not a time to neglect your dog's grooming. Brush her regularly to stimulate production of coat oils. Bathe her at least once a month using warm water, not hot or cold, and an oatmeal shampoo to moisturize the coat and treat dry skin. Use a sweet-smelling crème rinse if she is a longhaired or full-coated dog. Dry her thoroughly so she won't get chilled. A spritz of dog cologne makes a nice finishing touch.

- **Check for fleas and ticks:** Not only do they cause itching and discomfort, but those external parasites carry diseases that can be more harmful now because older dogs have lowered resistance, weaker immune systems, and thinner, more fragile skin.

- **Groom her regularly:** If Lucy is of a breed that requires professional grooming, put easy upkeep ahead of glamour. Keeping her coat trimmed short will mean easier home maintenance and less time spent at the grooming salon. Make sure your groomer is experienced and caring enough to groom your elderly dog. Senior dogs can be very difficult and challenging to groom. Some have trouble standing, and some strenuously object to having their faces brushed or clippered. They also stress out and tire easily, so having an understanding groomer who will get your dog in and out as soon as possible is a big plus.

- **Modify your home environment:** It's time to accommodate Lucy's second puppyhood. You may now need to confine her to the kitchen when you are not with her because of lapses in housetraining. Dig out those baby gates you used when she was a pup to keep your carpets from getting ruined. Your old girl tries her best but occasionally, accidents will happen. Because she sleeps so soundly, you may need to wake her for potty trips.

- **Medicate as necessary:** Have your vet prescribe medications to make her more comfortable. Sometimes a coated aspirin a day will do wonders, but if your senior citizen needs something stronger, there are many new medicines to help with joint pain, arthritis, and stiffness.

- **Take care of her teeth:** Loose teeth and gum disease can cause pain leading to loss of appetite and low energy. Dental problems can also make her cranky. Bacteria from tooth tartar can travel through her system, damaging the heart, kidneys, and liver. Keep brushing her teeth and get regular cleanings from the vet as well. Diseased teeth and gums cause bad breath, making it unpleasant to be near a dog in those final years when such companionship is more important than ever. If Lucy's halitosis keeps you at arm's length, use breath treats or spray to make your old friend nicer to be near.

Saying Goodbye

Losing a precious pet is one of the most traumatic events in the life of an animal lover. Your dog is your true companion, a huge part of your everyday life, and losing this family member can be overwhelming. Throughout its life, the little dog offers you emotional support, comic relief, and unconditional love. Although this parting is painful, it's also a time to reflect on the joyful bond you shared and to feel grateful that it has played such an important role in your life. No matter what the state of your dog's health, it is still vital to give your old friend lots of love every single day to let it know it is still an important member of your family. Lucy's senses may be impaired, but she is still aware of your voice and your touch.

Euthanasia

Sometimes you lose a dog through an accident or incurable illness, but sometimes you have to make a choice to let your dog go because it is suffering or its quality of life has deteriorated to the point that it's barely aware of its surroundings. Having a dog euthanized is one of the most difficult decisions you will ever have to make. It is also a decision that is yours alone. When your dog is gravely ill, your vet cannot tell you exactly how long it has to live. This is an emotionally loaded time, and vets know that dog owners may end up resenting their advice if they recommend ending a dog's life.

Essential

Some factors to consider in assessing your dog's quality of life are its ability to eat and drink and perform bodily functions, and to enjoy daily activities and family companionship. You must also determine whether any pain it is experiencing is being adequately relieved by medication.

You know your dog better than anyone else does. The one who will tell you when the time has come is the dog itself. The signs may differ. Some dogs will obviously be in pain, panting and shivering, while some will no longer take pleasure in the things they always loved to do. Some may stop eating or lose their ability to walk or control bodily functions such as urinating or moving their bowels. Some withdraw into their own world, sleeping all the time or having a glazed look as if they no longer know who you are.

When a dog is sick, it's time to sit down with family members and discuss what action you will take. Its terminal illness will likely make you face the same range of emotions as you would with the loss of any loved one: denial, anger, bargaining, depression, and finally, acceptance. It's a tough road, but at some point you will decide that the kindest thing you can do is to end your beloved dog's suffering and allow it to die with dignity.

The euthanasia procedure varies. Some vets will have you bring the dog to the clinic when things are quiet so you won't have to sit around waiting and you'll also have more privacy. Some will come to your home to allow the dog to be in the place it loved best. Typically, euthanasia involves an overdose of anesthesia to suppress brain activity and stop the heart. Some vets first administer a sedative like Valium first so there will be no struggle. The process is very quick, and the little dog literally goes to sleep. If you feel strong enough to be present, the best course of action is for you to accompany the dog into the treatment room and hold it in your arms to give your love and comfort as it leaves you.

Alert!

Burying the dog's remains yourself is not always an option because some communities do not allow it, even in your own backyard.

If your animal is dying of an undetermined illness, you may want the vet to perform a necropsy to determine the cause of death. Whether or not you do this, you will need to tell the vet if you want your dog to be buried in a pet cemetery or cremated, its ashes returned to you. You may decide to keep the ashes in an urn, bury them in the yard, or scatter them in a place that was meaningful to you and your dog.

Grieving

After your dog is gone, you need to allow yourself time to grieve. Don't suppress your feelings but find a way to work them through, either with family or friends or in a pet loss support group. You need someone to talk to who understands how much your dog meant to you and how sad you are feeling.

While grief is a personal experience, there is no need to go through it alone. Many forms of support are available, including pet bereavement counseling services, pet-loss support hotlines, local or online bereavement groups, books, and videos. Here are some ways to get the help you need and deserve:

- Ask your veterinarian or humane association to recommend a pet loss counselor or support group. The ASPCA offers comprehensive support for those dealing with the issue of euthanasia, grieving the loss of a dog, dealing with children in this situation, and helping other pets to cope. To find out about these services, call the ASPCA Pet Loss Support Program in New York City at (212) 876-7700, extension 4355, or the Pet Loss Hotline at (800) 916-1616. Enter the pin number 140-7211 and leave your phone number.
- Regional hotlines: Veterinary students throughout the country have set up the following pet loss support hotlines:
  - California: (916) 752-4200, staffed by University of California Davis veterinary students
  - Florida: (352) 392-4700, then 1+4080, staffed by University of Florida veterinary students
  - Illinois: (708) 603-3994, staffed by Chicago Veterinary Medical Association veterinarians
  - Massachusetts: (508) 839-7966, staffed by Tufts University veterinary students
  - Michigan: (517) 432-2696, staffed by Michigan State University veterinary students
  - New York: (607) 253-3932, staffed by Cornell University veterinary students
  - Ohio: (614) 292-1823, staffed by Ohio State University veterinary students

- Virginia: (540) 231-8038, staffed by Virginia-Maryland Regional veterinary school students
- Visit *www.petloss.com*, a Web site for pet lovers grieving over the illness or death of a pet. Here you will find personal support, thoughtful advice, information on its Monday Pet Loss Candle Ceremony, tribute pages, and healing poetry.
- Write about your loss in poetry or a journal.
- Make a donation to a humane society or rescue group in your dog's name.

The loss of a pet is often a child's first experience with death. You need to discuss feelings of guilt and fear that it will bring up with your child. Above all, tell the truth. Let your child know you are also feeling very sad as you help the youngster work through the grieving process.

Essential

Don't be ashamed to cry when your dog passes away. It is necessary to grieve before you can move on with your life.

For senior citizens, coping with the loss of a pet can be extremely traumatic, especially if they live alone. It may trigger memories of other losses, and remind them of their own mortality. It is important for them to take immediate steps to cope with their loss and regain a sense of purpose. Even if they feel they should not take on the responsibility of getting another pet, sometimes volunteering at the humane society will help them express their love for animals.

After losing your dog, it's usually not a good idea to rush right out and get another. No animal can replace the one you have lost. Give yourself time to grieve. For some, the process can last a few weeks, while for others it may take years. When memories of your dog bring a smile to your face and a warm glow to your heart instead of pain and tears, you'll know you are ready to have another little companion in your life.

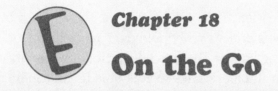

Chapter 18

On the Go

Little dogs love a lot of things—from pilfering the cat's food to digging holes in the yard—but most of all they like to be with their owners. It's hard to look at their plaintive eyes as you leave for work or a trip to the store. There is nothing quite as guilt-inducing as that "Are you leaving me again?" look as you grab the car keys.

The good news is you don't always have to leave little Scooter behind. It may take some creative thinking on your part, but turning your small dog into your traveling sidekick may be easier than you think.

The Ease of Traveling with a Small Dog

The smaller the dog, the easier it is to take with you. The smallest of the small (toy breeds and others under twenty pounds) can easily be toted in travel bags that look like big purses. These handbags for dogs are like soft-sided luggage with zippers and mesh sides so your little friend can breathe easy while in transit. Usually made of nylon, they come in a wonderful variety of colors and patterns so toting your pint-size dog is like having a new fashion accessory—and what a great conversation starter!

Every small dog also needs its own lightweight plastic or fiberglass pet carrier. If you're the outdoorsy type, you may also want to invest in a pet backpack for hikes with your dog safely aboard until you decide to let it explore the terrain on a leash.

While you're out on a road trip your little buddy can also ride along safely if you have a dog safety belt or special car seat made for small dogs. If your dog wears a harness, you can also improvise your own pet safety system by attaching it to one of your vehicle's own seatbelts. You wouldn't dream of driving children around without buckling them into car seats or seatbelts, and where safety is concerned, dogs are no different. A slam on the brakes can send your dog flying.

 Fact

In Europe, the public has a more laissez-faire attitude toward dogs. When traveling abroad, you spot small dogs everywhere, from restaurants to markets.

Once you reach your destination, finding accommodations that allow dogs is easier if your dog is on the small side too. Many hotels and motels

CHAPTER 18: ON THE GO

limit their canine accommodations to small dogs only. Airlines allow the smallest to travel right under your seat. From crates to beds to food dishes, small dogs require smaller accessories, so you won't need a separate suitcase to pack little Scrappy's stuff, either.

There are still lots of places where dogs of any size are not welcome, but you and your dog can be on the cutting edge of changing this situation. Making sure you are both considerate travelers will do a lot to make the dog's presence more acceptable for other people and their dogs.

Around Town

Just as every great journey begins with one small step, making little Sassy a seasoned traveler begins with taking her on everyday outings around town. Of course, the temperature outdoors must first be taken into account. If it's too hot or cold, for safety's sake, she'll have to stay home.

If you plan to tote her in her special handbag, it's a good idea to get her used to it before you embark. Start by practicing at home, placing her in the bag for a few minutes at a time, making sure she has a comfy mat inside. Some pet bags come already equipped with cushy fleece pads. Give her a treat while she's getting used to it and then go about your business with your household activities. Next, take her out in the yard and carry her around inside it, then reward her again.

It's fun to take a dog where you know it will be welcomed. Whether your little dog is in a bag or on a leash, the pet store is a good destination to begin travel training. Everyone there likes dogs, and you can let your little friend pick out her own treat as a reward for her good behavior. Tiny dogs in tote bags can go just about anywhere, from the bank to the post office to the flower shop, but leashed dogs are more restricted.

When you use a drive-up teller at the bank or get a cup of coffee at the drive-through window, the person who assists you will often offer a biscuit to your dog. Outdoor events like fairs, carnivals, and flea markets are also fun for small dogs and offer great opportunities for socialization as well.

No matter how short the trip, always bring a leash, bottled water, and a bowl (collapsible ones are great), plastic poop bags, spray cleaner, and paper towels. Better yet, keep your dog's travel kit right in the car so you'll always be ready to pick up and go.

 Alert!

When you go inside a store, never leave your little dog leashed outdoors where it could escape or get stolen.

Pet-Friendly Accommodations

You can find a wide variety of books outlining pet-friendly lodgings all over the country. Some are regional in scope, such as The Dog Lover's Companion to New England, by JoAnna Downey and Christian J. Lau. Plenty of online resources are also available.

The Web site *www.dogfriendly.com* offers comprehensive guides to hotels, motels, and bed-and-breakfasts throughout the United States and Canada where you and your dog will be welcome, as well as information on dog-friendly places to visit once you get there. At *www.pettravel.com*, you'll find a list of almost 20,000 pet-friendly accommodations all over the world. The Web site details immigration rules for over ninety countries regarding quarantine requirements, vaccinations needed, and travel regulations for all airlines at home and abroad. The Web site *www.petsonthego.com* lists 30,000 hotels, motels, and inns that welcome dogs worldwide, including such posh digs as The Four Seasons. You can also check *www.takeyourpet. com* for extensive information on pet-friendly lodgings, but you must pay to become a member. Substantial discounts on accommodations and other pet services are included if you decide to sign up.

Most resorts and hotels have Web sites that detail whether your dog will be welcomed. Florida's Disney World, for example, offers five kennels where your dog can stay while you're touring the park. Most open one hour prior to the park's opening and close one hour after it closes. Some are solely daycare facilities, while others offer overnight stays. At California's Disneyland, kennels are also available for day-care, but there are no overnight accommodations for dogs.

Fact

Realizing his own two dogs, a Lab and a Jack Russell terrier, would not be allowed at Starwood Hotels, CEO Barry Sternlicht changed the policy at Sheraton, Westin, and W hotels throughout the United States and Canada. The Starwood "Love that Dog" program now provides canine guests with custom-designed dog beds, oversize dog pillows, special dishes, temporary ID tags, and many other doggie perks and services.

As you travel with your dog, you'll find that some inns have specific pet-friendly rooms, some hotels require a security deposit, and all will require you to read and sign their pet policy. Some have restrictions on the number, type, and size of pets allowed. Other lodgings actively court people with pets. On Cape Cod, the quaint Wingscorton Farm Inn in East Sandwich advertises a private beach where dogs can run free. Not surprisingly, the Cypress Inn in Carmel, California, owned by screen legend and animal activist Doris Day, welcomes pets with open arms.

Ask if your pet-friendly room will be in a smoking area if this is of concern to you. Also find out if your dog must be crated if left unattended in the room. If you are staying in a hotel or motel, a ground-floor room would make nighttime potty runs easier. Make sure you use only designated areas on the grounds, and always be prepared to clean up after your dog before coming back indoors.

If your dog uses a litterbox indoors, place it in the bathroom to make cleanup easier. When you leave your dog in the room, turn on the radio or television to provide comforting background noise. If you expect the housekeeping staff to stop by, crate your dog for its own safety and the workers' peace of mind. When you go out, inform the front desk of your whereabouts, and give them your cell phone number in case they need to reach you. If your dog should damage any property, report it immediately and offer to pay for repairs.

Camping and Motor Homes

Most campgrounds and RV parks welcome pets, but you should always call ahead if you are not absolutely sure. Some have restrictions on the size and number of dogs you may bring. Some require you to keep your dog leashed at all times. There is usually no additional charge for pets beyond the regular campsite fee, but some will charge an extra dollar or two per night per pet.

There are numerous guidebooks on camping where pet policies are spelled out for individual camping areas, or you may check the Web site *www.gocampingamerica.com* and use their quick-search to locate a park that permits pets in your desired vacation spot. The Web site *www.camping-usa.com* will also furnish you with listings of pet-friendly campgrounds. When planning to visit any national park, check the National Park Service Web site, *www.nps.gov*, for specific information.

Many campers bring along an x-pen to allow their pets some outdoor freedom without the need to be leashed or tethered.

The Family Motor Coach Association (FMCA), which offers advice on traveling with pets in these vehicles on its Web site, *www.fmca.com*, notes that while some pets adapt to travel easily, others need to take many short trips before they are comfortable in the motor home. Because of health, environmental, or behavioral factors, some pets might never be ready, willing, or able to travel in a motor home. The FMCA online magazine recommends that you consider the following issues before traveling with your pet in a motor home:

- **Routines:** Some pets, especially dogs, tend to be creatures of habit. An animal used to a certain life at home may not appreciate having to alter its schedule to accompany the family on motor home trips. Consider your pet's welfare before bringing it along.
- **Space:** Motor-home floor plans today are more spacious than ever. However, pets accustomed to plenty of room to play will need to adjust to its tighter living quarters. City animals that like to romp in

urban parks might not like to be out in open trail country. Conversely, country animals used to more freedom might not adjust to being cooped up in the motor home.

- **Behavior:** Is your dog well trained? Is it housebroken? Does it come when called? How well does it do on a leash? Will it get motion sickness on longer trips? Your answers to these questions will determine whether RV travel is appropriate for your pooch.

- **Campground rules and manners:** Campgrounds and vacation spots expect your dog to be quiet. Some animals can become territorial about the motor home and may bark at strangers or other animals walking past their "house." You'll rarely have a secluded campsite, so relentlessly noisy or aggressive animals will not be welcome.

- **Being left behind:** Does your dog like to be alone? Some may bark, whine, or howl incessantly when you leave them to go visit a local attraction, one reason why many vacation destinations will not permit pets. No pet should ever be left outdoors unattended.

- **Temperatures:** On a hot day, the temperature inside a closed RV can exceed 100 degrees. Heat stroke kills many animals each year, simply because the owner left the pet inside an enclosed vehicle.

 Essential

Wherever you pitch your tent or park your RV, remember that your behavior with your dog will affect all other campers with pets as well. Most, if not all, campgrounds expect your dog to remain on a leash when outside the RV. Some may not permit pets to be tied outside to picnic tables or nearby trees. Check in advance to become familiar with a campground's pet regulations.

Camping with pets takes preparation and dedication, but for many campers the companionship and enjoyment derived from traveling with their beloved dogs overrides the extra considerations that their small companions require.

Alert!

Small dogs should not be subjected to extreme fluctuations in temperature. If your motor home or RV does not have air-conditioning, it would be safer to leave your dog with a friend or a pet sitter or in a kennel.

If you're camping with your dog, you'll need the following items:

- Pet ID (a temporary ID tag with your name, current location, and cell phone number)
- Insect spray and flea and tick repellent
- First aid kit including tweezers for tick removal
- The name and phone number of the nearest vet or emergency veterinary clinic, and a copy of your dog's medical records
- Grooming basics (brush, comb, dog shampoo, towels, nail clippers, and handheld hair dryer)
- Water bottles and dog dishes, including a collapsible bowl
- A sufficient supply of your dog's regular food and treats
- Chew toys, balls, and other favorite toys
- Crate and/or bed
- Sweater for cold weather
- An extra leash and collar
- A spiral tie-out stake for hooking up its leash or cable
- A flashlight for late-night potty outings
- Pet wipes, disposable poop bags, and a trash bucket with a lid
- A life vest for the dog if you plan to go boating

Boarding Kennels and Pet Sitters

If it isn't feasible to take your dog on vacation with you, you'll need to make other arrangements. Unless a friend or relative can take your dog, boarding and pet sitting are your two main options. Boarding a small dog can be a tricky proposition because many small dogs are so strongly bonded to their owners that they don't do well in the kennel setting. Some go on a hunger strike, refusing to eat or drink water, a serious threat to their health. Some become severely stressed in the kennel environment, especially in a traditional layout with many separate dog runs on each side of a main aisle. The noise of barks and howls and metal gates reverberates in such a cavernous facility and can be highly disturbing to a small dog that has rarely been away from home. If your budget allows it, pet sitting may work for you and your dog.

Boarding Your Dog

The best way to find a kennel is by word-of-mouth. Ask your small-dog-owning friends, your vet, groomer, or breeder if they have any recommendations. You may also check the Web site of the American Boarding Kennels Association (ABKA) at *www.abka.com* for a member kennel. ABKA accreditation indicates a certain level of professionalism and training on the part of the kennel owners. The organization also offers certification to members who complete its training programs and performs on-site evaluations of their facilities.

Some kennels have separate areas for their smaller boarders, and some board small dogs only. If you need to board your small dog at a kennel, make sure you first tour the premises, preferably making an unannounced visit. Make sure it looks and smells clean. Ask to see where your small dog will be housed. Its quarters should be large enough for comfort and free of any sharp objects. It should have a soft place to sleep, preferably its own bed you bring from home. For both safety and sanitary concerns, dividers should be in place between your little dog and its neighbors. The temperature must always be within certain limits, especially crucial for small dogs.

Kennel personnel should be friendly and willing to answer of your questions. They should also be able to provide a list of satisfied customers as a reference. The facility should have stringent rules regarding vaccinations. If it doesn't, your dog could be exposed to dangerous infections. A veterinarian must be on call at all times. Lastly, you may check on the establishment's business history with your local Better Business Bureau. Above all, when boarding a small dog, you should always have a trusted backup person available on very short notice to come to the kennel and take your small dog home if it gets too stressed or has any sort of health crisis in the boarding situation.

Alert!

Make sure your dog will not be exercised or allowed to play with any larger canines. If it is at all dog-aggressive, it should not get up close and personal with any other dogs, regardless of their size.

If you have determined that the kennel you have selected is clean, comfortable, and safe for your little dog, these hints may help make things easier on both of you when you leave him there:

- **A practice visit:** Just to make sure he will be okay, leave Barney for a night or two before you take a longer vacation. It will be a trial run for both of you.
- **Check his shots:** If Barney's vaccinations need updating, bring him to the vet a couple of weeks before you're scheduled to leave him. He should be immunized against rabies, distemper, hepatitis, leptospirosis, parainfluenza, parvovirus, and bordetella (kennel cough).
- **Medication:** If he is on any type of medication such as a heartworm preventative, make sure it will be given to him while boarded.
- **Toys:** Bring along his favorite toys, a blanket, and your old sweatshirt, preferably unlaundered, so your scent will be a comfort to him.
- **Food:** Keep his eating routine normal, and don't switch his food right before you go. That could add an upset stomach and diarrhea to his kennel stay.
- **Contact information:** Leave information on where you will be staying as well as the phone number of your vet and backup person.
- **No tears:** Try to remain calm and upbeat when you drop him off. No long dramatic parting scenes either. You know how your dog is tuned in to your emotions, so if you act heartsick and upset, he will too.

Using a Pet Sitter

Pet sitters offer another option if you must leave your dog at home. These canine companions are becoming more and more popular as dog owners realize that as long as they have a caring person looking in on it regularly and providing food, affection, and exercise, most little dogs will probably be happier at home. On their own turf they can follow their regular routine with no worries about the trauma often associated with being boarded. They won't be exposed to other animals, and your home will be more secure with someone coming and going in your absence.

 Essential

"Most pets adjust better to their owner's absence and experience less anxiety when they can remain in their home under the care of a loving professional," says Patti Moran, president of Pet Sitters International. "There's no stress of a new environment, new food, exposure to illnesses, or travel trauma for your and your pet when he/she can stay at home."

A reputable pet sitter is a bonded and insured professional, and it is the pet sitter's job to remember every aspect of your dog's care. If you do not know of a reputable pet sitter in your area, ask your vet or groomer or check the Pet Sitters International Web site at *www.petsit.com* to find a member near you.

You will need to get your dog acquainted with this new caregiver before you go away. Scheduling some midday walks is a good way to start. Make sure the sitter is aware of all your dog's idiosyncrasies, the toys, treats and games it loves, its favorite hiding places, its human and canine neighborhood pals, and the things that make it nervous or afraid. Be sure it has ID tags or is microchipped or tattooed and that its collar fits properly so it cannot escape while out for a walk. Let the sitter know where its health records are kept and how to contact the vet as well as a twenty-four-hour vet emergency clinic. Leave the number of the groomer as well in case your baby gets dirty or needs a flea bath while you're away.

Make sure the sitter knows where you can be reached. Leave sufficient food and regular medications if your dog needs them. Also leave a list of emergency phone numbers for your maintenance people such as the plumber, electrician, alarm company, and home handyman. Let the sitter know if any areas are off limits, and secure these places before you leave.

Because of the nature of their service and number of visits they must make, pet sitters will cost more than a boarding kennel. But for some small dogs, they provide the best possible care when you must be away.

Away You Go!

Now matter where you are going or what mode of transportation you'll take to get there, be realistic about your dog's ability to travel. If your little one is very young or old, not in the best of health, pregnant, or recovering from surgery, it may be best for all concerned to have her cared for by a friend, family member, pet sitter, or kennel rather than taking a chance on injuring herself or ruining your vacation. Even if your dog is in excellent health, start your travels together in small increments. An overnight or weekend trip is a great way for both of you to cut your teeth on this new experience together. If you are in doubt, ask your vet's advice.

Here are a few additional tips for you and your traveling four-footed friend:

- Trim your dog's nails before you go. It will have less chance of getting them caught on carpets or in its crate.
- Never take your dog on an escalator unless it is in its crate or being carried in your arms. Its leash, nails, or fur could easily become caught in the moving machinery.
- Feed your dog lightly before you embark, only about one-third of its regular portion. It can finish its meal once you've reached your destination.
- Don't let your dog stick its head out the car window.
- If you're driving, take breaks every few hours to allow both you and your dog to stretch your legs, take a comfort stop, and have a drink of water.

- Don't let your dog run loose at roadside rest areas. It could get lost, run into traffic, or get in a scuffle with another animal.
- Never leave your dog unattended in the car for any amount of time, especially during warm or cold weather, unless the heat or air-conditioning is left on. If the car is unlocked, your dog might get stolen.

Travel by Air

Air travel for pets is a risky and complicated affair, and it should not be undertaken lightly. Yes, smaller is better, but only the smallest dogs are allowed in the cabin with their owner. Most dog owners ship their dogs by air only if they have no other alternative. Before you do, weigh the pros and cons, and understand what air travel will mean for your little dog.

Rules and Regulations

The United States Department of Agriculture (USDA) regulates air transportation of dogs and requires that they be at least eight weeks old and weaned at least five days prior to flying. Compassion and common sense dictate that it's wiser to wait until a puppy is twelve weeks of age before taking it on a plane. In addition, if your small dog is ill, highly stressed, pregnant, or very old, it's inadvisable to transport it by air.

Before you purchase your tickets, you need to check with your airlines for any restrictions that may apply to your dog. Not every airline can or will accommodate travel for dogs. It is necessary to find out which airlines will and the policies they have in place before your travel plans are finalized.

 Fact

At the time of this writing, a new airline specifically for traveling pets and their owners was slated to begin operation soon. You can check out their Web site at *www.companionair.com* for current information.

Most airlines will only allow one dog per person. If you have two dogs small enough to travel in the cabin with you, you'll need to purchase a seat ticket for the second pet. (On an airplane, no one rides free except airline personnel.)

Airlines have strict rules concerning how many dogs can travel on any given flight. When booking your reservation, be sure to ask the whether any other animals will be boarding as well. This will alert the reservation person and keep you and your dog from getting bumped off your flight.

When it comes to dogs, airlines have three options for travel: cabin, checked baggage, or cargo. While size and weight restrictions vary among airlines, if your dog weighs more than fifteen pounds, the latter two options are generally the only ones available, and they are not really advisable unless you have no other option. In checked baggage, you would be on the same flight as your dog. The combined total of its weight and that of its crate must not exceed a hundred pounds. In the cabin, your dog will be with you and must fit entirely under the seat in front of you, with the carrier size stipulated by each airline.

Pet Carriers

Airlines adhere to strict codes concerning the size and type of pet carrier they allow. For dogs less than fifteen pounds—the usual cutoff weight for traveling in the cabin with you—major airlines require the following:

- Your carrier may be a hard plastic, metal, or soft-sided.
- It must have adequate ventilation on three sides.
- It must be leakproof.
- You must be able to fit it under the airline seat, and it must be no larger than seventeen inches in length, sixteen inches in width, and ten and a half inches high. For small jets or prop planes, size restrictions may call for an even smaller carrier.

Your dog's crate must both meet the airline's standards and be large enough for the dog to lie down comfortably, turn around, and stand freely. It must be labeled "Live Animal—This Side Up," and include your name, address, and telephone number in case the dog gets lost in transit. Another label should bear your dog's name, breed, destination, and flight number. You might even personalize it: "Hi! My name is Angus. I am a Scottish terrier going to Los Angeles on American Airlines Flight 222. Thank you for taking good care of me." Include the name, address, and telephone number of your planned destination, a contact name and number, as well as any special instructions for baggage handlers. Your best bet is to get it used to this travel crate ahead of time, both at home and in the car.

Alert!

Certain small breeds such as the Boston terrier, Lhasa apso, Pekinese, pug, and shih tzu are at risk when transported by air because these short-muzzled breeds are more susceptible to breathing difficulties caused by the thin air at high altitudes.

Before You Fly

Inquire about other cargo on the flight to make sure that there are no substances that would be dangerous to your dog, and insure your dog for at least $10,000. The cost will be minimal, and it may mean greater attention will be given to your dog.

All major airlines require a certificate from a veterinarian stating the dog is healthy, suitable for flying, free of parasites, and current on vaccinations. If you are traveling overseas, you must check the destination country's health certificate and quarantine requirements. Your airline will assist you with this information. Make sure you have copies of your dog's health and rabies certificates before you leave for the airport. Bring a leash or harness with you, as most airports require that the dog be removed from its carrier at the security checkpoint so that the carrier may be put through the X-ray machine. Confirm the check-in and arrival locations for shipping the dog; they may differ from passenger departures. Also inquire about cutoff times for acceptance of your dog on the flight. USDA regulations provide that your dog may be tendered no more than four hours before flight time unless you have made special arrangements. Once aboard, don't be afraid to inquire whether your dog has also been loaded.

During the Flight

Your dog will not be allowed out of its carrier, so make sure it has a chance to relieve itself before you board the plane. You should also ensure that your dog is wearing a collar with ID tags in case it escapes. Never muzzle your dog, as its ability to breathe and regulate its temperature by panting would be severely compromised.

Secure a leash to the outside of the crate, and have two empty food and water dishes inside. The USDA requires that you have fed and watered your dog within the last four hours, and the airline will require you to sign a certification to this effect. Do not feed it a full meal at that time, however, as a full belly might make your dog uncomfortable during the flight.

 Essential

If the flight will be a long one, attach extra food, water, and any required medication to the outside of the crate along with any special instructions and a twenty-four-hour history of feeding, watering, and medication.

Obviously, a nonstop flight would be best. If your flight is not a nonstop, check on your dog during the layover. If the layover is long or the temperature a factor, confirm that the dog has been unloaded for the layover and is not allowed to remain in the cargo hold or out in the sunlight on the tarmac. If the layover is long enough, you may claim your dog, take it for a walk, and give it some water before reboarding.

The USDA prohibits the shipment of animals where temperatures at either the origin or destination of the flight are below 45 degrees or above 85 degrees. Many airlines are even more stringent, not allowing dogs to travel as either checked baggage or as cargo during the hottest summer months. The concern is that if the airplane has to sit on the runway for an extended period, the cargo compartment may overheat. Even though the embargo exists most airlines will accommodate animals on flights that leave after 9:00 P.M. and before 6:00 A.M.

Alert!

When traveling by air, the use of sedatives or tranquilizers is not advisable since their effects on animals at high altitudes are unpredictable. Never give a pet a sedative unless advised to do so by your vet.

When it comes to air travel for your dog, the bottom line is this: Being shipped with checked baggage in the cargo bay is risky and it's not fun for your dog. If you are relocating, you may have no choice. But if you are taking a long vacation, you'll have to decide whether the pleasure of having your dog with you once you get to your destination outweighs the stress factors associated with this mode of travel.

Chapter 19
Therapy Dogs

If you decide to train yourself and your small dog for therapy work in hospitals and nursing homes, you will both be making an invaluable contribution to your community. This volunteer activity makes a big difference in the quality of life of the ill, physically and mentally challenged, elderly, and isolated. Therapy dogs are now recognized members of the health care profession, bringing joy and comfort to millions every day.

How to Get Started

There are hundreds of therapy-dog groups around the country. Some do their own training and certification, while others require certification by one of the national organizations. Local groups generally have agreements with medical or residential facilities that use their volunteers. If you have a particular facility that you would like to visit, ask about its pet-therapy policy and you will be guided to the necessary testing, training and certification.

 Essential

Sometimes a mind that has been locked in its own prison of isolation for years can miraculously reawaken through the simple act of connecting with a pet.

The first time a therapy dog visits a facility, most people are happily surprised. Smiles light up their faces, and regardless of the age, illness, or physical condition of the residents or patients being visited, the therapy dogs are happy to see them, too. Such joy and warmth is the usual reaction of most people to dogs. But for those who are institutionalized, often deprived of companionship and love, it is always heartening to witness the reaction provoked by cuddly canines with wagging tails.

Therapy Dogs International, Inc.

According to Therapy Dogs International, Inc. (TDI), these four-footed therapists give something that medical science can't produce without the use of drugs. "It has been clinically proven that through petting, touching, and talking with the animals, patients' blood pressure is lowered, stress is relieved, and depression is eased," advises the organization's Web site, *www.tdi-dog. org*. TDI is a nonprofit organization. There is no charge for its visitations. All funds are derived from associate membership dues and contributions.

Could your small dog be a TDI therapy dog? Well, first it needs to be examined by a certified TDI evaluator and be at least one year of age. "The dogs must respond to hugs and caresses from strangers and not be spooked by clanging bedpans, wheelchairs, odd-looking medical apparatuses, hospital smells, or the quick and erratic movements of some elderly patients," advises TDI's literature. The prospective therapist must pass both the AKC's Canine Good Citizen Test (CGC) and a temperament evaluation to demonstrate its suitability to become a TDI therapy dog. In addition, TDI requires its health record form to be completed and signed by a vet.

Fact

In 2004, over 14,000 dogs and approximately 12,200 handlers were registered with TDI, active in every state and in Canada. These dogs come in all shapes and sizes. Some have pedigrees, some come from breed rescue or the local shelter, and they include both purebred and mixed-breed dogs.

To find out about getting a preliminary evaluation from TDI for your dog, check out the Web site. After you and your dog have passed the testing requirements, you will receive a TDI application for registration from your evaluator. In addition to the stringent requirements attesting to your dog's health, you will also need a letter of recommendation from your vet and letters of recommendation from any institutions you are planning to visit.

Pet Partners

The Delta Society (*www.deltasociety.org*) is another major source of training and certification for therapy dogs through its Pet Partners program, established in 1990. It provides training and screening for people who want to visit hospitals, nursing homes, and other facilities with their animals. Currently, over 6,400 Pet Partners teams operate in all fifty states and four other countries, helping more than 900,000 people each year.

Successful completion of its Pet Partners course, in either an instructor-led classroom or home-study format, is required for registration. The course is usually presented in a day-long workshop where you will receive the Pet Partners Team Training Course Manual and practice visiting skills. Taught by Delta-licensed instructors, the courses are scheduled throughout the year in locations all over the country.

Next you must have your vet complete a health screening for your dog, attesting to its physical well-being, lack of parasites, and its up-to-date immunization record. Then a team evaluation process will determine how well you handle your dog, how it responds to you as its handler, and how you interact with the evaluator and others involved in the process. Think of it as a temperament test for humans! Your dog's behavior and responsiveness will be evaluated as well. After you have both passed these tests, you will receive a signed and dated copy of your test forms that include the date when you submit your completed registration packet to the Delta Society.

Once you have received your badge and certificate of registration from the Delta Society, you and your dog are officially a Pet Partner team and are permitted to conduct visits as such. In order to remain active as a registered Pet Partner with all the benefits it entails, you and your dog must be re-evaluated every two years. Registered Pet Partners are covered by liability insurance when they are performing therapy work.

Bright and Beautiful Therapy Dogs, Inc.

Bright and Beautiful Therapy Dogs, Inc., is another a nonprofit organization that evaluates, tests, trains, qualifies, and supports therapy dogs to be used for loving support in nursing homes, hospitals, psychiatric wards, and in other facilities where such dogs are needed. To train your dog to be a canine therapist, both you and your dog must first pass the Bright and Beautiful Therapy Dogs, Inc., therapy-dog certification analysis given by one of their evaluators. When you pass the test, you are sent a kit containing a registration form signed by a certified evaluator; your ID card and a name badge with your dog's picture stating it is a therapy dog; a 2-million dollar accident and liability insurance policy for coverage while doing therapy work; a bone -shaped ID stating: "I Am a Therapy Dog"; a Bright and Beautiful Therapy Dog leash; an official certificate; and a bumper sticker advising other motorists: "Transporting Therapy Dogs—Please Don't Tailgate."

This organization encourages you to make your own evaluation to see if you and your dog are suited to this kind of work. The quiz is light-hearted but it helps you determine your dog's suitability. The following is a partial list of the questions you are asked:

1. How does your dog react to rolling shopping carts, roller blades, or skateboards?
   A. He calmly watches with curiosity as they move past.
   B. The eyes glaze over, the mouth foams, and with curled up lips he barks and growls furiously.
2. How do you and your dog handle the unexpected?
   A. Appropriately, just like Lassie.
   B. Does Cujo come to mind?
3. How does your dog behave at the vet or groomer?
   A. He compliantly agrees to whatever fate awaits him.
   B. They meet us at the door with a muzzle.
4. Have you and your dog had any formal training? How about at-home training?
   A. Yes, we have been through at least beginners and we still practice at home.
   B. We're perfect, we don't need no stinkin' training.
5. Do people cringe at the sight of your dog?
   A. No, they smile sweetly and pat him fondly.
   B. Is that what they're doing? Oh.
6. Does your dog like children?
   A. Yes, he wags his tail and wants to go play—gently. He knows not to jump up and scare little ones.
   B. Yes, baked, broiled, or boiled; he doesn't care.

If you score mostly A responses, you and Bowser are ready. If, however, you score even one B response, you should consider a training course before venturing out to do therapy work with your dog.

All kidding aside, pet-therapy visits are important work. As much as medical experts know about caring for the sick, they can still learn more from a little dog whose quiet presence with a patient can lower the blood pressure, get those endorphins flowing, and banish stress and pain.

As the owner of a small dog, you already know all the joy and unconditional love that such endearing creatures can bring into your life, so if your dog is suited for this kind of work, why not share this healing presence with someone less fortunate? Passing along this magical connection is one of the greatest gifts you and your small dog can give.

E Chapter 20

Just for the Fun of It

In general, small dogs are people magnets. If this is your first dog, you'll be surprised by how many perfect strangers will stop to admire your dog and chat with you. Sure, you may encounter some people who are not dog-friendly, but most will have a positive reaction to your clean, cute, and friendly little dog. Of course there are places you won't be allowed to go—indoors at restaurants, supermarkets, and some stores—but in the majority of public and private places where people congregate, bringing your dog along is worth a try.

At Home

You probably already know many of the dog-friendly places where you can take your pooch in your own city or town. When you're ready to venture beyond the local park, it's always a good idea to call an establishment you plan to visit ahead of time to check their current policy.

Start by dining al fresco with your dog. Make sure Bubba does not bother other diners by bringing along some yummy treats of his own. Of course, keep him leashed at all times, and use the opportunity to put training commands such as "Down" and "Stay" into practice. If you are turned away, try not to take it personally. It's best to respond graciously, both for your own sake and for other dog owners like you who are eager to show people that well-mannered dogs should be welcomed wherever their owners go.

Away from Home

Provincetown, on the tip of Cape Cod in Massachusetts, is a quaint summer colony with a decidedly bohemian flavor. Here you will find dogs everywhere, on the job with their owners in antique shops and art galleries, at sidewalk cafés like the Café Blasé on Commercial Street, people-watching with locals and vacationers, and proudly parading down the narrow streets. In Provincetown, a well-groomed dog in a trendy leash, collar, stylish bandanna, or colorful bow is a surefire status symbol.

 Fact

In Boston's dog-friendly South End, dogs are welcome outdoors at restaurants like The Dish, The Red Fez, Gallia, the Salty Dog Seafood Grille, and the Wisteria House Chinese Restaurant, as well as in outdoor cafés along Newbury Street in the Back Bay, and at the Kinsale Irish Pub near Government Center.

Dogs are celebrated in Southern California. Trainer Janine Pierce, who works out of locations in Canoga Park and Granada Hills, has assembled a comprehensive e-guide to dog-friendly locations on her Web site, at *www. j9sk9s.com.* Her listings include four full pages of restaurants, cafés, and coffeehouses in the Los Angeles area plus eight more pages of every kind of retail establishment imaginable, from hardware stores and car washes to Tiffany's on Rodeo Drive (which allows leashed dogs under fifty pounds). There is even a hairstylist, Salon Paul/Florent at Laurel Canyon, where dogs are welcome to visit and wait while their owners get groomed. Another fun suggestion she offers is a stroll with your dog down the Hollywood Walk of Fame.

Some restaurants even put dog food on the menu. The Park Bench Café in Huntington Beach, California, has two sections, one specifically for people with their dogs. Since owner Mike Bartusick instituted the policy six years ago, his dog business has grown fivefold, the dog menu now boasting a dozen selections. His eatery's policy has strict rules: no dogs on chairs; and no dogs eating off the table, from your fork, or from your plate.

Susan Gilbert, author of the e-book *How to Take Your Small Dog Everywhere—From Around the Corner to Around the World (www.firstclass pettravel.com)*, is a San Diego resident whose delightful and comprehensive account of her travels with Spencer, her ten-year-old Yorkie, is chock-full of hints to make travel easy and fun for you and your small dog. When you download it, you'll also get a free ten-part course featuring hints on traveling with your dog, a subscription to Spencer's e-zine, and a pet-friendly hotel and restaurant guide.

In her own hometown, Gilbert lists several pet-friendly restaurants that she and Spencer have frequented, offering a thumbnail review of each: The Parkhouse Eatery, Trattoria La Strada, Point Loma Seafoods, Café Italia, Terra Restaurant, Pacific Fish Co., and the Gulf Coast Grill all allow patio dining with your dog. In nearby La Jolla, the Beach House Brewery and Girard Gourmet are equally pet-friendly, she advises.

At *www.citydog.net* you'll find City Dog guidebooks available for seven major U.S. cities: New York, Los Angeles, San Francisco, Chicago, Atlanta, Detroit, and Washington, D.C., as well as a national guide to wonderful places specifically for dogs, highlighting attractions such as boat and carriage rides, museums, restaurants, parks, beaches, and lodgings.

Dog Camps

If your idea of a perfect vacation is more rustic than staying at a hotel and ordering room service, camping with your dog may be your idea of nirvana. Dog camps allow you to spend time with people like you who are unashamedly crazy about their dogs and these getaways vary widely in focus. Some are for the serious competitor where you and your dog can work on perfecting your skills at obedience, agility, and other canine sports. Some are more laid back, offering activities ranging from the competitive to the just plain silly, while some are actually in-service seminars for professional trainers.

As yet, there are just a handful of dog camps nationwide, but they attract a loyal following. To find out more about dog camps, check out *www.dog patch.org* or *www.dogplay.com*.

🐕 Essential

Because yours is a small dog, it's important to ask if there will be enough activities suitable for smaller canines to make it a good bet for you and Bowser. Ask for references from other small-breed owners, too.

Camp Gone to the Dogs

Vermont's Camp Gone to the Dogs is perhaps the best-known dog camp. Started by Honey Loring in 1990, it draws dogs and their owners from all over the world, many returning year after year. Held at two locations, its big summer camp with 200 campers in residence is held on the campus of Marlboro College in Marlboro, while the Mountaineer Inn in Stowe hosts summer and fall sessions with half as many attendees. Loring's camps offer something for everyone, with lessons in herding, hunting, obedience training, agility, hiking, swimming, dock diving, freestyle dancing, conformation handling, skateboarding, and Tellington Touch, a massage technique for reducing tension and changing canine behavior. There are also workshops on canine massage, first aid, and even spinning dog hair into yarn. Loring's quirky sense of humor is reflected in her contests in tail-wagging, kissing, and hot-dog retrieving.

While you and your dog may choose from as many as fifty activities each day, you can also opt to kick back and do as little as possible. (Loring rewards your right to relax by issuing certificates to those who participate in less than two activities per day.) Check out the camp at *www.camp-gone-tothe-dogs.com*.

Camp Winnaribbun

Camp Winnaribbun, on the shores of Lake Tahoe in Nevada, was started by trainer and handler Lory Kohlmoos in 1995. With sessions held in August and September, it focuses on leisure and learning with a decidedly Western flavor. Away from it all on thirty-three secluded acres, here campers may participate in a wide range of activities, among them obedience, agility, herding, tracking, homeopathy, the psychology of dogs, and first aid, plus swimming lessons, games, crafts, photo sessions, and massage therapy. At night, campers gather around a roaring fire to eat S'mores, tell tales, and gaze at the stars. Accommodations are rustic. Campers sleep in log cabins with bunk beds, use a central shower, and bring their own linens and sleeping bags.

Camp Dances with Dogs

Now in its eleventh year, Camp Dances with Dogs promises to be "a freewheeling exploration of dogs and our relationships to them." Hosted by well-known proponent of holistic health and humane training advocate Suzanne Clothier of Flying Dog Press, the camp will be held at a new location in 2005, The Natural Gait, a sprawling horse farm and conference center near Harper's Ferry, West Virginia. Open to just thirty campers at a time, its brochure points out that it's not your everyday dog camp. "We don't give a hoot about perfect scores, or precision heeling. We're not competitive (at least at camp!) but we do believe in developing the relationship that allows the dog/handler team to strive for their own personal best. It's all about the dance of relationship between dog and human," Clothier explains. To be accepted here, you must fill out a lengthy questionnaire.

Alert!

Your dog's activity level is an important consideration when considering a dog camp. Some small dogs are city slickers, not the best candidates for swimming, hiking, and other strenuous outdoor pursuits, especially in warm weather.

Held for one week in August, this camp offers a full menu of activities on training, tracking, retrieving, performance, correcting behavior problems, holistic pet care, and water work, plus lots of fun and games. There is no carved-in-stone daily plan for camp week. "If you'd like to throw away your watch for a week, and relax into a human being instead of a human doing, and rediscover the joys of lying on your back with your dog watching clouds float overhead, then this might be the right camp for you," advises Clothier's Web site *www.flyingdogpress.com*. For lodging, the camp offers log cabins and lodges as well as camping in your own tent or RV.

Other Fun Stuff

You've spent lots of time teaching your small dog its manners to make your life easier at home and in your travels. Mastering obedience commands was your dog's mandatory education, but teaching dog tricks is like recess—it's just for fun. Like any training, your dog will learn when you reward it for doing what you want it to. If you want Bruiser to fetch, for example, you'll praise him like crazy and give him a treat when he brings back the ball or toy. Your happy attitude is vitally important in teaching tricks, so try to shape the dog's behavior with positive reinforcement only—no loud and crabby "No's," please. This is playtime. Learning tricks and playing games are not mutually exclusive. They both make use of your small dog's keen intelligence, and provide enjoyable downtime as well.

Learning Tricks

Practice the tricks described in this section two or three times a day, and perfect only one trick at a time.

To teach him to shake hands, your dog will first need to know the "Sit" command. Gently take his paw and give the command you have chosen, offering the treat with the other hand. Repeat this a few times to make sure he gets the message.

Essential

Use simple one-word commands like "Paw" or "Shake" when you want the dog to shake hands or "Dance" when you want him to stand up or twirl around on his hind legs. The more you babble on when instructing little Badger, the less he will understand.

If your dog is one who loves to jump up on people, it will be easy to teach him to dance. When he gets excited and stands up to get to you, hold his paws and tell him "Dance!"

Praise him, offer a treat, and set his front feet back on the ground. Once he masters standing without you holding on, use the treat to get him to turn in a circle. Most small and toy dogs have no trouble standing up, so this is a cute trick for them to learn.

Another appealing trick is bowing. You can teach it by slowly moving the treat down to the floor in front of your dog. He will follow it and when his head is down to the floor, give the "Bow" command. Eventually your little trickster will be bowing on command like the little ham he is, treat or no treat.

Small dogs love to announce their presence through barking, so the "Speak" command is a natural. Get Spunky excited—you know how—and give the command, rewarding him for barking.

Games

Playing games with your dog is fun too. The most basic one involves hiding a favorite toy and asking him, "Where's the toy?" or telling him, "Get the toy!" Make it simple for starters, letting him see you hide the object under a pillow or blanket. When he returns it triumphantly, make a big happy fuss.

If your little dynamo is led around by his nose, he can play tracking games right at home. Make him sit while you hide a tasty treat in the next room, then tell him to "Go get it!" Play the game some more when you're out in the yard, making him sit while you hide treats in the grass, behind the shed, or on the porch. Make finding the treats increasingly harder so he'll have to tap into those ancient hunting instincts to find the object of his search.

Hide-and-seek is another fun game. At first, hide yourself in an obvious place, like under a blanket where he can see you, and call him with "Where's Mommy?" He will dig under that blanket with his nose and paws to find you, so have that treat ready to reward him. One of your children can hide in another room or somewhere in the yard, and he'll have to use his scenting and tracking abilities to find them, much to everyone's delight.

Dogs love the thrill of the chase, too. But since chasing people or children might encourage unwanted aggression, it's better to have them chase a squeaky toy, ball, or stick, and to get a reward and lots of praise for bringing it back. This can be tied into the "Fetch" command.

Small dogs are highly intelligent. They can learn to ring a bell when it's time to go potty, put their toys back in the toy box, get their own leash when it's time for a walk, balance cookies on their noses, give a kiss or a hug, shake their heads "Yes" or "No," and go wake up the kids in time for school. They can even be taught to chime in when you sing "Happy Birthday." The happy reaction these tricks and games generate will be its own reward for your little crowd-pleaser.

Costumes and Other Apparel

Pets are at the very heart of family life, so it's easy to understand why people love to include them in all aspects of their lives, including holidays and other celebrations. According to the latest poll by the American Pet Products Manufacturers Association (APPMA), 54 percent of dog owners purchased holiday gifts last year for their four-legged friends. Doting owners remembered 9 million of their best friends with special Valentine presents and treats as well, and 44 percent of owners who travel for business or pleasure make it a point to pick up souvenirs for their furry family members back home.

It should come as no surprise that people love to dress up the family dog for Halloween, Christmas, a birthday party, or an Easter parade. The pet industry has responded to this trend by marketing more and more costumes for our furry friends.

Fact

Many of the short-and smooth-coated breeds—Italian greyhounds, Chinese crested (the hairless variety), miniature pinschers, and Boston terriers among them—really do need coats and sweaters to protect them when they go outside in the winter months.

"As long as pet owners use good judgment and make sure their pet is comfortable in costumes or party situations, pets can really benefit from the added attention and affection they'll get for being so festive," says Bob Vetere, APPMA's chief operations officer and managing director.

Rubies Costume Company, online at *www.rubiesny.com*, offers a distinct line of pet costumes including such characters as a cowboy and Batman. It also offers Halloween bandannas for dogs featuring such sayings as, "Does tricks for treats."

At *www.halloweenmart.com*, your dog has almost as many costume options as you will, including devils, witches, pirates, cowboys and cowgirls, clowns, and jailbirds, plus Rambo-style army fatigues and jester collars with bells. The national pet supply chains Petco and PetSmart stock up on pet costumes in time for Halloween as well.

You can make Rover safer if you take him trick-or-treating with lighted dog products from Tobz Corporation, producers of lighted leashes, collars, and harnesses in four glowing colors, visible from more than 1,000 feet. They are washable, water-resistant, and the battery is included. Check them out at *www.tobz-style.com*. A lighted collar from PolyBrite (*www.polybrite.com*), is not only illuminated by a battery, it's also reflective, making it twice as safe for your canine trick-or-treater.

Then there are Pet Blinkers from Flipo Group, Ltd. (online at *www.flipo. com*). Attached to your dog's collar, their bright flashes will make people notice your little sidekick and keep him safer in the dark.

Alert!

Remember: No trick-or-treat candies or Easter basket sweets for little Fido. Sugar and chocolate are harmful to dogs. Your favorite doggie bakery or pet supply store will have lots of healthier holiday treats made just for him.

Just like those ubiquitous reindeer antlers for dogs at Christmas, there are bunny ears in time for Easter at all pet stores. Taking Munchkin to a costume party? Now you can dress him up as a canine Elvis impersonator. Fox & Hounds (online at *www.foxandhounds.com*) has teamed up with Elvis Presley Enterprises to produce the Elvis Presley line of pet accessories. Its Hound Dog Collection includes blue suede collars, leather canine jackets, Jailhouse Rock T-shirts and caps, sunglasses, sequined jumpsuits, white leather Vegas collars, even peanut-butter-and-banana treats modeled after the king's favorite snack. At *www.yuckles.com*, you can find page after page of dog costumes, from a canine bride and groom to superheroes like Superman, Spiderman, and Batman. And don't forget the Santa suit for Christmas!

When dressing up your dog, make sure the costume isn't so constricting as to make walking difficult, and be careful not to obstruct vision. The way your dog reacts to wearing a costume may depend on how happy and encouraging you are about the idea. Just be careful not to let the festivities frighten your little dog or allow him to run away in all the excitement.

Unusual dog apparel is not just about holiday costumes. In addition to its full line of pet products and accessories, The Pampered Pup in West Palm Beach, Florida, offers a full line of doggie designer duds, including a princess dress and a ballerina tutu for your special four-legged girl. (Check them out online at *www.thepamperedpet.com*.)

Thinking of having little Cookie in your wedding party? There are brides-maids' dresses for dogs in satin and lace and a whole spectrum of colors here as well. And if the pooches themselves are the ones getting hitched, there are tuxes and top hats for dashing canine grooms as well as a splendid array of wedding dresses for their brides, off-the-rack or custom-made.

Canine Collectibles

Dog lovers adore art objects that feature their own breeds or other dogs they admire. From China plates to cookie jars, stuffed toys, jewelry, num-bered prints, arts and crafts-loving canine aficionados collect them all. The range of items considered collectible covers just about everything. Cups and plates, teaspoons, welcome signs, rugs, advertising memorabilia, walking canes, bookends, snuff boxes, umbrella handles, cookie jars, stuffed toys, salt-and-pepper shakers, magazines, matchbooks, cigarette cards, movie memorabilia—you'll even find dogs on postage stamps.

Limited-edition collectible plates and figurines from the Bradford Exchange, Royal Doulton, or Lladro have an investment value well beyond their beauty. Then there are the superb dog figurines and statues made by companies like Mortens Studio and Royal Doulton, the blue dog plates from Denmark, and an incredible range of jewelry as well. At major dog shows, you will find lots of vendors of dog collectibles and gift items for dog lovers.

To acquaint yourself with this vast marketplace, you could purchase numerous books on the topic at online book vendors like Amazon.com or BarnesandNoble.com. You can also subscribe to the Canine Collectibles Courier, online at *www.erinrac.com*. This site provides information about availability and market prices on the items that pique your interest, and its free online classified ads are fun to browse. And there's always eBay, where dog collectibles are popular sellers.

At Pug Manor (*www.pugmanor.com*), the adorable pug mug can be found on T-shirts, tote bags, dog sweaters, mouse pads, magnets, luggage, and purses. You could even order a psychic reading for your pug or down-load some "pug music" for your wrinkly-faced dog to enjoy.

Fact

You may search out collectibles for your breed online by using keywords specific to the breed. The keywords "pug collectibles," for example, turned up 1,314 Web sites to explore!

Dog collectibles will take your love of dogs to a whole new level. Whether it's a trendy purse emblazoned with your dog's likeness and a sprinkling of rhinestones or a vintage French art deco figurine to display in your home, your canine collectibles will express an important part of your personality and add to your delight in having a small dog of your own.

Appendices

Appendix A

Clubs and Organizations

Appendix B

Additional
Reading and Resources

Appendix A
Clubs and Organizations

American Kennel Club
> 260 Madison Avenue
> New York, NY 10016
> ✆(212) 696-8200
> ✍*www.akc.org*

American Society for the Prevention of Cruelty to Animals
> 424 East 92nd Street
> New York, NY 10128-6804
> ✆(212) 876-7700
> ✍*www.aspca.org*

Animal Protective Foundation
> 53 Maple Avenue
> Scotia, NY 12302
> ✆(518) 374-3944
> ✍*www.animalprotective.org*

Best Friends Animal Society
> 5001 Angel Canyon Road
> Kanab, UT 84741-5000
> ✆(435) 644-2001
> ✍*www.bestfriends.org*

Massachusetts Society for the Prevention of Cruelty to Animals
> Boston Animal Care and Adoption Center
> 350 South Huntington Avenue
> Boston, MA 02130
> ✆(617) 522-5055

Metro South Animal Care and Adoption Center

1300 West Elm Street Extension
Brockton, MA 02410
✆(508) 586-2053
✍*www.mspca.org*

Doris Day Animal Foundation

227 Massachusetts Avenue NE, Suite 100
Washington, DC 20002
✆(202) 546-1761
✍*www.ddaf.org*

PetRescue.Com, Inc.

P.O. Box 531057
Debary, FL 32753-1057
✍*www.petrescue.com*

Appendix B
Additional Reading and Resources

General Publications and Web Sites

Dog Watch–The Newsletter for Dog People. (Torstar Publications).

Benjamin, Carol Lea. *Mother Knows Best*. (Hungry Minds, Inc., 1985).

Jester, Terry. *Living with Small and Toy Dogs*. (Alpine Publications, Inc., 1996).

Kalstone, Shirlee. *How to Housebreak Your Dog in 7 Days*. (Bantam Books, 1985).

Kriechbaumer, Armin. *Small Dogs: A Complete Pet Owner's Manual*. (Barron's Educational Series, Inc., 1994).

Monks of New Skete. *The Art of Raising a Puppy*. (One Leg Up Products, 1992).

Rice, Dan, DVM. *Small Dog Breeds*. (Barron's Educational Series, Inc., 2002).

Siegal, Mordecai and Margolis, Matthew. *I Just Got a Puppy, What Do I Do? How to Buy, Train, Understand and Enjoy Your Puppy*. (Fireside, 1992).

Wilcox, Bonnie, DVM and Walkowicz, Chris. *The Atlas of Dog Breeds of the World*. (T.F.H. Publications, 1989).

www.canismajor.com

www.cavaliersonline.com (an e-zine devoted to the cavalier King Charles spaniel)

www.citydog.net (loaded with information about living with dogs in the city)

www.dogbitelaw.com (includes information about dog bites and their legal ramifications)

Canine Health Resources

For information on specific health problems, or on genetic conditions particular to individual breeds, please conduct a Web search using appropriate keywords. In most cases, the AKC Web site (at *www.akc.org*) provides a link to the chapter for all recognized breeds. From that link, current and reliable health information is easily available.

American Animal Hospital Association

12575 W. Bayaud Avenue
Lakewood, CO 80228
✆ (303) 986-2800
✐ *www.healthypet.com*

The American Veterinary Medical Association

1931 North Meacham Road, Suite 100
Schaumburg, IL 60173
✆ (847) 925-8070
✐ *www.avma.org*

Canine Eye Research Foundation

Purdue University
Lynn Hall
625 Harrison Street
West Lafayette, IN 47909-2026
✐ *www.vet.purdue.edu*

Animal Eye Care Clinics

1221-B Avenida Acaso
Camarillo, CA 93012
✆ (866) 393-8387
✐ *www.eyevet.com*

Animal Wellness Center
2115 112th Avenue NE #100
Bellevue, WA 98004-2946
☎(425) 455-8900
✍www.holistic-pet-care.com

Humane Society of the United States
2100 L Street NW
Washington, DC, 20037
☎(202) 546-1761
✍www.hsus.org

Pet Health and Nutrition Web Sites

✍www.animalessentials.com
✍www.bravorawdiet.com (a commercial raw diet; includes plenty of information on raw diets in general)
✍www.caninehealthnutrition.com
✍www.fda.gov (online home of the U.S. Food and Drug Administration Center for Veterinary Medicine)
✍www.hsus.org
✍www.iams.com (commercial site with information on feeding at all stages of life)
✍www.petloss.com
✍www.petplace.com (includes information on pet aging and loss)
✍www.thepetprofessor.com
✍www.petwellness.com (the Novartis Animal Health site, a good resource for health information of all kinds)
✍www.puplife.com
✍www.webvet.cornell.edu

Training and Obedience

✍www.goldenretriever.com (includes a good article on housetraining "special" dogs)
✍www.inch.com/-dogs (the American Dog Trainers Network Web site)

✐*www.minpin.org* (includes useful information for training that clever breed, the min-pin)

✐*www.veterinarypartner.com* (includes articles on clicker training and correcting destructive behavior)

Doggie Travel Web Sites

✐*www.dogfriendly.com*

✐*www.firstclasspettravel.com* (Susan Gilbert's subscription site for tips on travel with small dogs)

✐*www.petsonthego.com*

✐*www.pettravel.com*

✐*www.takeyourpet.com* (The Starwood Hotel chain's pet policy)

✐*www.wdwinfo.com/tips_for_touring/kennels.htm* (the Walt Disney World kennel program)

Camps and Camping

✐*www.camp-gone-tothe-dogs.com*

✐*www.camping-usa.com/campingwithpets.html*

✐*www.campw.com*

✐*www.coyotecom.com/dogcamp.html*

✐*www.dogpatch.org/doginfo/camps.html*

✐*www.dog-play.com/camps.html*

✐*www.flyingdogpress.com*

✐*www.fmca.com* (the Family Motor Coach Association Web site)

✐*www.newrver.com* (includes information about RV travel with pets)

Dog Sports and Activities

Bright and Beautiful Therapy Dogs, Inc.

✐*www.pet-therapist.com*

Canine Freestyle Federation

✍*www.canine-freestyle.org*

Delta Society Pet Partners Program

✍*www.deltasociety.org*

North American Flyball Association

✍*www.flyball.org*

Therapy Dogs International, Inc.

✍*www.tdi-dog.org*

United States Dog Agility Association

✍*www.usdaa.com*

Index

A

Affenpinscher, 8, 17–18, 155
Age of dog, 49
Agility training/competition, 205–6, 282
Aging, 136–37, 228
  death and, 235–38
  life expectancy and, 228–29
  senior citizens, 232–34
  stages of life and, 229–32
Air travel, 251–55
AKC. *See* American Kennel Club (AKC)
Allergic reactions, 145–46
Alpha dog exercises, 210–12
American Eskimo, 7, 28, 155
American Kennel Club (AKC)
  agility training/competition, 206
  breed standards, 16–17
  contact information, 66, 276
  popular breeds, 14–16
  registration, 78
Anemia, 137
Animal behaviorists, 203
Animal shelters, 56–57, 97–98
Animals, other, 11–12, 77–78, 218

Apartments, small dogs and, 47
APDT, 203
Appetite loss, 128
Arthritis, 136
Atopic dermatitis, 131
Australian terrier, 33–34, 155

B

Baby gates, 87
Barking problems, 220–22
Beds, for dogs, 87
Beds, puppies on, 183
Behavior, 97–98
  abnormal, 129
  puppies, 97
  temperament and, 46–47, 73–74
Behavior problems, 209–24. *See also* Obedience training (at home); Obedience training (formal)
  aggression, 216–18
  barking, 220–22
  biting, 212–15
  chewing, 215–16
  digging, 219
  getting help for, 223–24
  hyperactivity, 219–20

preventing, 210–12
  running away, 219
  separation anxiety, 222–23
  thinking like a dog for, 212
Bichon frise, 7, 28–29, 154, 155
Bich-Poo (bichon frise/poodle), 15
Biting, 212–15
Boarding dogs, 247–49
Body language, 226–28
Bolognese, 14, 155
Border terrier, 6, 34, 155
Boston terrier, 7, 34–35, 47, 50, 131, 154–55
"Bow" command, 269
Breed rescue organizations, 64
Breeders, 65–79
  AKC help, 66
  breeding rights and, 75–76
  buying process, 71
  choosing puppy, 73–78
  finding healthy dog, 71–73
  following advice of, 74–75
  medical histories and, 16
  multiple dogs from, 77–78
  overview, 65–67
  paperwork, 78–79
  puppy mills, 60, 61
  questions to answer from, 70
  questions to ask, 69–70

H

I

J

K

L

THE **EVERYTHING** SERIES!

BUSINESS & PERSONAL FINANCE

Everything® Budgeting Book
Everything® Business Planning Book
Everything® Coaching and Mentoring Book
Everything® Fundraising Book
Everything® Get Out of Debt Book
Everything® Grant Writing Book
Everything® Home-Based Business Book
Everything® Homebuying Book, 2nd Ed.
Everything® Homeselling Book, 2nd Ed.
Everything® Investing Book, 2nd Ed.
Everything® Landlording Book
Everything® Leadership Book
Everything® Managing People Book
Everything® Negotiating Book
Everything® Online Business Book
Everything® Personal Finance Book
Everything® Personal Finance in Your 20s and 30s Book
Everything® Project Management Book
Everything® Real Estate Investing Book
Everything® Robert's Rules Book, $7.95
Everything® Selling Book
Everything® Start Your Own Business Book
Everything® Wills & Estate Planning Book

COOKING

Everything® Barbecue Cookbook
Everything® Bartender's Book, $9.95
Everything® Chinese Cookbook
Everything® Cocktail Parties and Drinks Book
Everything® College Cookbook
Everything® Cookbook
Everything® Cooking for Two Cookbook
Everything® Diabetes Cookbook
Everything® Easy Gourmet Cookbook
Everything® Fondue Cookbook
Everything® Gluten-Free Cookbook

Everything® Grilling Cookbook
Everything® Healthy Meals in Minutes Cookbook
Everything® Holiday Cookbook
Everything® Indian Cookbook
Everything® Italian Cookbook
Everything® Low-Carb Cookbook
Everything® Low-Fat High-Flavor Cookbook
Everything® Low-Salt Cookbook
Everything® Meals for a Month Cookbook
Everything® Mediterranean Cookbook
Everything® Mexican Cookbook
Everything® One-Pot Cookbook
Everything® Pasta Cookbook
Everything® Quick Meals Cookbook
Everything® Slow Cooker Cookbook
Everything® Slow Cooking for a Crowd Cookbook
Everything® Soup Cookbook
Everything® Thai Cookbook
Everything® Vegetarian Cookbook
Everything® Wine Book, 2nd Ed.

CRAFT SERIES

Everything® Crafts—Baby Scrapbooking
Everything® Crafts—Bead Your Own Jewelry
Everything® Crafts—Create Your Own Greeting Cards
Everything® Crafts—Easy Projects
Everything® Crafts—Polymer Clay for Beginners
Everything® Crafts—Rubber Stamping Made Easy
Everything® Crafts—Wedding Decorations and Keepsakes

HEALTH

Everything® Alzheimer's Book
Everything® Diabetes Book
Everything® Health Guide to Controlling Anxiety

Everything® Hypnosis Book
Everything® Low Cholesterol Book
Everything® Massage Book
Everything® Menopause Book
Everything® Nutrition Book
Everything® Reflexology Book
Everything® Stress Management Book

HISTORY

Everything® American Government Book
Everything® American History Book
Everything® Civil War Book
Everything® Irish History & Heritage Book
Everything® Middle East Book

HOBBIES & GAMES

Everything® Blackjack Strategy Book
Everything® Brain Strain Book, $9.95
Everything® Bridge Book
Everything® Candlemaking Book
Everything® Card Games Book
Everything® Card Tricks Book, $9.95
Everything® Cartooning Book
Everything® Casino Gambling Book, 2nd Ed.
Everything® Chess Basics Book
Everything® Craps Strategy Book
Everything® Crossword and Puzzle Book
Everything® Crossword Challenge Book
Everything® Cryptograms Book, $9.95
Everything® Digital Photography Book
Everything® Drawing Book
Everything® Easy Crosswords Book
Everything® Family Tree Book, 2nd Ed.
Everything® Games Book, 2nd Ed.
Everything® Knitting Book
Everything® Knots Book
Everything® Photography Book
Everything® Poker Strategy Book
Everything® Pool & Billiards Book
Everything® Quilting Book
Everything® Scrapbooking Book

All Everything® books are priced at $12.95 or $14.95, unless otherwise stated. Prices subject to change without notice.

Everything® Sewing Book
Everything® Test Your IQ Book, $9.95
Everything® Travel Crosswords Book, $9.95
Everything® Woodworking Book
Everything® Word Games Challenge Book
Everything® Word Search Book

HOME IMPROVEMENT

Everything® Feng Shui Book
Everything® Feng Shui Decluttering Book,
    $9.95
Everything® Fix-It Book
Everything® Homebuilding Book
Everything® Lawn Care Book
Everything® Organize Your Home Book

EVERYTHING® *KIDS'* BOOKS

All titles are $6.95

Everything® Kids' Animal Puzzle & Activity
    Book
Everything® Kids' Baseball Book, 3rd Ed.
Everything® Kids' Bible Trivia Book
Everything® Kids' Bugs Book
Everything® Kids' Christmas Puzzle
    & Activity Book
Everything® Kids' Cookbook
Everything® Kids' Crazy Puzzles Book
Everything® Kids' Dinosaurs Book
Everything® Kids' Gross Jokes Book
Everything® Kids' Gross Puzzle and
    Activity Book
Everything® Kids' Halloween Puzzle
    & Activity Book
Everything® Kids' Hidden Pictures Book
Everything® Kids' Joke Book
Everything® Kids' Knock Knock Book
Everything® Kids' Math Puzzles Book
Everything® Kids' Mazes Book
Everything® Kids' Money Book
Everything® Kids' Nature Book
Everything® Kids' Puzzle Book
Everything® Kids' Riddles & Brain Teasers Book
Everything® Kids' Science Experiments Book
Everything® Kids' Sharks Book
Everything® Kids' Soccer Book
Everything® Kids' Travel Activity Book

KIDS' STORY BOOKS

Everything® Fairy Tales Book

LANGUAGE

Everything® Conversational Japanese Book
    (with CD), $19.95
Everything® French Phrase Book, $9.95
Everything® French Verb Book, $9.95
Everything® Inglés Book
Everything® Learning French Book
Everything® Learning German Book
Everything® Learning Italian Book
Everything® Learning Latin Book
Everything® Learning Spanish Book
Everything® Sign Language Book
Everything® Spanish Grammar Book
Everything® Spanish Practice Book
    (with CD), $19.95
Everything® Spanish Phrase Book, $9.95
Everything® Spanish Verb Book, $9.95

MUSIC

Everything® Drums Book (with CD), $19.95
Everything® Guitar Book
Everything® Home Recording Book
Everything® Playing Piano and Keyboards
    Book
Everything® Reading Music Book (with CD),
    $19.95
Everything® Rock & Blues Guitar Book
    (with CD), $19.95
Everything® Songwriting Book

NEW AGE

Everything® Astrology Book, 2nd Ed.
Everything® Dreams Book, 2nd Ed.
Everything® Ghost Book
Everything® Love Signs Book, $9.95
Everything® Numerology Book
Everything® Paganism Book
Everything® Palmistry Book
Everything® Psychic Book
Everything® Reiki Book
Everything® Tarot Book
Everything® Wicca and Witchcraft Book

PARENTING

Everything® Baby Names Book
Everything® Baby Shower Book
Everything® Baby's First Food Book
Everything® Baby's First Year Book
Everything® Birthing Book
Everything® Breastfeeding Book
Everything® Father-to-Be Book
Everything® Father's First Year Book
Everything® Get Ready for Baby Book
Everything® Get Your Baby to Sleep Book,
    $9.95
Everything® Getting Pregnant Book
Everything® Homeschooling Book
Everything® Mother's First Year Book
Everything® Parent's Guide to Children
    and Divorce
Everything® Parent's Guide to Children
    with ADD/ADHD
Everything® Parent's Guide to Children
    with Asperger's Syndrome
Everything® Parent's Guide to Children
    with Autism
Everything® Parent's Guide to Children with
    Bipolar Disorder
Everything® Parent's Guide to Children
    with Dyslexia
Everything® Parent's Guide to Positive
    Discipline
Everything® Parent's Guide to Raising a
    Successful Child
Everything® Parent's Guide to Tantrums
Everything® Parent's Guide to the Overweight
    Child
Everything® Parent's Guide to the Strong-
    Willed Child
Everything® Parenting a Teenager Book
Everything® Potty Training Book, $9.95
Everything® Pregnancy Book, 2nd Ed.
Everything® Pregnancy Fitness Book
Everything® Pregnancy Nutrition Book
Everything® Pregnancy Organizer, $15.00
Everything® Toddler Book
Everything® Tween Book
Everything® Twins, Triplets, and More Book

All Everything® books are priced at $12.95 or $14.95, unless otherwise stated. Prices subject to change without notice.

PETS

Everything® Cat Book
Everything® Dachshund Book
Everything® Dog Book
Everything® Dog Health Book
Everything® Dog Training and Tricks Book
Everything® German Shepherd Book
Everything® Golden Retriever Book
Everything® Horse Book
Everything® Horseback Riding Book
Everything® Labrador Retriever Book
Everything® Poodle Book
Everything® Pug Book
Everything® Puppy Book
Everything® Rottweiler Book
Everything® Small Dogs Book
Everything® Tropical Fish Book
Everything® Yorkshire Terrier Book

REFERENCE

Everything® Car Care Book
Everything® Classical Mythology Book
Everything® Computer Book
Everything® Divorce Book
Everything® Einstein Book
Everything® Etiquette Book, 2nd Ed.
Everything® Inventions and Patents Book
Everything® Mafia Book
Everything® Philosophy Book
Everything® Psychology Book
Everything® Shakespeare Book

RELIGION

Everything® Angels Book
Everything® Bible Book
Everything® Buddhism Book
Everything® Catholicism Book
Everything® Christianity Book
Everything® Jewish History & Heritage Book
Everything® Judaism Book
Everything® Koran Book
Everything® Prayer Book
Everything® Saints Book

Everything® Torah Book
Everything® Understanding Islam Book
Everything® World's Religions Book
Everything® Zen Book

SCHOOL & CAREERS

Everything® Alternative Careers Book
Everything® College Survival Book, 2nd Ed.
Everything® Cover Letter Book, 2nd Ed.
Everything® Get-a-Job Book
Everything® Guide to Starting and Running
     a Restaurant
Everything® Job Interview Book
Everything® New Teacher Book
Everything® Online Job Search Book
Everything® Paying for College Book
Everything® Practice Interview Book
Everything® Resume Book, 2nd Ed.
Everything® Study Book

SELF-HELP

Everything® Dating Book, 2nd Ed.
Everything® Great Sex Book
Everything® Kama Sutra Book
Everything® Self-Esteem Book

SPORTS & FITNESS

Everything® Fishing Book
Everything® Golf Instruction Book
Everything® Pilates Book
Everything® Running Book
Everything® Total Fitness Book
Everything® Weight Training Book
Everything® Yoga Book

TRAVEL

Everything® Family Guide to Hawaii
Everything® Family Guide to Las Vegas,
     2nd Ed.
Everything® Family Guide to New York City,
     2nd Ed.
Everything® Family Guide to RV Travel &
     Campgrounds

Everything® Family Guide to the Walt Disney
     World Resort®, Universal Studios®,
     and Greater Orlando, 4th Ed.
Everything® Family Guide to Cruise Vacations
Everything® Family Guide to the Caribbean
Everything® Family Guide to Washington
     D.C., 2nd Ed.
Everything® Guide to New England
Everything® Travel Guide to the Disneyland
     Resort®, California Adventure®,
     Universal Studios®, and the
     Anaheim Area

WEDDINGS

Everything® Bachelorette Party Book, $9.95
Everything® Bridesmaid Book, $9.95
Everything® Elopement Book, $9.95
Everything® Father of the Bride Book, $9.95
Everything® Groom Book, $9.95
Everything® Mother of the Bride Book, $9.95
Everything® Outdoor Wedding Book
Everything® Wedding Book, 3rd Ed.
Everything® Wedding Checklist, $9.95
Everything® Wedding Etiquette Book, $9.95
Everything® Wedding Organizer, $15.00
Everything® Wedding Shower Book, $9.95
Everything® Wedding Vows Book, $9.95
Everything® Weddings on a Budget Book,
     $9.95

WRITING

Everything® Creative Writing Book
Everything® Get Published Book
Everything® Grammar and Style Book
Everything® Guide to Writing a Book Proposal
Everything® Guide to Writing a Novel
Everything® Guide to Writing Children's Books
Everything® Guide to Writing Research Papers
Everything® Screenwriting Book
Everything® Writing Poetry Book
Everything® Writing Well Book